MODERN AMERICAN HISTORY ★ A
Garland
Series

Edited by
FRANK FREIDEL
Harvard University

FROM NEW DEAL
TO NEW ECONOMICS ★ The American
Liberal Response to
the Recession of 1937

Dean L. May

Garland Publishing, Inc.
New York & London ★ 1981

Library of Congress Cataloging in Publication Data

May, Dean L.
  From New Deal to new economics.

  (Modern American history)
  Bibliography: p.
  Includes index.
  1. United States—Economic policy—1933–1945.
I. Title. II. Series.
HC106.3.M2777   338.973   80-8466
ISBN 0-8240-4862-8   AACR2

All volumes in this series are printed on acid-free,
250-year-life paper.
Printed in the United States of America

For
Cheryll, Timothy,
Caroline and Thaddeus

CONTENTS

A common view of President Franklin D. Roosevelt's second term observes that a series of events, notably the court packing plan, the sit-down strikes, and the ill-conceived attempt to "purge" congressmen in 1938, stymied the New Deal, forcing liberals to fight against increasingly confident conservatives.

Dean May's concise study of the Recession of 1937-1938 offers a broader perspective that focuses on the continuing centrality of economic problems during the late 1930's. The Recession, he shows, provoked protracted and profound debate among Roosevelt's advisors. At issue was not only economic policy, important though that was, but also the very future of American liberalism and democratic government. Those engaged in the debate, occurring when authoritarian regimes were threatening to engulf the West, advanced moral and political as well as economic arguments. Roosevelt, they insisted, must not only end the Recession; he must sustain capitalism and political freedom. May shows clearly the importance of these arguments to an understanding of the changing course of liberalism in the 1930's.

In describing the debates, May focuses on the major contestants, Henry Morgenthau, Jr., Secretary of the Treasury, and Marriner S. Eccles, chairman of the Board of Governors of the Federal Reserve System. In such a battle of wills Eccles seemed doomed to failure. A Mormon banker from Utah, he was an outsider in Washington. He was outspoken and undiplomatic. Morgenthau, by contrast, was an old personal friend of Roosevelt, with whom he ate lunch every Monday. But Eccles possessed several advantages. One was his ability to see the Recession in its broadest terms; his memoranda perceptively pointed to the potentially devastating impact of the Recession on Roosevelt's political fortunes and on the future of democratic government. Another was his friendship, developed since 1933, with important New Dealers like Harry Hopkins. Most important, Eccles had a plan to end the

Recession--compensatory fiscal and monetary policies--whereas Morgenthau could urge only balanced budgets. Roosevelt, though a fiscal conservative, was temperamentally an activist. Moreover, FDR had lost virtually all patience with leading bankers and corporate spokesmen. May's book, indeed, suggests that the anti-business thrust of Roosevelt's "second New Deal" of 1935 was deeply-felt and lasting.

Thanks mainly to the influence of Hopkins, Eccles won the war of wills, and Roosevelt embarked on a policy of increased public spending in April, 1938. May reminds us that this policy may not have caused the slow recovery which followed; market forces may have been more important. But the reliance on government spending, May insists, was of great significance in setting a pattern for future economic policy in America. He argues that the spending program of 1938 involved more than temporary pump-priming, more than political expediency; it revealed the New Deal's acceptance of a different kind of liberalism. This focused less on making structural changes than on employing macroeconomic insights to increase national income. Though it agreed with Keynesian insights, it depended hardly at all on the theoretical writings of academic economists. Rather, it reflected the political influence of Marriner Eccles and his friends.

Some readers may believe that the ideas of men like Eccles did not really receive official support until World War II, or later. But May's argument is cogent. He uses to great advantage the voluminous papers of Eccles in Utah and of Morgenthau at the Roosevelt Library in Hyde Park, and displays a sensitive awareness of personality. The result is a provocative study of policy-making and of economic thought, set in the broad contest of the frightening world that faced the United States in the late 1930's.

James T. Patterson
Brown University

The present study does not fall neatly into any of the categories normally used in labeling historical monographs. In focusing upon the Recession of 1937, it is in some respects an economic history. A central theme is the struggle for influence with President Franklin D. Roosevelt, which raises questions of interest to political historians and to students of public policy making processes. The decisions made during the crisis had enormous social consequences for America, and in this sense the study partakes of some elements of social history. It is, however, primarily an intellectual history, though of a particular type. In the conclusion to his General Theory John Maynard Keynes maintained that "the ideas of economists and political philosophers, both when they are right and when they are wrong, are more powerful than is commonly understood. Indeed the world is ruled by little else." The image thus evoked of an idea going out to conquer single-handedly the world has a certain appeal to those of us who trade each day in the commodity. Yet why is it that certain ideas, like those of Keynes' own General Theory, are at times taken so avidly into a society as to command the whole field of vision for decades while others, which in their internal logic would appear equally compelling, are not?

I have been preoccupied with this question as I have attempted to follow as closely as sources permit the struggle leading to a New Deal decision to increase government spending in the wake of the Recession of 1937. And this study has convinced me that the enormous subsequent influence of the ideas of the General Theory was as much a consequence of the exigencies of that historical moment as of the elegance of the theory itself. The Recession of 1937 precipitated a crisis for New Dealers--persons who saw the event in both an internal political context and a world context, concluding that the fate of democratic, liberal values in America and in the West hinged upon a successful resolution of the matter. The crisis evoked what Herbert Stein has called a "struggle for the soul of FDR" in which Treasury Secretary Henry Morgenthau, Jr. and Reserve Board Chairman Marriner S. Eccles, each heading government agencies specifically charged with responsibility for economic affairs, were principal combatants. Personality, background, Washington connections, and received notions about the federal budget, government spending, and depression economics; all mingled in the process by which Morgenthau and Eccles fixed upon certain policy recommendations and then sought to urge their adoption by the President.

The decision to increase spending in April 1938 did not resolve the crucial questions raised by the Recession. Once signs of recovery could be seen, however, important figures in both the New Deal and the Liberal academic community found a coherent and satisfying explanation of what had happened, first in a tract prepared by a small group of American Keynesians, titled An Economic Program for American Democracy, and finally in the General Theory itself. With almost audible sighs of relief they took to themselves the ideas that brought light and under-standing to one of the darkest, most perplexing moments in their public experience. The firmness of their attachment to Keynesian economics since that time was not thus a product of the compelling logic of the ideas themselves, but of particular historical circumstances--of fears and anxieties of the time--which the ideas seemed to resolve, giving American liberals as Eccles put it, "assurance that we can go forward in the future."

Chapter one delineates the crisis precipitated by the Recession. In chapter two Henry Morgenthau, Jr., whose relationship to FDR and whose personality traits did much to shape his approach to the crisis, is introduced. In addition, the reform movement which shaped the attitudes of Morgenthau's generation towards the federal budget is examined together with its effects upon Hoover and Roosevelt as they sought to combat the Great Depression. Chapter three reviews Marriner S. Eccles' background indicating which aspects of his past shaped his approach to the Recession and influenced his favoring resumption of government spending. His relationship to Roosevelt was of considerable importance, and is discussed in this chapter. Chapter four explores both the theory and practice of government spending in depression prior to 1937 in order to understand the notions which Hoover and Roosevelt drew from and which Eccles attempted to recast during the crisis. Chapter five follows Henry Morgenthau, Jr., in his efforts to commit the Administration to balancing the budget, first, as consequence of a recovery underway, and then, as recession became evident, as an instrument of recovery. Chapter six describes, how, after a long spring spent in policy limbo, the President decided to resume spending. This decision, however, did not seem to provide the "program" for which Roosevelt's well-wishers had hoped. The transformation of that policy decision into a "program"--a coherent foundation for New Deal policies generally--is explained in chapter seven, together with the consequences of that process for our present generation.

During the several years since I first began to see the Recession of 1937 as a touchstone which might reveal the means and meaning of Keynes ascent to dominance in America economic thought, I have incurred many debts. Frank Freidel and Ernest R. May encouraged me at a difficult time and Freidel has read and offered suggestions for improving the manuscript. John L. Thomas, James T. Patterson, and Barry D. Karl gave early versions of the study a thorough working, teaching me much of the historian's craft in the process. I am grateful to Professor Patterson for taking the time to write a foreword for the book. John Morton Blum kindly read the manuscript, offering several helpful suggestions. Leonard Arrington's insights have contributed much to my understanding of the milieu in which Eccles grew up. Needless to say, I have not always followed the advice given, and assume full responsibility for the conclusions I have come to.

Others have helped greatly in giving me access to materials necessary for the study. The staff of the Franklin D. Roosevelt Library has greatly expedited my research, providing efficient access to their collection. The Eleanor Roosevelt Foundation made possible one last visit to Hyde Park to check on papers of Harry Hopkins and Henry Morgenthau, Jr. not accessible earlier. Likewise the staff of the Butler Library at Columbia University, especially those in the Columbia Oral History Office, have been most helpful. Marriner S. Eccles took time to discuss his career with an historian whose work he did not fully appreciate or understand. He and his secretaries Lee Durrant and Erma Hogan were most helpful in giving me ready access to his papers. Paul M. Sweezy shared with me documents pertaining to An Economic Program for American Democracy. The family of Henry Morgenthau, Jr. and the Marriner S. Eccles Foundation gave permission to use photographs of each.

Several have provided invaluable service in typing, proofing, and otherwise expediting the production of this volume. Jeffrey Purcell, wherever he may be, shepherded the manuscript through typing, copying, and proofing at a critical juncture. Charles M. Hatch, and Dale, Jeanne, and Lou Sneddon labored far beyond the call of duty in preparing the final draft for printing. I am grateful to the editors of the

Journal of Mormon History for permission to use sections of chapter 3 previously published by them.

Others have contributed in a more general, but most important sense. Van L. Perkins helped make decisions leading me in this direction. Maris and Mary Vinovskis and Tamara K. Hareven are probably not aware of how much they have contributed to this effort. My wife Cheryll has gone patiently through the entire labor, helping me to refine concepts and ideas, critically reviewing my prose style, and giving vital encouragement in difficult moments. She, together with Timothy, Caroline, and Tad know all the world need to learn about combatting Great Depressions.

Dean L. May
Salt Lake City
July 17, 1981

I am convinced that the success of our whole
program and the security of our people demand that
we adjust all expenditures within the limits of my
Budget estimate.

FDR   April 1937

If government activities are fully maintained,
there is a good prospect of our becoming an eighty
billion dollar country in a very short time. With
such a national income, present tax laws will
yield enough each year to balance each year's
expenses.

FDR January 1939

CHAPTER ONE

THE RECESSION OF 1937--
"A CRISIS EXTERNAL AND INTERNAL"

INTRODUCTION

Between April 1937 and January 1939 New Dealers underwent a significant transition in their thinking on national fiscal policy and its relationship to economic recovery.[1] In April 1937 President Franklin D. Roosevelt urged Congress to help him hold down expenditures in the face of declining tax revenues. "A balance of actual income and outgo" was so high a priority that the President was willing to forgo advancement of domestic social reforms in order to achieve it.[2] Twenty months later, in his annual message to Congress, Roosevelt condemned an "approach to government investing and government income" which "calls for the elimination of enough activities of government to bring the expenses of government immediately into balance with income of government." Such a course, he continued, would "invite disaster."[3]

Contained in the President's changed view of proper fiscal priorities was a new definition of social and economic doctrine for the New Deal. Between April 1937 and January 1939 a preponderance of New Dealers concluded that the most characteristic and successful of the New Deal anti-depression policies had been and should continue to be the stimulation of the economy through government expenditures.[4]

Contemporary observers sensed the turn the New Deal had taken, as a cartoon in a December 1938 <u>Washington Star</u> illustrated. The cartoon depicted the New Deal band being led by Marriner S. Eccles. Band members Roosevelt, Hopkins, and Ickes were playing their respective parts with great gusto. "Merrily we must Spend Our Way, Spend Our Way, Spend Our Way." The one "sour note" came from Henry Morgenthau, Jr., who was sitting on the back row facing the opposite direction blowing his tuba in obstinate discord, "deficit Keeps a Growin' Big, Growin' Big, Growin' Big."[5]

Eccles had been playing his spending tune since at least 1933, when as a prominent Utah banker he was asked to testify before Mississippi Senator Byron "Pat" Harrison's famous "Depression Clinic" of that February.[6] And Morgenthau's outspoken opposition to deficits dated back at least to the time his old friend and neighbor, Franklin D. Roosevelt asked him to take over the duties of the Secretary of the Treasury in the fall of that year. But during 1938 Eccles' position clearly began to emerge as the one which would come to characterize the economic thought of later New Dealers.

The months during which the Eccles' view on fiscal policy rose to a dominant position among New Dealers were turbulent ones for the Roosevelt Administration. The election triumph of 1936 was placed under an early cloud by the national outcry against Roosevelt's efforts to reorganize the Supreme Court. The President's Quarantine Speech of October 1937 underscored the growing importance to Americans of ominous international events. The extra "reform" session of Congress, convened November 15, failed to pass any of FDR's recommended legislation. Many observers interpreted the Congressional elections of 1938 as a repudiation of the President's attempted "purge" of dissident Democrats in Congress. Roosevelt enjoyed some successes during the period, but contemporary writings of New Dealers nonetheless show a distinct sense of devolution--a sense which was sharpened by uncertainty as to the President's successor should he choose not to run for a third term, and doubts that another figure could command the prestige to keep the New Deal powerful and intact.

The Sour Note
C. K. Berryman Cartoon in <u>Washington</u> <u>Star</u>
December 4, 1938

Overshadowing these events, however, was the dramatic economic downturn now known as the Recession of 1937. In a six month period between August 1937 and January 1938 the economic indicators registered as sharp a drop in industrial production as had occurred in the thirteen months following the stock market crash of 1929. Stock prices showed an equally dramatic decline. After a fairly sharp break in April 1937 the Dow Jones averages rallied during the summer to a level nine points below the all-depression high of 129.9, reached in March of that year. September brought another break, which administration officials at first bravely viewed as a normal seasonal readjustment. But the decline did not level out and was accentuated by sharp waves of selling in mid-October. By early November it was widely feared that another major depression was underway. All salient indices--industrial production, stock price averages5, employment, payrolls, and income payments--had turned sharply down and showed no signs of leveling out. A short respite at the end of December brought a brief hope that the bottom had been reached. But the decline resumed again after the holidays and did not touch bottom until April. From peak to trough stock prices had fallen 58%, employment 28%, and both payrolls and industrial production 43%.[7]

Such figures are eloquent in themselves, but only a conscious effort to see the Recession through eyes of the 1937 New Dealers can afford a sense of its full meaning. Just when it appeared that five long years of enormously costly effort might be rewarded by a return to 1929 prosperity the structure collapsed. Indices plunged more steeply than ever before to a trough of unknown depth. It was by any measure a deeply disturbing experience.

This sudden economic downturn stimulated the high-level policy debate from which Eccles' position emerged victorious. When the President referred in January 1939 to the resumption of "government activities" as a "common sense" response to the Recession he glossed over what had been a critical struggle within the New Deal. As Thurman Arnold might have put it, the Recession caused New Dealers to sever themselves from a wide-ranging set of old "symbols" and attach themselves to new ones. It was a painful process--a process which a single generation of men undertake only when goaded by the need to resolve a particularly distressing crisis.[8]

The Recession threatened the New Deal far more fundamentally than did the domestic political setbacks of 1937 and 1938. These could be seen as consequences of assaults from external forces hostile to specific aspects of the President's program. A southern senator who opposed a wages and hours bill might seem selfish and wrong-headed, but his opposition need not cause New Dealers to consider the possibility that they had erred in any fundamental way. They could still see themselves holding the citadel of humanitarian values and morally correct principles against a siege of alien forces. Far from suggesting error, such opposition confirmed New Dealers in their belief that what they were doing was fundamentally right.

The threat which the Recession posed was quite a different matter. It was a systemic phenomenon with no readily identifiable cause, affecting the whole economy with generally harmful results. It was as if a plague had fallen across the land, striking those who defended the New Deal as well as those who attacked. There seemed no convincing escape from the suspicion that the source of the infection might lie within the citadel itself. Friends and compatriots were regarded with suspicion. All past policies were questioned. There was even an occasional haunting fear that in some unguarded moment a heresy had been uttered for which the gods of this land now exacted retribution. Never had it seemed more necessary to seek safety in close adherence to old and familiar creeds.

The New Dealer looking outward in 1937 faced international and domestic situations which added ominous dimensions to the economic crisis. He saw the success of the new totalitarian states of Europe and Asia as a challenge to American democratic values. He also saw the growing strength of political opposition at home as a challenge, but to New Deal values. The economic recession made the two external threats sometimes appear as one. The logic of the situation suggested that continuing economic stagnation might discredit the New Deal. This, in turn, could diminish the strength of Roosevelt's leadership, seriously threatening liberal democracy in America, and perhaps in the world.

To the New Dealer looking inward other aspects of the crisis appeared equally disquieting. The Recession suggested that Roosevelt's followers did not possesss the key to economic recovery--indeed it was conceivable that some administration policies might be endangering the economy. If the destiny of the New Deal was not bound up with its success in bringing the nation out of depression then wherein did that destiny lie? Could there be discerned in its past a form and substance which bespoke a distinctive mission in American history independent of success in bringing economic recovery? From what source could corrective policies be drawn and how could such form and substance be given the New Deal?

For those who identified with the administration these questions took upon themselves a deeply personal meaning. If the New Deal was without form and substance then how could an official such as Morgenthau assure himself that his own commitment and exertions had been purposeful? What had been the meaning of the recent years of strenuous personal investment? The New Dealer's interpretation of the meaning of his own past commitment was thus influenced by external events. The two entered into one another in such a way as to give the recession crisis a compass as general as the fate of democracy in the world and as specific as the individual observer's sense of personal worth. Whatever resolution the intensive searching of 1937 and 1938 was to achieve would need to deal with both internal and external aspects of the crisis the Recession had brought. The crisis is for this reason worthy of closer examination in its external as well as its internal dimensions.

OUTWARD DIMENSIONS OF THE NEW DEAL CRISIS

Historians commonly divide Roosevelt's presidency into two distinct segments. The first deals with the reform and recovery measures designed to bring the nation out of the Great Depression. The second deals with the policies which prepared the nation for war, the President's leadership during the war, and the conferences which began the planning for a post-war settlement. Curiously enough, one seldom gets the sense, in moving from histories of the New Deal to histories of our involvement in the war, that domestic and foreign concerns at any point had a significant influence upon one another.[9] Historians generally have seen the connection as negative--the President's concern for one prevented his acting upon concerns for the others. They give the impression that at some point in 1938 or 1939 international events became so pressing as to absorb most of the time and attentions of FDR and his chief aides, diverting them from further pursuit of domestic programs. At this point the New Deal simply stopped growing.[10]

Though this overall picture accurately reflects the main tides of activity within the Roosevelt administration, it nevertheless needs qualification. Events in Europe during the recession period, far from diverting attention from domestic problems, amplified the perceived importance of successfully solving these problems. When the Recession struck, the Spanish Civil War had already presaged a possible division of Europe into warring fascist, communist, and democratic nations. The democracies, weakened by economic and political turmoil, seemed hardly a match for the regimented efficiency of Germany and Italy. The brutal bombing of the civilian population of the Basque town of Guernica in northern Spain by aircraft of Germany and Italy in April 1937 quickly became an event of ominous international significance.

In some not-clearly-specified way New Dealers felt the preservation of democracy in Europe was dependent upon America's success in dealing with the economic and social problems at home. Though it was not yet known what role America might play in a general European war, administration officials believed that at least as an example to nations attracted to fascist or communist ideologies America must prove that a liberal democracy was capable of solving the economic crisis and bringing about social justice for its citizens. Roosevelt's partisans thus gave expression once again to the traditional self-image of America as city on a hill--to the pious hope that the mere preservation of a prosperous free democracy in America might cause the beleaguered forces of liberalism in Europe to look and take heart, thereby gaining the strength to preserve their own liberties. New Dealers also knew that only a reinvigorated economy could produce reserves of material resources upon which European democracies might one day need to draw, but the memory of America's involvement in World War I was still too fresh for them openly to discuss such ideas in Washington.

Underlying much of the anxiety about the ominous turn in European affairs was an acknowledgment by many Americans of the sobering possibility that eighteenth century political forms were in fact incapable of dealing with the economic and social problems of a twentieth-century industrial state. The President himself had alluded to this fear in an address delivered September 17, 1937, before it was suspected that the downturn might lead to a major recession. Roosevelt acknowledged that the methods of the "the challengers," communists and fascists alike, had helped their people obtain material benefits. This fact made it essential that America's "constitutional, democratic form of government," take steps to raise the standard of living of its people to satisfactory levels. Only through success in this endeavor "can we insure against internal doubt as to the worthwhileness of our democracy." These concerns had caused the President to conclude that "there is a crisis in American affairs which demands action now, a crisis particularly dangerous because its external and internal difficulties reinforce one another."[11]

Not the least threatening aspect of the Recession from the New Dealers' point of view was the possibility that it might discredit the Administration, preparing the way for political reverses in 1938 and 1940. Marriner S. Eccles underscored this point in a memo he prepared for the President on October 31, which began with the proposal that present conditions threaten to repeat "the vicious deflationary circle of 1929-32."[12]

The sting of an explicit comparison between 1929 and 1937 must have been especially painful for a president who had recently built a presidential campaign on the contention that his election had brought a complete break with both the policies and the economic conditions of the Hoover administration. Again and again during the campaign of 1936 the

American people had been asked if they wanted to return to the conditions of early 1933. The voters seemed to answer that question with a resounding "No." But now Eccles was suggesting that America was in danger of going backwards, and under the banner of the New Deal. To the New Deal community there could be no more chilling prospect.

Treasury officials were equally concerned about the political implications of the Recession. Shortly before Eccles' memo was being prepared in the Federal Reserve, high level discussions in the Treasury department centered on the same problem. As Herman Oliphant, an assistant to Secretary Morgenthau put it:

> We've sat here long enough and taken enough of this stuff in our face to know that the people that are trying to block his [the President's] reforms--they wouldn't be satisfied with anything short of just turning the whole thing back to them and letting them do as they please with it.

"You can't satisfy them," Morgenthau added indignantly.13

The most immediate prospect for "turning the whole thing back to them" lay in congressional elections to be held just a year from the onset of the Recession. The court reform and executive reorganization issues had already demonstrated that Roosevelt's old magic with congress, even among those elected under his aegis, might be fading. A major recession at this time would further diminish the advantage young Democratic congressmen might have gained from identifying with the President. At the same time, it would strengthen the hopes and resolves of outspoken conservatives in the Democratic as well as the Republican parties. It would damage the President's prospects of working effectively with the present Congress and pave the way for further additions in the 1938 elections to what was already an incipient anti-New Deal coalition.14

The comments of both Oliphant and Eccles suggest how closely the aims of political power and pursuance of social reform in America were identified in the minds of New Dealers. Eccles feared the repercussions of continued recession "on our whole social, political and economic structure." Oliphant felt the Recession was the product of a deliberate effort to "block" the President's reforms. As they saw it, the only alternative to the New Deal would be a retrenchment on reform and the turning of power "back" to men who would use the federal government to further their own interests. They knew that the preservation of a congressional majority sympathetic to the President's programs was essential to a preservation of their reforms. The Recession threatened the well-being of Americans through the immediate consequence of fewer jobs and increased human needs. But the possibility that the Recession might bring again to power men whose philosophy did not allow government to minister to such emergency needs extended the nature and the scope of the crisis.

There was, however, a political question implicit in the recession crisis larger than the control of congress. No one knew whether the President would run for a third term. Few of his partisans saw a viable successor. The 1940 elections promised to be critical in determining whether men sympathetic to the New Deal would continue to have power in the executive branch of government. Many feared the Recession would so discredit the New Deal that even FDR himself might not be able to win in 1940. For example, Harold L. Ickes, Secretary of the Interior was asked in November 1937 for his views on politics in America in the next twenty years. Ickes replied that "at that time the bough would be inclined as the twig is bent in 1940," an opinion he said the President had expressed to him two and one-half years before.

Ickes' thoughts as recorded in his diary on November 21, 1937, are representative of a widespread feeling that the fate of the New Deal values in America might depend on the elections of 1940. "I think that the present business situation is part of the fight for control that lies in the immediate future,"he wrote. "It is conceivable that in the near future we might have a return to prosperity if the President should forego, or practically so, all of his social and economic program." Ickes concluded, however, that even the President's capitulation would not bring lasting gains. If FDR were to retreat in his social and economic program, "it would be only a few years to a much greater economic crash which would result in social revolution."[15]

In this passage Ickes defined the perplexing situation which confronted the President in attempting to secure both recovery and reform. Business leaders claimed that the economy would fail if the President did not roll back his reforms. And New Dealers were convinced that business would ultimately fail if the President did roll them back. Before 1937 New Dealers had doggedly pursued their reforms, pointing to recovery as proof that businessmen's fears were unfounded. The Recession threatened this course of action in two fundamental ways. It provided plausible evidence that there might be some truth in the businessmen's contentions. And it raised the possibility that even if Roosevelt wished to continue reform he would not have the political power to do so, or to designate a successor who would be able to do so. Either way, as New Dealers saw it, the American people would lose. In their view, the Recession paved the way for a future return to power in congress, the presidency, or both, of representatives of big business-- men who had little concern for social justice and human values.

Confronted by the Recession, then, New Dealers were brought to assume a more thoroughgoing defensive posture than they had hitherto found necessary. Looking outward in the effort to identify their enemies, they fixed upon the drama of competing nations in Europe and distilled it into ideological abstractions which were then used in defining the domestic scene. According to Morgenthau, the President on November 8, 1937 said that "in his conferences with the bankers at Hyde Park he had discovered that many of them would really like to see the United States a Fascist nation, with the expectation that they would be in control."[16] Few in America possessed a clear and consistent definition of fascism. To Roosevelt and his party at the time the essential feature was control of government by major financial and industrial concerns. Their opponents saw the defining characteristics to be unchecked executive power maintained by demagogic appeal to the masses. Both groups showed the extreme suspicion which emerges when ideological opponents perceive that momentous decisions are hanging in the balance. It seemed that the course of this recession might determine the fates of men at home and abroad for generations to come.

The issues ultimately reduced themselves to a necessary choice between two abstract concepts, "liberty" and "prosperity". Disturbingly, the new dictatorships seemed to rest their power upon a willingness of their peoples to exchange liberty for prosperity. If prosperity were not insured at home, Americans might one day make the same choice. Roosevelt and his opponents set different limits to the meanings of the two ideals; they disagreed on how they were to be achieved and sustained; but both parties affirmed that these ideals had always been central to the promise of American life and as such must be preserved. The real questions was whether America, which had so long offered an abundance of both, would find a means of preserving the two intact. It was impossible, in the face of renewed recession, to answer the question in the affirmative without doubt and hesitation. But events in Europe underlined the compelling need for America, if she would preserve her historic identity, to find that affirmation. New Dealers were convinced that the answer must lie somewhere within their own experience. The circumstances forced them to look inward, asking themselves what they had done wrong as well as what they had done right. Though external threats abroad and at home had aggravated the crisis brought by the Recession, it seemed in the final analysis that a resolution could be found only through a penetrating search within.

Yale Law Professor Thurman Arnold's 1935 book, Symbols of Government, had dealt at length with precisely the problems that the Recession precipitated within the New Deal community. On the surface the book was an effort to analyze the role of the law in American political, social, and intellectual life with the same irreverent distance Thorstein Veblen had employed in his examinations of American economic institutions. But the book in addition was an apology for the New Deal--specifically an explanation of why the New Deal had no underlying philosophy to provide guiding principles for its policies. The problem, as he saw it, was that the collapse of America's economic system caused men, who during flush times had no need to correlate their behavior and their ideals, to refer back to those ideals in the effort to discover what might have gone wrong. The ideals thus took on new significance precisely at a time when men needed to free themselves from old dogma in order to deal effectively with pressing practical problems. Such "symbols of government" as budget balancing, rugged individualism and the Constitution became important at the worst possible time, confusing and confounding those who were attempting to evolve a new set of symbols appropriate to changed conditions and changing needs. As Arnold put it:

> When, . . . institutions fail to exercise the social
> control which we expect of them, and we rely on
> principles to tell us how to fill the gaps, both our
> actions and our principles appear chaotic and con-
> fused. Yet we can never completely escape trying to
> follow our symbols of government, even though we
> know they are leading us in all directions at
> once.[17]

In Arnold's view, the apparent chaotic nature of New Deal policies should not cause alarm. Such apparent chaos was a necessary part of evolving a new and more useful set of "symbols of government."

Arnold was attempting to account for ideological problems confronting Americans in general during the mid-1930's. He wrote his book before the Recession of 1937 struck. The dynamic he described, however, is almost precisely what happened within the New Deal between the fall of 1937 and the spring of 1939. By 1937 New Dealers had evolved their own set of "symbols"--ideas they passed among themselves as a common part of their interpretation of the mission of the New Deal in America. "Wall Street," "big business," and "trickle-down spending" became as important a set of symbols for them as did "That Man," "confiscatory taxes," and "WPA" for their opponents.

Implicit in the set of New Deal symbols was what amounted almost to a philosophy of American history. Roosevelt's followers saw in the nation's past a recurrent process wherein the powerful and wealthy constantly sought to establish themselves in the seats of power so they might use the prerogatives of government for their own aggrandizement. Usually successful and dominant, they occasionally had been dislodged by great champions of the "little man"--such as Jefferson, Jackson, or Wilson. But in each earlier case the wealthy and selfish had been successful in moving back into power after a comparatively short period of government in the interest of the people. The New Deal had entered American history in its most critical moment--a time when government by and for the rich had collapsed under its own excesses and brought the nation to a standstill. What dramatist could imagine a more brilliant scene than Roosevelt's assumption of power in March 1933? The inaugural address, the banking crisis, the fireside chats, the hundred days of recovery and reform legislation, all signaled the beginning of a new era, when men in Washington would concern themselves with the needs of all the people in a humane and moral climate. By 1937 New Dealers were convinced that they had built a sound recovery, necessary social re- forms, and a political base which would assure that the privileged would not be able again to put government to their own uses.

Until 1937, New Dealers, despite their vision of America's past, had felt no compelling need to articulate clearly their program or to root it firmly in that past. Roosevelt's call had been to break with tradition, to offer Americans a New Deal, to experiment boldly and persistently in attempting to solve the nation's social and economic difficulties. Most of Roosevelt's followers took him at his word. They constructed their definition of the New Deal largely from qualities opposite to those they saw in Hoover's presidency. The New Deal was what Hoover Republicanism was not. Where Hoover favored big business, the New Deal favored the little man. Where Hoover bullied the poor with tanks and soldiers, the New Deal offered them food and jobs. Where Hoover failed to act, the New Deal was restless with activity. And most fundamental of all, where Hoover brought deepening depression, the New Deal brought recovery. "Early in 1933", Morgenthau stated in a passage common to hundreds of speeches by Roosevelt and his partisans, "after three years of progressive deterioration, our whole economic mechanism was demoralized. . . . Today the situation is greatly changed."[18]

The New Deal community, like Morgenthau, came to see March 1933 as the beginning of all that was good or important in American history. All past was prelude--all future extension of the present. So long as recovery continued the New Deal seemed a whole unto itself--past, present, and future found there a definition. Though Federal budgets were not yet balanced and social equity not yet extended to all, the continued recovery offered assurance that one day these things would be accomplished. If questions, doubts or failures arose they could quickly be swept under the rug of continued recovery or attributed to the selfish action of those fighting the President's will. As Arnold observed, "The very success of the institution prevents anyone questioning its underlying theory."[19]

The President himself had encouraged the tendency to tie the New Deal identity to continued recovery. During the 1936 campaign, FDR frequently contrasted the paralysis of March 1933 with the subsequent New Deal progress. He repeatedly attributed the paralysis to Hoover's inaction and the recovery to his own policies. He thus used his enormous prestige and popularity to teach the American people that recessions will respond if government officials take proper corrective measures. The President, in bringing home this point, had apparently not considered what the important lesson, once taught, might suggest to Americans if the recovery he had brought should falter.

Once Americans had learned that proper government action brings recovery they could readily be persuaded that depressions might be a consequence of improper government action. In November 1937, the weekly reports of industrial production, each dropping below those of the previous week, were relentless reminders of the possibility that some aspect of past New Deal policy had been harmful to the economy. Whatever the causes, they urged the necessity of early government action to avert intolerable consequences. The President's close friend and confidant, Felix Frankfurter, spoke for many New Dealers when he urged FDR to action in a letter of November 10. "Whenever, since March 4, 1933, the public mind has been confused," he wrote, "you alone had the power to give it composure and coherence." He pointed out that the nation was again entering a period when "the so-called leaders of business and finance . . . are trying to infect the general public with their own panicky and short-sighted disquietude." As in the past, Frankfurter told his friend, the great body of Americans were looking to FDR for assurance.

> They would be glad to hear . . . at firsthand and
> from your own lips that you are not panicky, that
> you know better than any of the croakers that there
> are difficulties and what they are, that nobody is
> more concerned to do what can be done towards
> remedying difficulties, that you have a well-defined
> direction toward objectives to which you will adhere

because they are the objectives of national well
being.

In Frankfurter's opinion, the Recession made it "essential" that the
President fill the atmosphere with his "robust energy and contagious
confidence in the working out of our difficulties through sensible
effort in the general direction in which you have been going."[20]
    In this letter, Frankfurter expressed perfectly the thoughts
troubling New Dealers as the Recession became apparent. The letter
really offered more than just an admonition to action. Behind his brave
advice Frankfurter sought assurances not only for the public, but for
himself, and perhaps for the President as well. The Recession, after
all, could not so easily be laid at the feet of the President's enemies.
It was just possible that the President was panicky, that he did not
know what was wrong, and that he had no well-defined direction, no clear
objectives towards which to move. This was certainly Morgenthau's
impression when he saw FDR just two days before Frankfurter wrote his
letter. The President, Morgenthau wrote in his diary that day, is
"fighting like a cornered lion . . . he does not want to be tamed and
still, on the other hand, he does not know where he can put his strength
at this particular juncture to bring about recovery."[21] With
devastating effect the Recession had brought down the sense of mastery--
of "composure and coherence"--which had once characterized the New Deal.
Eccles spoke for them all when he told Morgenthau on November 4,
"Nothing is more important than this [recession] situation . . . I mean
it's here, and there isn't anything else, there's just nothing--I mean--
as far as I'm concerned, I don't think that we could possibly spend our
time to any better advantage no matter how much it takes, than
considering immediately just what the present problem is."[22]
    The Recession of 1937, then, broke the lull of self-confident
assurance the slow, steady pace of recovery had brought. It cut the New
Deal adrift and sent the President's top advisors scurrying in search of
new and better moorings. Secure ties to the American past and clear
visions of her future were needed. The search was confused by the need
each felt to find an explanation of the Recession and a proposed remedy
which would not indict his own past policies or the general policies of
the Administration. Self-conscious introspection characterized an
administration which until that time had possessed an abundance of smug
self-confidence. This introspection took place in an atmosphere where
"both actions and principles" appeared "chaotic and confused." New
Dealers could not escape trying to follow their symbols of government,
even though those symbols were leading "in all directions at once."
    From all this activity an underlying unity of purpose emerged.
Indeed, the President's lieutenants were searching for more than just a

policy to counter the Recession. The word they used again and again was "program"--a concept which included far more than just a proposal to increase government spending or to balance the budget. Whatever action was taken, it must be part of an overall definition of just what the New Deal had been and where it was going. Moreover, it must promise consistent, coherent solutions to a broad range of problems confronting the economy. Many New Dealers hoped there would be no more piecemeal and haphazard congeries of policies but that all would be subsumed under a program with a clearly stated underlying philosophy. As Morgenthau prepared for a November 1937 speech before the Academy of Political Science he told his aides he wanted to explain

> that I know what I'm talking about, and know where I'm going. Now if they ask me today, I don't know-- I don't know what the President's done. He doesn't know, because nobody's ever laid this out for him . . .

> But what I am trying to get him to do is to lay out a program for the next three years that he is in. . . . One of the real reasons that people in this country are so frightened is that they don't know. They don't know where we're going.[23]

Harold L. Ickes described a cabinet meeting of November 5 as being "different from those earliest ones," in 1933. "Then the President had pretty well thought out his program. Now it is clear that he is greatly disturbed over the business and economic situation and doesn't know quite which way to turn."[24] Treasury officials early in 1938 hoped with many others that the Administration would counter the Recession with "a program rather than the adoption of unrelated and sporadic measures."[25]

The internal crisis the Recession had precipitated thus made many New Dealers sense the need of an articulated coherent New Deal program. If old symbols could not provide a key to understanding and dispelling the present distress then new symbols must and would be found. Henry Morgenthau, Jr. and Marriner S. Eccles were the most important of those advisors who took upon themselves the task of providing the President a way out of the recession crisis. Morgenthau was at the peak of his influence as an advisor on economic policy at the time the Recession struck. Drawing from a heritage he shared with Roosevelt, he was the first to confront the problem of reconciling the promise of a balanced budget--a symbol from the New Deal past--with the spending policies made necessary by past and present exigencies.

CHAPTER TWO

**MORGENTHAU AND THE FEDERAL BUDGET—
"THE BASE OF THE WHOLE RECOVERY PLAN"**

MORGENTHAU AND ROOSEVELT

Accounts by contemporaries suggest that of all Roosevelt's close advisors Henry Morgenthau, Jr. was least likely to hold out against an opposing tide of New Deal opinion on important policy questions. Harold Ickes was among those who felt that Morgenthau had few firm opinions of his own and was openly obsequious in the presence of Roosevelt. On November 15, 1934 Morgenthau came to a White House conference attended by the President, Harry Hopkins, and Harold Ickes, armed with reports designed to discourage plans for a major public works program. After presenting a pessimistic financial picture, he produced with considerable flourish a further statement prepared for him by the eminent Chicago economist, Jacob Viner, indicating, according to Ickes, that "what he was prepared to offer would cut all the ground from under the proposed public works program for the next few years." The intended moment of truth turned into a complete rout when the President and Ickes broke into laughter at what Ickes called in his diary a "ridiculous" and "absurd" argument. Louis Howe then entered the room and the President insisted, over Morgenthau's protest, that the statement be read to the end so Howe might share in the merriment. Ickes observed that the Viner argument "had made no impression at all on the President . . . although Morgenthau had thought it perfectly devastating." When Roosevelt's reaction became clear to Morgenthau, however, he "swung clear around. He was strongly in favor of the public works program and was willing to do anything he could to put it in effect." The experience convinced Ickes that Morgenthau "was willing to waive his own opinions and fall in with the President's suggestions even, although [sic] he did not agree with them."[1]

Though Ickes was well known for a lack of generosity in his opinions of Washington peers, such experiences were not uncommon with Morgenthau. The Secretary, well-supplied with recommendations from his experts, comes prepared for final battle. Ill-equipped to defend the arguments his staff has prepared, he is ineffective in countering the President's attack upon his position. So confronted, he comes quickly to the President's side--never having given his opinions the benefit of sound defense. Certainly such demonstrations did not inspire the observer to confidence.

Ickes was not alone in concluding from such demeanor that the Secretary's abilities were inadequate for the resolute and independent-minded discharge of the responsibilities of his high office. Paul W. Ward wrote in The Nation that Morgenthau, the "most loyal Cabinet member" had "no fixed convictions or anything beyond a resolve to keep his department honest as well as efficient" and that consequently his public role had been reduced "to that of a White House errand boy."[2] Impressions similar to Ward's were not uncommon in press commentary on the Secretary.

However, Morgenthau was by no means the obsequious bumbler that such accounts seem to suggest. Transcripts of Treasury staff meetings make it clear that when surrounded by his trusted subordinates the Secretary frequently presented his views with sound, determined arguments, parried effectively when challenged, and launched vigorous counter-attacks against those opposing his views. His unimpressive manner on other occasions seems to have been primarily a product of a deep-seated lack of confidence in his own abilities. It appears that Morgenthau was placed under intense emotional pressure when he felt his

18

performance was being judged by others important to him. In such situations he often was unnerved to the point that his fears of disapproval provided their own justification. He did not work well under pressure.

Seeing Morgenthau perform only under the anxiety which their presence created, colleagues and reporters were inclined to discount his abilities. The President, who for long periods favored the Secretary with a relationship closer than that extended to his other advisors, undoubtedly had a more accurate understanding of Morgenthau's competence. Nevertheless, one suspects that the close association of the two men--to some an annoyance and a mystery--was as much a product of a peculiar and particular compatibility of personality as it was of Presidential trust in the Secretary's advice on matters of policy.3

The two had been neighbors in Dutchess County, New York since shortly after Morgenthau had purchased a farm there in 1913. Over the years, the families had become close to the point of intimacy. Morgenthau's candid record of his attitudes and activities throughout his public career, however, suggests that his affinity to the President was more than simple friendship. The relationship was both strengthened and complicated by traits of personality formed early in his life.[4]

The youth of Henry Morgenthau, Jr. was beset by personal anxieties which the financial ease assured by his father's wealth could not dispel. Born May 11, 1891, young Henry was the long-awaited scion of a family dominated by a confident, assertive father. By the time of his son's birth the senior Morgenthau had built a solid foundation of family wealth through extensive investments in New York real estate. Both father and mother, Josephine Sykes Morgenthau, engaged in social causes, lending their support to the Henry Street Settlement, the Bronx House, and the improvement of fire safety conditions in the poorer areas of the city. The elder Morgenthau was also an active supporter of the Ethical Culture Church, which provided an outlet for his religious and ethical interests sufficiently ecumenical to imply no disrespect for the traditions of his German-Jewish ancestors.

Young Henry had two older sisters, and his birth was to be followed by that of yet a third. Thus, a particularly heavy burden of parental and especially paternal expectations came to rest upon the only son, a son who bore his father's name. However, Henry, Jr. was not suited in talent or temperament to become the hard-driving master of family empire which his father wanted him to be. He was shy where his father had been assertive. He was delicate in health where his father had been robust. He was uninterested in scrambling for academic or social prominence. He adored his father, yet seemed profoundly intimidated by him. In later years he recalled that "mother felt weak when father walked into the room. He was electric, a bundle of nerves and ambition." It is highly likely that in this, as in so many other instances, Morgenthau was projecting--enjoying the luxury of candidly expressing his own feelings by attributing them to others. The historian John Morton Blum relates that Josephine Morgenthau, a devotee of opera, wanted young Henry to cultivate his fine singing voice. Her husband, however, considered singing "sissy", and encouraged him instead to learn to play the cello. The incident is typical. As Henry, Jr.'s wife was later to recall, "his father tried to regulate his life and to dominate his thoughts--he kept him too much with him and away from companions his own age."[5]

Morgenthau did poorly at Phillips Exeter, finding it necessary to supplement his preparation at Sachs Collegiate Institute in New York City with private tutoring before he was admitted to Cornell in 1909. His father encouraged him to study architecture because of its possible relation to real estate development. Henry, Jr. soon found that he was not interested in architecture, and after three semesters he left college to try his hand at other ventures. He worked as a timekeeper with a construction company, as a machinist with a typewriter company, and as a bank teller. In all of these enterprises the influence of his father was strongly evident, all three being with businesses in which his father had considerable involvement. Even Morgenthau's subsequent sojourn at the Henry Street Settlement, an experience which had considerable impact on him, was undoubtedly a consequence of his father's connections and interest in the project.

In 1911, at the age of 20, Morgenthau went to Texas to convalesce from typhoid fever. His exposure to farm and ranch life in Texas was to be of great importance. Upon returning he announced to his father that he had decided to become a farmer, a gesture which clearly expressed the strength of his desire to begin an independent and autonomous life. After a brief return to Cornell as an agriculture major, followed by a trip with a government agriculture expert to observe farming practices from New York to California, he purchased several hundred acres, close to home, in the Hudson River Valley. In explaining his decision Henry recalled of his father that, "He was crazy to have me in business with him. He would say to my poor mother, 'Josy, you can have the girls, let me have the boy.' In a desperate move to get out from under him I moved to the country."[6] In 1913 at the age of twenty-two, Morgenthau took up farming and sought during the next decade-and-a-half amidst apple orchards and cattle imported from the West, to become his own man.

In April 1916 Morgenthau married Eleanor Fatman, a charming and intelligent Vassar graduate of almost precisely the same social background. The two had been delivered by the same doctor, played together in Central Park as children, and had attended the same primary school in New York City. Morgenthau and his wife were devoted to the three children born to their marriage enjoying a close and affectionate relationship with young Henry, Robert, and Joan.

Overseeing the smallest details of his extensive farming operations with indefatigable energy, Morgenthau soon developed a reputation as a progressive, successful agriculturalist. He became an active advocate of farmers' cooperatives and developed programs for dealing with French agricultural problems during the war. In 1922 he began publishing the American Agriculturalist, which soon became a leading farmers' journal in New York State.

Morgenthau was also active in politics. Through his father, he became acquainted with leading figures of the Democratic party, including Woodrow Wilson. The senior Morgenthau was finance committee chairman for the Democratic National Committee in 1912 and again in 1916, and served as ambassador to Turkey during the war. Henry, Jr. represented his father at the 1914 Democratic State Conference in Saratoga, New York, where he tried, without success, to encourage support for a progressive ticket. Though devoted to his farm, he could hardly escape involvement in the local and national political concerns of progressive Democrats which occupied the bulk of his father's time.

Within two years of moving to Dutchess County, Morgenthau had made the acquaintance of Franklin D. Roosevelt, a long-time resident, nearly ten years his senior. Morgenthau developed a relationship with Roosevelt over the years which had come, by 1928, to exercise an influence upon the younger man nearly as powerful as that of the senior Henry Morgenthau. It was as if Morgenthau, troubled by a lingering sense that he had not fulfilled his father's expectations, chose to see in FDR an alternate father--an older man who would cheerfully and unreservedly accept him as he was.

The two met in 1915 at Hyde Park. On that occasion, Roosevelt, already prominent in national as well as local politics, tried unsuccessfully to persuade Morgenthau to run for sheriff. Later, while in Europe, he instructed his secretary Louis Howe to inquire after Morgenthau. "I was apparently solicitous about you," the President later commented, "but I do not know why."[7] Sharing a common interest in building rural strength in the Democratic party to counter New York City control, the two men found frequent occasion for meetings which deepened their friendship. Morgenthau visited Roosevelt often during the latter's convalescence from poliomyletis.

In 1928, when Roosevelt was elected Governor of New York, Morgenthau became a regular consultant to his friend on agricultural matters in the State. In 1930, the triumphantly re-elected Governor appointed his friend State Conservation Commissioner, and Morgenthau began a long career as official advisor and confidant to Roosevelt. After the appointment Eleanor Morgenthau sent Roosevelt a remarkably insightful letter--almost prescient in light of the relationship which developed between the two men. "Henry always goes about his work with a real feeling of consecration," she wrote, "but the fact that he is working under you and for you, fills him with . . . enthusiasm . . . The part which pleases me the most is that while you are moving on in your own work . . .. It also gives Henry a chance to grow, so that your friendship can continue to be cemented by a community of interest as well as by the deep affection with which he holds you."8

When Roosevelt was elected to the presidency, Morgenthau's interest in agriculture and his successful publishing of the American Agriculturalist had caused him to hope that he would be appointed Secretary of Agriculture. His disappointment at being passed over in favor of a midwestern Progressive, Henry A. Wallace, did not prevent him, however, from enthusiastically accepting his assignment as head of the Federal Farm Board. Morgenthau planned and carried out the transmutation of the Hoover agency into the Farm Credit Administration, a new unit designed to consolidate responsibility in agricultural matters that had previously been divided among several different departments of the Government. He served successfully in this capacity until November 13, 1933 when the President asked him to become acting secretary of the treasury to replace the ailing William Woodin. When it became clear in January that Woodin would not be able to return to his official duties, Morgenthau was made secretary. He served in that position until June 1945, when two months after the President's death, he resigned his office and ended his public career. From the time he had chosen to purchase a farm in Dutchess County in 1913 his most conspicuous successes had been products of his friendship with FDR. The record of his service to Roosevelt suggests that from their relationship he gained the filial satisfactions denied him as a youth.

Morgenthau's greatest rewards came from pleasing FDR and his unhappiest moments came when he felt Roosevelt was not appreciative of his efforts. He became depressed when he felt Roosevelt was not seeking or was ignoring his advice. He seemed never so elated as when he felt he had done needed service for "the boss." When his staff presented him with an idea which he especially liked, he occasionally indicated his excited approval with the peculiar and suggestive exclamation, "That's Papa!" Morgenthau's sense of accomplishment and well-being were inextricably connected with his assessment of the level of Roosevelt's esteem for him. The great object of his public career was to serve Franklin D. Roosevelt well and faithfully.9

Morgenthau's apparent need for an approving father figure found a complement in Roosevelt's oft-noted tendency to assume a father role in his dealings with top members of his administration.10 Secretary of Labor Frances Perkins recalled, for example, Roosevelt's impatience with rumors that he was not well enough to be a candidate in 1944. "Apparently," he said, "Papa has to tell them." Frequently after press conferences he would ask his staff, "How did Papa do?" Roosevelt's fathering tendency seems to have provided an ideal reciprocal for Morgenthau.

Another aspect of Morgenthau's personality relevant to the Recession crisis was his deep compassion for the poor and underprivileged. Perhaps his early insecurity made him especially sensitive to the suffering of others. Whatever the reasons, he exhibited throughout his public career the impulsive humanitarianism common among the President's close advisors. One illustrative incident occurred in October 1937 as staff members began to report the onset of a possible recession. The Secretary interrupted a report by his aide Steve Gibbons on growing unemployment and the resulting privation. "Listen, Steve," Morgenthau interjected,

> there's no use giving me this stuff. I'll let George [Haas] read it. . . . Somebody in this town has got to keep his feet on the ground, and getting isolated cases of hard luck stories just doesn't help me. . . . And I just--if you don't mind, the personal individual cases--it just upsets you. . . . It doesn't do me one iota of good, and it only upsets me.[11]

During the ensuing weeks he spoke bravely to his staff of the importance of going about their tasks "quietly and calmly" and trying to back up their conclusions "with facts, and not all this emotional stuff." Yet the record reveals that Morgenthau was offering his staff advice that could be more appropriately directed to himself. Morgenthau is often seen, as the economic reports became more ominous, excitedly urging a calm staff not to become excited.

Not until November 3rd of 1937 did Morgenthau come to the conclusion that the indices pointed unmistakably toward a renewal of the Depression. That night he wrote the President a letter expressing his concern. "I hardly need tell you," he concluded, "that the first to feel another depression will be the 1/3 undernourished, etc. This cruel process has already begun. Mr. President, what can we do to stop it?"[12] The Secretary's first impulse, upon concluding that another depression threatened, was to see the event in terms of the human suffering it would bring. Morgenthau's own comfortable material circumstances did not limit his sensitivity to the miseries which privation brought to others.

Also important to the recession crisis was Morgenthau's scrupulous sense of the need for honesty and morality in the conduct of governmental affairs. Morgenthau's effort to save for the public record virtually every document that passed through the Treasury during his tenure, even to verbatim transcripts of phone calls and departmental meetings, seems significant. It suggests an almost compulsive desire to assure that the purity of his public life would one day be revealed through the exacting scrutiny of biographers and historians. As he put it in his mandate to John Morton Blum who edited the diaries for publication, he wanted a historian "to tell the whole story. I am willing to let the chips fall where they may."13

When Roosevelt, as Governor, had appointed Morgenthau Conservation Commissioner he recommended that Morgenthau try to mend fences with Tammany Hall. Instructed to shake hands with the head of the organization, Morgenthau later commented that "this was very repulsive to me, but FDR was insistent."14 Strongly opposing the appointment of less than competent persons to public office for political reasons, he wrote in his diary that "I made up my mind that I am not going to aid the politicians, and I am going to tell them politely, but firmly that I cannot accept their candidates. I believe in the long run that they will respect me for it."15

Morgenthau's insistence that his own public life be characterized by transparent honesty and uncompromised candor carried over into his conduct of Treasury business as well as into his broader designs for the whole New Deal. Indeed, at times his devotion to the President seemed to find expression in a wish to nudge his friend into strict adherence to the Secretary's own sense of moral rectitude. Roosevelt once gave Morgenthau a photograph of the two of them seated together in an automobile. The President signed it, "To Henry, from one of two of a kind."16 In some situations it seemed that Morgenthau wished to insure the literacy of the inscription by urging the President to comply with his own ideal of right conduct in public affairs.

Morgenthau's personality was more important in shaping his response to the Recession crisis than were the ideas of economists advising him or his awareness of the political exigencies raised by the Recession. His first response was a tender humanitarian concern--an empathy for the suffering of others so strong that he was visibly upset by the mere recounting of problems of the poor. His sense of moral rectitude caused him, nevertheless, to urge upon Roosevelt a policy which would restrict the amount of funds available for relief. He recommended this policy because it possessed the virtue of being honorable--redeeming promises the President had long made to the American people. The Secretary's devotion to Roosevelt went well beyond that which a close friendship normally builds. But convinced that his friend was being tempted toward policies which would defer indefinitely the redemption of a long standing and fundamental New Deal promise, he persisted in his advocacy of a balanced budget.

To Him from me two of a kind

Franklin Roosevelt

Morgenthau and the President

It may seem paradoxical to the mind nurtured in post-New Deal orientations of political, social, and economic ideology in America that Morgenthau, the humanitarian, should have become the New Deal's most persistent advocate of a balanced budget. Since Roosevelt's presidency many Americans have come to assume that budgetary restraint is necessarily a correlative of moral insensitivity and social irresponsibility. Few would have subscribed to this point of view in 1937. It was still common to see government finances as problems of proper administrative procedure, bearing little necessary relationship to social policy. The eventual widespread diffusion of the idea that budgetary policy is really in effect social policy was one of the significant consequences of the New Deal response to the events of 1937-38. Morgenthau's initial reaction to the Recession was typical of an older New Deal—a New Deal that responded with impulsive sympathy and did not choose ameliorative policies on the basis of their ideological consistency or purity. But the forces brought into play by the Recession were working upon Morgenthau as they were working on other New Dealers, causing him, with others, to be more and more uneasy with the seeing incoherence and lack of ideological underpinning which characterized past New Deal measures.

The generation of progressive Americans to which Morgenthau and most New Dealers belonged had witnessed the establishing of a federal budgeting system a scant two decades earlier. The discussion leading to that estabishment had attached to the budget a set of associations which entered deeply into the policy debate raised by the recession crisis.

THE BUDGETARY REFORM MOVEMENT IN AMERICA

During the decade 1910-1920, American politicians hotly debated whether and how the government should rationalize the management of its fiscal accounts. Progressive reformers, Woodrow Wilson among them, urged that a federal budgeting system be established. Morgenthau's friend, then Assistant Secretary of the Navy, Franklin D. Roosevelt, spoke publicly of the need to include budgetary reform with other recommendations he made for improving governmental machinery. In 1922 Roosevelt planned a book on governmental reform, titling one chapter, "The Crying Need of a National Budget."[17] Budget reform became an issue in New York State politics, particularly between 1910 and 1915. In 1915, the year after Morgenthau participated in the state Democratic conference at Saratoga, a state budgeting system was incorporated into proposed constitutional reforms, only to be rejected by the voters in November, partly because of intense opposition by Tammany leaders.[18] Through the activities of progressive Democrats, with whom he identified, and through his friend, Roosevelt, Morgenthau had ample opportunity to follow and become involved in the debate over budget reform.

Important public figures had advocated a systematic keeping of government accounts since early in the Republic. The initial effort of Alexander Hamilton to establish a regular government accounting procedure under the executive had failed--victim of congressional jealousy, partisan politics, and public apathy. During the nineteenth century, various methods of keeping government accounts were employed, but the responsible agencies were always within congress, either in a single committee or divided among committees. The House Ways and Means Committee assumed major responsibility for fiscal accounts until 1865. In that year a Committee on Appropriations was created, exercising considerable power until 1885, when its duties were divided among several committees, apparently as a rebuke to the chairman, Samuel J. Randall. Responsibility for governmental receipts and expenditures continued to be relatively decentralized and subject to the intrigues of congressional politics well into the twentieth century.[19]

Two obstacles delayed the reform of federal accounting procedures. During most of the nineteenth century the level of national concern about the issue was so low that congress had little inducement to legislate in the matter. The nineteenth century experience with financing the federal government taught Americans that growing prosperity always brought sufficient revenues to amortize whatever temporary indebtedness a war or depression might necessitate. Discussion of fiscal problems was as likely to center upon how to deal with embarrassing surpluses as upon how to repay indebtedness. In the 112 peacetime years before World War I a surplus was reported for 82 years. Deficits, recorded for 30 years during this period, tended to be much smaller than surpluses in proportion to total expenditures. In only six years did the deficit amount to more than one-fourth of expenditures.[20]

Equally important in delaying budget reform was the fact that attempts inevitably foundered on a constitutional issue unrelated to the general desirability of a budgeting system--the question of separation of powers. Hamilton's argument that the president should have a good deal of latitude in determining the specific uses of funds fell victim to those same forces which helped kill the Federalist party. The idea that the executive should prepare a master plan for the allocation of all public funds did not again gain currency until the early decades of the twentieth century. Lacking a ready gauge of the annual surplus or deficit, and confident that accounts would always balance in the long run, Americans were not inclined to worry about the system of federal finance. Morgenthau's generation was the first to see the balancing of the federal budget as a critical national issue.

Because the Treasury was enjoying surpluses when the reform movement began, advocates of a national budgeting system argued that blessings far more significant and pervasive than fiscal solvency would result from the reform. For a full decade they contended that a national budget would open the way to a thorough overhauling of the American governmental process. One prominent spokesman for the movement, W.F. Willougby, assured the public that "the movement for the adoption of budgetary systems by our governing bodies is an integral and essential part of the whole greater movement for the accomplishment of governmental reforms generally."21 Congressman Henry Temple of Pennsylvania asked Franklin D. Roosevelt during House hearings on budget reform in 1920 if one of the benefits would not be to "throw light on the necessity of the . . . complete reorganization of the United States?" Without hesitation the Assistant Secretary of the Navy affirmed "I go just as far as that."22 A budgeting system, Roosevelt said, would be the "opening wedge" for accomplishing needed changes in government operations. He asserted that in twenty years men would look back upon "this period of running the government as the dark ages, there are going to be so many changes. . . . The next great step," he maintained, "is to put the Government on a business basis."23

Budget advocates emphasized that full disclosure of public accounts would make government more open, more honest, and more democratic. A properly prepared budget, wrote Willoughby, "at once serves to make known past operations, present conditions, and future proposals, definitely locates responsibility and furnishes the means of control." It would "automatically . . . result in better administration or at least make it possible for all interested parties to determine, without the necessity for special investigations, whether affairs were being efficiently and economically administered or the reverse."24 Speaking of a proposed budgeting system for New York State, Louis Marshall of the New York Times wrote in 1915 that "if this fiscal plan is adopted, then the public will know who is responsible for any abuse which may arise... The radiant light of publicity will henceforth illumine our State finances, which have hitherto been shrouded in darkness."25 The arguments of the reformers were admirably suited to appeal to men who felt, as did Morgenthau, that an open, honest government was ipso facto a well-run government, firmly under popular control.

Arthur E. Buck and Frederick A. Cleveland, authors of a major document in the budget reform movement, were among those who stressed the idea that a budget would assure the success of the general reform movement. In the initial chapters of their book, The Budget and Responsible Government (1920), they discussed in detail the institutions and traits of the national character necessary to insure popular control of government, explaining how American government had degenerated from original Jeffersonian principles and practice in this regard. Lacking institutions which would guarantee popular control, American government had been captured by "bosses," irresponsible, self-serving political parties, and elitist do-gooders. The proliferation of social ills and unrest had been the inevitable consequence. Budget reform, the authors asserted, would eliminate the entire chain of mismanagement and abuse.[26]

It is significant, however, that former President William Howard Taft, in writing an introduction to the Cleveland and Buck volume in 1920, chose to emphasize the economies a budget would assure over the promise of democratic reform. By 1920 advocates of budget reform still expected general benefits from their proposal, but the need to service the debt of World War I had given new significance to the movement, adding a more visible, immediate argument to its case. Budget reform was "critically important," Taft maintained, because "for years we shall have to raise enormous amounts" to service the war debt. Budget reform would permit retiring of the debt without the danger that the "stifling weight of taxation" might interfere with prosperity.[27]

After three years of unprecedented war deficits, followed by the depression of 1920-21, Congress finally created a central budgeting authority under at least some measure of executive control. President Warren G. Harding signed the Budget and Accounting Act into law in June, 1921. A decade of controversy had taught proponents to expect much from their reform; corruption would be eliminated; economy and efficiency would characterize a government previously distended by the largess and the granting of privilege; the people would be fully informed on all activities of their government; a strengthened executive would have the initiative in allocating public funds where they would be most beneficial to the whole population; the tendency of a government assuming greater responsibilities to become overburdened with the weight of new bureaucracies would be checked. The Budget and Accounting Act promised to realize the fondest hopes of progressive reformers.

Henry Morgenthau, Jr., was in his early twenties when the budget reform movement began to attract national attention. In 1914, at the age of twenty-three, he supported progressive Democrats at the state party conference. He was twenty-five when the Democratic party first wrote a proposal for budgetary reform into its platform in 1916, and nearly thirty when the party finally gave its unqualified support to the creation of a budgeting agency under executive control.[28] His father was deeply involved in national political issues during the period, probably bringing the controversy to his son's attention. Even in the unlikely event that the younger Morgenthau had not come in contact with budget reform through his father, there can be little doubt that he was exposed to the main issues through his friend, Franklin D. Roosevelt. Morgenthau, ever alert to cues from Roosevelt, could hardly have escaped being aware of the arguments Roosevelt used in advocating a national budgeting system.

Evidence that the budget reform movement influenced Morgenthau is circumstantial but strong. Given his personality and his associations at an impressionable age, it would be remarkable were he not convinced, with others, that the budget opened the way to cleaner, better government. For those sharing the perspective and experience of Roosevelt and Morgenthau the national budget was not an archaic remnant of social or economic "orthodoxy" but rather a treasured progressive instrument for reforming the governmental process in America.

Also importantly, the budgeting act provided America for the first time with a single annual statement of fiscal accounts for the federal government. The preparation of a budget was a necessary precondition for making generalizations upon the health of the nation from the state of its finances.

During the prosperous twenties most Americans came to see the annual budget statement as a gauge of national well-being. However, in the wake of the Great Depression, surpluses melted into deficits causing an important change in the interpretation government officials placed upon the budget. A balance had earlier indicated health. One would expect that an imbalance would have been seen accordingly as an indicator of illness—an alarm device suggesting that something in the system was out of order and needed correcting. As the depression deepened, however, Hoover, with others, began to see the deficits not as indicators, but as active agents in the complex of forces prolonging economic stagnation. No one had suggested earlier that surpluses caused or prolonged prosperity. But curiously, the deficits of the early 1930's came to be seen as active agents in prolonging the Depression. In proposing that a balancing of the budget would bring recovery public officials seemed close to suggesting that shaking down the mercury of the thermometer would reduce the patient's fever.

During the administration of Herbert Hoover balancing the budget came to be seen by many Americans not just as a goal which would indicate that the desired end, prosperity, had been achieved, but rather as a positive means of helping to achieve that end. Morgenthau was to subscribe to this point of view in 1937. Eccles rejected it from 1930 on, insisting upon every possible occasion that budget deficits were but symptomatic of severe maladjustments in the economy as a whole and would take care of themselves once the real problems were overcome. The budget messages of Hoover and the 1932 campaign speeches of both Hoover and Roosevelt provide insight into how Americans came to see deficits as active agents in prolonging economic stagnation.

FEDERAL BUDGET POLICIES UNDER HOOVER AND ROOSEVELT

President Hoover delivered his first budget message December 4, 1929. The economic decline since the Crash in October had caused him to fear that proposed "additional activities" of the government might jeopardize "either the balanced condition of the Budget or the continuation of the benefits of reduced taxation." He did not, however, indicate whether, if forced to make a choice, he would reduce taxes or balance the budget. His message left the impression that the question was still open and that a balanced budget would not automatically be chosen over the "increase in prosperity of business brought forth by tax reduction."

During the next twelve months it became obvious that the economic decline was cutting into all sectors of the economy with unprecedented severity.[29] Accordingly, in the next annual budget message (prepared for December 1930 delivery), the President explained that because of the depression, receipts would be smaller than anticipated and expenditures considerably larger, changing the budget for fiscal 1931 from a previously expected surplus of $122 million to a deficit of $180 million (the actual figure when accounts were closed after June 30th was $462 million).[30]

The President did not consider this deficit a serious matter. He took pains to point out that it would be less than five percent of the total government expenditures. So small a deficit could readily be met by drawing upon the positive balance in the general fund and, if necessary, "by temporary borrowing by the Treasury." The large surpluses of the past eleven years Hoover explained, were evidence that "we can confidently look forward to the restoration of such surpluses with the general recovery of the economic situation, and thus absorption of any temporary borrowing that may be necessary."[31] The deficit for 1931 was made more palatable by a planned balance for fiscal 1932, based upon a presumed recovery and upon repeal of the tax cuts of 1928. In recommending a "discontinuation of the tax cut" Hoover made one of his earliest references to the balanced budget as a highly desirable national goal: "I am confident, he said, "that the sentiment of the people is in favor of a balanced budget. I am equally confident that the influence on business of having the financial affairs of the Federal Government on a sound basis is of the utmost importance."32

This (1930) budget message was noteworthy for two reasons: first, the President maintained that the proposed deficit was not potentially harmful in its effects upon public confidence, and hence upon expected recovery. He felt a temporary deficit, financed by borrowing if need be was perfectly acceptable during a period of economic distress. This was, of course, a small deficit, expected to be of only one year's duration, but Hoover's reference to the rapid retirement of the incomparably larger World War I debts (totalling $23 billion for the three years 1917-1919) suggested considerable latitude might remain for increasing depression indebtedness without doing harm to the economy or to public and business confidence.33 The arguments Hoover mustered to justify this relatively small deficit could conceivably have been used to justify much larger deficits, as Roosevelt later demonstrated.

Second, in spite of these reassurances, Hoover felt obliged to express his confidence that the people favor a balanced budget and that it is of "utmost importance," because of its possible effects on business to have the financial affairs of the federal government on a sound basis. He did not specify what, in fact, a "sound basis" might be, but the implication was that at some unspecified level and duration of federal deficits public confidence would ebb and serious economic consequences would follow. In one paragraph the President assured the nation that a specific present deficit need cause no alarm and in the next he warned of unspecified dangers of a future deficit.

It is significant that the warning occurred in a paragraph where its obvious function was to prod the public and congress into accepting a return to higher tax levels. Hoover's first public references to the dangers of an unbalanced budget in fact were employed to create support for unpopular policies--policies which otherwise would have been very difficult to effect when dealing with an unfriendly, Democratic congress. Taken as a whole, the December 1930 budget message leaves the impression that the President was trying to preserve for himself the option of moving in whichever direction future needs might prompt. The possible choice of a government deficit financed by borrowing seems not yet to have been entirely ruled out.

Circumstances forced the President to make that final choice the next fall, when it became clear that the expected recovery had failed to materialize. In his December 1931 budget message Hoover announced that:

> We are now face to face with a situation where for
> the first time the current revenues of the Govern-

ment under our existing laws have fallen below the
amounts required to meet the absolutely necessary
expenses. This brings the question directly before
us of the course that shall be pursued.[34]

The press, as recently as June 1931, had carried reports that no tax
increases were planned and that Hoover expected to finance the
government's expenditures by borrowing until the depression was over.[35]
But the budget message put a quick end to such speculation. Hoover
declared that without tax increases sufficient to keep the deficit
within manageable limits "public confidence" and the "stability of the
Federal Government" would be lost. Proposed tax increases would minimize the deficit but could not hope to balance the budget in fiscal
1932. The President promised a balanced budget in fiscal 1933, except
for the amount required for statutory debt retirement (which Hoover had
always hitherto included as a regular part of the budget) and again for
fiscal 1934 including the debt retirement payment. The budget message
emphasized in its final paragraphs that maintaining the integrity of the
federal government "is a necessary factor in the rebuilding of a sound
national prosperity." For the first time, a president was asserting
that a balanced budget, seen since the mid-twenties as a passive indicator of national economic well-being, was now a necessary active agent in
bringing economic recovery.

Until the campaign of 1932, Hoover was the most prominent active
apostle of this new doctrine. Finding the argument useful in promoting
increased taxes, he employed it again in the spring of 1932 against the
flood of public works and other spending measures being proposed in
congress. In a press conference of January 8, 1932, the President
lashed out against advocates of major spending programs. "We cannot
squander ourselves into prosperity," he said. The primary national goal
must be to bring recovery and "the reduction in governmental expenditures and the stability of government finance is the most fundamental
step towards this end."[36] By May, he was asserting that balancing the
budget "is indispensible to the restoration of confidence and to the
very start of recovery."[37]

Finally, in the heat of the 1932 campaign, Hoover maintained that
the very proposal of spending programs in congress "undermined public
confidence and delayed all efforts of the Administration . . . to save
the country." Recovery, Hoover said, "began the moment when it was
certain that these destructive measures of this Democratic-controlled
House were stopped."[38] The point was finally being made that the whole
economy responded directly to the public assessment of prospects for a
balanced budget.

There would certainly have been concern over the deficits even had

Hoover chosen not to make them a major issue. The first deficit of the Great Depression was far larger than any previous peacetime deficit, totalling $462 million. The 1932 deficit was nearly six times as large--almost $3 billion.39 The deficits of World War I, however, had been significantly larger, $9 billion in 1918 and over $13 billion in 1919. Yet post-war prosperity had made it possible by 1930 to retire nearly one-third of the debt outstanding on July 1, 1920.40 Experience taught that deficits substantially larger than those of 1931 and 1932 could be managed without dire consequences. It would seem that the widespread fear of deficits could not be attributed entirely to their size. These were peacetime deficits, of course, but there was no logical reason to suspect debts caused by the depression would be more difficult to repay in the long run than those caused by war. Concern was no doubt heightened by the fact that the new budgeting system, for the first time, reported the deficits at a given time and place for all to see.

The natural concern Americans had over unprecedented peacetime deficits did not necessarily lead to Hoover's further conclusion. It is one thing to be alarmed at growing deficits and to hope that the budget can be balanced. It is another to say that the deficit is retarding recovery and that the budget must be balanced before recovery will come. Roosevelt was to have this interpretation of the depression thrown up to him by prominent members of the business community in a litany which reached a thundering crescendo when the Recession 1937 seemed to confirm the belief. Observing the growth of the idea in 1933, economist Jacob Viner charged that Hoover's budget balancing campaign

> had made it dangerous to increase the debt substan-
> tially because of the adverse effect it would have
> on the morale of a proud public taught to measure
> the stability of government by the financial record
> for a single year or short period of years.41

Businessmen's fears of federal deficits, he maintained, had been largely a creation of Hoover and his Secretary of the Treasury, Ogden Mills.

As the 1932 campaign approached, Roosevelt could not resist springing the snare Hoover had laid for himself. Under Hoover the budget had moved from a surplus in fiscal 1930 amounting to 22.5 percent of total expenditures to a deficit in fiscal 1932 which was 58.7 percent of expenditures.42 Roosevelt had only to employ Hoover's arguments to make a prima facie case for the contention that even by its own lights the Hoover administration was retarding recovery. Hoover directed his rhetoric during the campaign more against the spending inclinations of the democratic congressmen than against the presidential candidate, hoping apparently that Roosevelt would be found guilty by association. Roosevelt spoke against the extravagance of Republican government. The two of them, each with his own variations, gave the public a thorough schooling in the doctrine that a balanced budget must be a necessary part of any recovery program.

Once in office, Roosevelt presented a recovery "plan" which in its fiscal aspects, reinforced the arguments both candidates had pressed in the campaign. Beginning with the budget submitted January 1934 (the first budget prepared by the Roosevelt Administration) the Treasury divided expenses into "general" and "emergency" categories. Regular revenues, even as estimated in 1934, were sufficient to meet the "general" or normal expenses of government operations. Roosevelt interpreted the enormous $10.5 billion deficit projected in this budget as solely the product of a crisis inherited from the previous administration.[43] Through stringent economies (symbolized by the Economy Act of 1933), he claimed to be balancing the budget except for the imbalance left him by Hoover. The "plan" was that as recovery progressed, this deficit would be erased from both ends-by declining expenses as the need for recovery and relief expenditures diminished and by increased taxes as the government reaped its share of a rising national income. The January 1934 message indicated that the Government would plan to balance the whole budget in the fiscal year ending in June 1936. In the meantime fiscal solvency as a precondition to recovery could be said to have been achieved. The $10.5 billion deficit projected for fiscal 1934 made it relatively easy for Roosevelt to show declining deficits in subsequent years. Except for this deficit, the Roosevelt budget was "in balance."

Politically, the plan was masterful. The balancing of the budget was interpreted solely as a problem of removing the Hoover legacy. The proposal, however, was not a plan for achieving recovery, but rather an indication of how the public might best measure the pace of recovery. Roosevelt was using and hence reinforcing the by then prevalent public assumption that a balanced budget was the most reliable indicator of the state of the economy. In effect, he was announcing that the public need only watch his annual progress towards a balanced budget to see how close to recovery the New Deal was striking. When the budget showed a positive balance the Hoover deficit would have been eradicated and recovery achieved. By careful manipulation and presentation of the budget the President would be able to show each year that progress was being made according to the "plan" he had announced in 1934.

The campaign of 1936 served for the most part to reinforce the lessons of the campaign of 1932. The roles were, of course, reversed and Roosevelt's opposition was now able to take the offensive in criticizing him for failure to deliver on his promise to balance the budget. But where Hoover, in the absence of positive economic progress had been forced to cast his achievements in terms of traditional American ideals and national character, Roosevelt was able to point not only to general economic progress, but also to specific acts which had entered tangibly and positively into the lives of most Americans. In his major campaign address on fiscal policy he deliberately refreshed public memory of his handling of the banking crisis by announcing that there had not been a single national bank failure during the last twelve months. He pointed with pride to the CCC programs, work relief efforts, and conservation measures.

In taking the offensive, Roosevelt was in fact suggesting that achievements other than a balanced budget might reliably indicate the state of affairs in the nation. At one point he proposed that " . . . rise and fall of national income," was "an index of the rise and fall of national prosperity," as well as an index "of the prosperity of your government." Emphasizing that a high level of national income was needed to provide tax revenues for running the government, he concluded that if national income were to keep rising at present rates, "the receipts of the Government, without imposing any additional taxes, will within a year or two, be sufficient to care for all ordinary and relief expenses of the Government--in other words, to balance the budget."[44] Roosevelt, through a wish to put his best achievements first, was beginning to suggest that America's economic well-being might be indicated by national income as well as by a balanced budget--a new direction which was to become significant during the debate initiated by the Recession of 1937. For the moment, however, a balanced budget remained for the President as for his opponents, the test by which his success in the crisis would ultimately be measured. In October 1936 Roosevelt ignored Morgenthau's request that he publicly promise a balanced budget for fiscal 1938--postponing that final vindication of his policies to an indefinite "within a year or two."[45] Could he have seen a year or two into the future, his optimism would no doubt have been even more guarded.

Mrs. James Roosevelt, the President's mother, unwittingly posed the question which was to become increasingly discomforting to New Dealers during the late 1930's. Daniel Bell, recently appointed Acting Director of the Budget, was introduced to the President's mother during his first visit to the family estate at Hyde Park. "Oh, Mr. Bell," she said, "I'm so glad to meet you. So many of my friends ask me when Franklin is going to balance the budget. My dear Mr. Bell, when is Franklin going to balance the budget?"[46]

Certainly Mrs. Roosevelt's question became a dominant concern of Bell's superior in the Treasury, Henry Morgenthau, Jr. as the Administration moved into its second term. Morgenthau was determined to balance the budget because the achievement would offer visible, indisputable evidence that the President's plans for both reform and recovery had been successfully completed. The old progressive association of an ordered budget with governmental reform probably influenced Morgenthau's thinking as well, causing him to believe that this one great achievement, if consummated, would silence the President's critics and precipitate a spontaneous resolution of the problems which continued to plague the New Deal. Concerned above all with the moral tone of Roosevelt's administration, Morgenthau saw in balancing the budget the one symbolic act which would affirm that the government was honest, and therefore worthy of trust and confidence.

The "when" of Mrs. Roosevelt's question was particularly apt. Seldom did New Dealers divide themselves on the question, "Should the budget be balanced?" The critical question was "When should the budget be balanced?" Beginning in 1934 a small but significant procession of New Deal figures left the Administration at various times according to their respective judgments as to how many successive years of deficits and how high a level of indebtedness a peacetime government could safely sustain. Morgenthau, in speaking of Budget Director Lewis Douglas' 1934 resignation, explained that those staying with the Administration differed from those who left "not over whether a balanced budget was our ultimate goal, but over what sacrifices of relief and reform we were prepared to make inorder to get it right away."

Morgenthau maintained later that in 1934 he had been opposed to rigidly orthodox ideas about the absolute indispensability of a balanced budget,"--ideas which "interfered with the Administration's program."[47] Though the recollection exaggerates his liberality on the issue, Morgenthau remained loyal to the President, successfully financing relief and recovery programs while continuing to exercise his influence in behalf of a balanced budget. By the spring of 1937, recovery had progressed sufficiently that the "plan" of 1934 seemed within a hair's breadth of realization. Tax revenues were running above estimates and relief and recovery costs were down. Morgenthau sensed that the time had come at last to make his move, beginning a campaign to limit expenses in all departments sufficiently to permit at least a "cash balance" for fiscal 1938 and a balanced budget, including debt retirement, for fiscal 1939. To his delight, the fear of inflation had brought even such persistent spenders as Hopkins and Eccles to concur momentarily in his judgment that conditions were ripe for a balancing of the budget. "This was the moment," Morgenthau concluded (in a metaphor which, considering the President's condition, must remain a classic of insensitivity), "to . . . throw away the crutches and see if American private enterprise could stand on its own feet."[48]

CHAPTER THREE

MARRINER S. ECCLES—"PRACTICAL MEN
MUST DO SOME THINKING"

A WESTERN BANKER IN WASHINGTON

Shortly before Marriner S. Eccles left Washington in August 1937 for his annual visit to Utah, he met at the White House with Louis Brownlow, Charles E. Merriam, and Luther Gulick, of the President's Committee on Administrative Management. Eccles impressed Gulick with his "concern over the difficulty of keeping the private economy going concurrently with the introduction of large elements of public control," a task which in Gulick's opinion was "the central problem of American economic and political life." While the two could agree in defining the problem, the brevity of their correspondence suggests that fundamentally

different approaches towards a solution prevented a constructive inter-
change of ideas. On July 7, Gulick sent Eccles a paper by the English
economist, Josiah C. Stamp, which, Gulick maintained, dealt with the
problem in "an extraordinarily fruitful fashion." Five days later
Eccles wrote a polite reply, offering an opinion (prepared by a trusted
member of his staff, Lauchlin Currie) that Lord Stamp had stated the
problem effectively but offered little in the way of a possible solution. There was apparently no further correspondence between the two
men.[1]

It is not surprising that Eccles displayed little interest in a
paper titled "The Administrator and a Planned Society." He had already
formed firm opinions on how best to introduce elements of public control
into the economy without frightening the business community--opinions
which rejected Stamp's thesis that the solution lay in better public
administration and more careful social planning. Eccles had long emphasized the need to develop tools for effective use of fiscal, monetary
and tax policies in order to control the general level of economic
activity. This approach appealed to Eccles because it minimized the
need of what he called "direct control"--government regulation of the
activities of individual financial, commercial, and industrial firms.
To Eccles the "planned society" discussed by Stamp smacked of totalitarianism, precisely the evil his own program was designed to avert.

The following spring, Eccles wrote a letter To Frederic A. Delano,
chairman of the National Resources Committee, indicating the limited
intent of policies he had proposed:

> Unless I am entirely mistaken about the temper of
> the American Electorate, it will not go back to a
> policy which, however well suited to pioneer days,
> would only magnify the swings of unhealthy booms and
> ruinous depressions under modern conditions. . . .
> We should be concentrating all of our attention on
> understanding and developing the difficult technique
> required of government in attempting to use its
> powers for the moderation of the greater excesses
> inherent in the system we want to preserve.[2]

Though convinced that a return to "pioneer days" was neither possible
nor practical, Eccles by no means wished to inhibit the functioning of
the market as chief allocator of goods and services in the economy or to
dampen the spirit of free entrepreneurial activity. He wanted only to
control extreme fluctuations in the business cycle, leaving businessmen
as free as possible from direct government intervention in their activities. Freedom of enterprise should be touched by as little social

planning as modern conditions would permit. Eccles' long public service was characterized, more than anything else, by the wish to preserve as much as possible of the liberal democratic capitalism which had made his father wealthy and nurtured his own considerable fortune.

When Eccles spoke of pioneer days, the reference carried for him a concrete meaning arising from his own personal and family experience. His grandfather, William Eccles, had been converted to Mormonism in Scotland in 1842. It was twenty years before Eccles, aided by the Mormon Perpetual Emigrating Fund, was able to bring his large family to the new Mormon kingdom in the Great Basin. His oldest son, David, was fourteen at the time. Mormon agents funded, planned, and supervised the entire trip from Liverpool to Salt Lake City, running a cooperative immigration network which became widely recognized as a model of efficiency in an era when the miseries of overcrowding, illness, and exploitation were the common lot of poorer immigrants.[3]

In Utah, young David soon became the mainstay of the family, working as a lumberjack in Oregon, a teamster and coalminer in Wyoming, and a sawyer in Utah. Eventually he saved enough to undertake timber cutting contracts on his own, and finally to purchase his own sawmills. Quick to respond to the economic needs of an isolated pioneer community, he employed capital gained through early entry into the lumber industry in developing mining, railroading, heavy construction, and banking. While building industries vital to the Mountain West, Eccles amassed a sizable fortune for himself and his two families, leaving an estate at the time of his death in 1912 of over $7 million.

Marriner Eccles, oldest son in the family of David Eccles' second wife, Ellen Stoddard, later made pointed reference to the fact that his father's fortune did not rest on windfall discoveries of oil or precious minerals, but rather "was built through courage, hard work, self-denial, thrift, and a clear view of the kind of economic development that could succeed in a new area." "Thrift" and "hard work," the younger Eccles wrote, were the "magic words of his [father's] career." "He had built his works by himself, owned many of them outright, and ran them all in a direct and personal way. He saw no reason why other men could not or should not re-create themselves in his image, providing, of course, they were left free to use their wits and will without governmental interference."[4]

An important aspect of the economic environment which nurtured David Eccles' spectacular success was not mentioned in the reminiscences of his son. The economic and social ideology of the Mormon leadership in the nineteenth century attenuated the ruggedness of individualism characteristic of other frontier settlements. In the territory of Utah a centralized planning authority, the Mormon church hierarchy, imposed an order upon the settlement process which contrasted sharply with the anarchic character of other frontier communities.

For half a century thousands of Mormons responded obediently to "calls" from Brigham Young and his successors to cooperate in founding new, remote settlements and launching enterprises needed for economic self-sufficiency such as the culture and processing of cotton, sugar beets, and silk. Many new converts, coming as immigrants arrived destitute in Utah. Under Young's leadership the church assumed the responsibility of caring for the annual tide of immigrants, most arriving in the fall, too late to commence planting on their own. Shunning direct relief, Young offered the able-bodied jobs on public works projects--temples, churches, city walls and canals.[5] In assuming these responsibilities, church leaders helped develop two distinctive attitudes among the Mormons regarding the role of the central authority in the temporal affairs of the people. Many faithful Mormons came to believe that the church had a right and duty to plan and direct the economic development of the region even when this went against the immediate interests of individuals. They also came to expect the church to provide the needy with jobs and the basic necessities of life. These ideas continued to be of influence among Mormons long after the death of Brigham Young.

Marriner's father, David, grew up in this tradition. He was loyal to the Mormon church throughout his life, advancing to the high office of "Seventy" in the Mormons' lay priesthood. Following the counsel of church leaders, he took a second wife, Marriner's mother, in what the Mormons called plural marriage at a time when federal officials were zealously imprisoning polygamous Mormons. Several of his children, Marriner among them, fulfilled two-year missions for the church with his help and encouragement. The elder Eccles did not attend church regularly and did not accept offices in the church. He did accept civic responsibilities at the suggestion of church leaders, holding the office of alderman and then mayor of the city of Ogden as the church-supported Peoples' party candidate.[6] His children were on familiar terms with the President of the church, staying in the home of Church President Joseph F. Smith's first wife, "Aunt Julina," when they visited Salt Lake City. Eccles himself had frequent associations with top church officials, especially Heber J. Grant, who succeeded Joseph F. Smith as church president. Eccles tithed throughout his life, and made substantial commitments of his wealth to sustain church enterprises even when they did not, in his judgment, appear promising.[7]

Two of Eccles' enterprises, sugar factories in Ogden and Logan, were founded by him as community projects in keeping with the church leaders' wish to encourage cooperation in home industries. Most of his fortune was built, however, through individual entrepreneurial ventures fully in the spirit of his contemporaries, the Rockefellers and the

Carnegies. Once asked to fulfill a preaching mission for the church, he respectfully declined, arguing that he was of more worth as a provider of jobs than he would be as a missionary. Ecclesiastical leaders recognized the importance of that contribution. David O. McKay, who became the ninth President of the church, speaking at Eccles' funeral, acknowledged that "a man who can produce a million dollars and at the same time contribute a million dollars to the wealth of the community is a public benefactor. Such a man was David Eccles."[8]

Successful as a capitalist, Eccles nonetheless retained a sense of obligation to ideals and interests greater than his own. Like non-Mormon pioneers who participated in the rapid economic development of other new regions, the senior Eccles would notice that his own enterprises not only built, but were built upon, the general growth of the whole community; that to anticipate and fulfill profitably a community need is to admit the interdependence of those engaged in civilizing a wilderness. But he could not help noting further that room was found for his own free-wheeling entrepreneurial endeavor to exist and grow amongst the various cooperative and communal experiments of the Mormons and even in an economic environment where Church leaders were attempting to provide central planning for balanced economic growth. The boy Marriner grew up believing, like his father, that freedom of enterprise was a powerful agent of economic development. Yet he could hardly escape noticing as well that a degree of central planning and control did not cause the flower to wither and fade.

Another distinctive aspect of David Eccles' experience in early Utah is significant for its possible influence upon Marriner. The developing Utah economy provided an excellent opportunity for perceptive observers to gain a macroeconomic perspective on the dynamics of economic growth and development. In a manner close to the "desert island" example which economists are fond of using in illustrating their basic concepts, the isolated, burgeoning Utah economy simplified and clarified fundamental economic processes. It was clear that homes for a rapidly-growing population could not be built without a local lumber industry. But timber required roads and railways into the mountains, and the developing of power resources through coal mining or heavy construction in the building of dams and waterways. Machinery and equipment must be acquired, either from the East or through the founding of native basic industries. Capital was necessary for purchase of machinery abroad and for the development of manufacturing at home. Banking and financial enterprises were needed to minimize the grudging dependence upon eastern money markets. Problems raised by the constantly adverse regional balance of payments tuned the keen observer to notice the effects of monetary dependence and government subsidy on economic development.

The Eccles family enterprises included nearly all the industries essential to a new economy--lumber, transportation, mining, heavy construction, utilities, insurance, livestock, and sugar. An Eccles could not move in one of his enterprises without being made aware of the fact that such action affected the others. Young Marriner, bright and acute in observing things going on about him, would readily have gained a sense of the interrelatedness of economic events and decisions which other businessmen with fewer diversified interests in a more developed economy could easily miss. Marriner's family and religious background provided fertile soil for his later development of a rationale recommending government action to stimulate the sluggish national economy of the 1930's.

Marriner Eccles was born eight months before Henry Morgenthau, on September 9, 1890, in Logan, Utah. To avoid prosecution under federal anti-polygamy statutes, the father settled his second wife in Baker, Oregon, where he had extensive logging and sawmill operations. Dividing his time among his business pursuits and his two families, one in Ogden, Utah and the other in Oregon, David Eccles was frequently absent from the home. Marriner's mother raised her nine children largely by herself, involving them in the activities of the local Mormon church. Though the father was seldom at home, he nonetheless was a strong influence on the children, taking an active, affectionate interest in their development and training. Convinced that the practical experience he himself had received offered distinct advantages over book learning, he did not encourage his children to go to college. A neighbor's son, returning from an Eastern institution, confirmed Eccles' prejudices with his modish dress and lack of industry. Eccles was fond of pointing out this "educated fool" to his children as an example to be avoided.[9]

The elder Eccles went to great pains to insure that his own wealth would not sap the resourcefulness and ambition of his children. Hoping to steer young Marriner clear of the vices of idleness, David offered the eight-year-old child summer employment at five cents an hour carrying boxes in a family-owned factory. Eccles recalled that:

> When I held in my hand the first fifty cents for a day's labor, my father offered a plan whereby I could be taught to follow in his footsteps and become a capitalist by curtailing the consumption of my current income. At the outset of that first summer he said that if I saved my money until I had one hundred dollars he would sell me one share of Oregon Lumber Company stock at its par value.
> 'It's worth much more than that', he explained with great care, 'and if you come to own a share you

will be a capitalist'.

By the end of his third summer the boy had saved the one hundred dollars
and "was sold the share of stock as promised and became a capitalist at
the age of eleven." "The feat," Marriner remembered, "won a treasured
compliment from my father, which was multiplied many times over in the
compliments I paid myself. I've never ceased being a capitalist since
then."[10]

Marriner's formal schooling was completed at the age of nineteen,
with his graduation from the high school level of Brigham Young College
in Logan, Utah, where the family settled after prosecution of polygam-
ists declined. Shortly thereafter he received a "call" from the Mormon
church to fulfill a two-year "mission" in Scotland. Upon completion of
these duties, Eccles joined two Utah friends, also recently released
from their missions, in a grand tour of pre-war Europe. He had been
home but a short time when the unexpected early death of his father in
December 1912 cut short his youth and plunged him deeply into the practical world of financial and business affairs.

Upon his father's death, Eccles, at age twenty-two, assumed management of the two-sevenths of his father's estate which fell to him and
his eight younger brothers and sisters as children of his father's
second wife. (The other five-sevenths fell to David Eccles' first wife,
Bertha Jensen, and her twelve children.) Eccles managed his family's
smaller share of the estate so successfully that by 1920 he was able to
take over a considerable portion of the family enterprises once under
the control of his older half-brothers. He described his success with
undisguised relish in a chapter of his memoir titled "Joseph and his
Brothers." By 1928 he could name over thirteen corporations and
business establishments of major importance in the Mountain West in
which he, as president of Eccles Investment Company, had a significant
voice. Satisfied with the general climate of prosperity upon which he
had built so successfully, he recalled that he "had no time to reflect
on where I stood or how long I could stay there. If asked for an
opinion, I bowed to the East and paraphrased the latest statement of
someone like Ogden Mills and Andrew Mellon in the government, or of
Albert Wiggin, Charles Mitchell, and J.P. Morgan on Wall Street."[11]
Though not active in politics, Eccles tended to follow the McKinley
Republican leanings of his father.

The Great Depression took a particularly heavy toll of financial
institutions in the Mountain West, but Eccles exercised consummate
judgment and considerable daring in guiding his family's fortunes safely
through the storm with a minimum of loss. Fighting as he was to keep
his banks open, he began to observe that the action taken by individual
banks to remain solvent had the general effect of tightening the credit

structure, depressing prices and wages, and making it even more difficult for the banks' debtors to repay the loans and mortgages being
called in to keep the banks financially sound. "Seeking individual
salvation," he later wrote, "we were contributing to collective ruin."12
By 1931 he had formulated from such insights opinions on the causes of
the Depression and possible remedies which set him dramatically apart
from most prominent members of the American business and financial
community.

Encouraged by a group of close friends and associates, Eccles in
1931 began to offer his unorthodox views to Utah audiences. He also
began to attend lectures at the University of Utah by visiting notables,
meeting among others the Chicago economist and later Senator from
Illinois, Paul H. Douglas, and early in 1933 the noted publicist, Stuart
Chase. Chase was interested in Eccles' views, asking the Utah banker
what specific policy proposals he would recommend to the new
administration. Apparently impressed with Eccles' reply, Chase
concluded the discussion by recommending that Eccles find a larger
audience. Utah Senator William H. King had already invited Eccles to
speak before the Senate Finance Committee's "Depression Clinic" in
February. Upon hearing that Eccles would be coming to Washington, Chase
offered to arrange a meeting with Professor Rexford Tugwell of Columbia,
a prominent member of the President-elect's "Brain Trust."

In February 1933 Eccles left Utah to preach his new-found economic
gospel in "Egypt." "It was one thing," he wrote, to offer such views,
"on my home ground and quite another thing to repeat [them] . . . in the
intellectual East, where the Baruchs, Taylors, Atterburys, Duffields,
Houstons, and Weirs--'with the monotony and persistance of Old Cato'--
clamored for a balanced budget, as did the President of the United
States."13

At the time, Eccles was a youthful forty-three years of age, proud,
independent, and self-assured. He was slim, of less-than average
height, but his piercing dark eyes, aquiline nose, and quickness of mind
and manner seemed to make his physical stature unimportant. He possessed his father's gift for cutting through details and reducing complex
matters to their essentials. Once he grasped what he felt was the
essence of a problem, he did not allow his attention to wander from it.

Eccles' direct, abrupt manner did not help him in the delicate
diplomatic maneuvering essential to high government office. The Banking
Act of 1935 undoubtedly would have passed Congress more readily had
Eccles, in drafting the bill, been more sensitive to the proprietary
interest of Virginia Senator Carter Glass in the Reserve System. Eccles
began his Governorship of the Reserve System by alienating its longtime
research director, Emmanuel Goldenweiser, appointing a treasury
department associate, Lauchlin Currie, assistant to Goldenweiser, and

then allowing Currie to undercut Goldenweiser's authority by maintaining closer ties with himself.[14] The difficult relationship which developed between Eccles and Morgenthau after Eccles moved to the Federal Reserve could have been improved had Eccles taken greater pains to deal diplomatically with a man jealous of his prerogatives and insecure in his grasp of affairs over which he had authority. His brusque manner did not fit readily into the wary, cocktail party style in which much Washington business is done. Peppery in language and appearance, Eccles characteristically convinced others by unassailable arguments rather than through more gentle modes of persuasion. He was not a diplomat.

At the author's first meeting with Eccles in 1969, his initial greeting, from behind a large walnut desk, was "So you want to be a historian, do you?" To the positive response he replied, in dead earnest, "That doesn't seem like a fruitful way for a young man to spend his life." Eccles' dislike of anything he considered wasteful recurs frequently in his writings, a legacy no doubt of his father, whose Scottish thrift became a legend in the family. To Eccles, the most galling aspect of the situation in 1937 was the enormous waste of resources, which, but for the Depression, could have been put to productive use. He recommended public employment of those made jobless by the catastrophe,

> not so much because of social or humane considerations, although these are pertinent, but rather because I consider it an inexcusable economic waste to have capital, raw materials, and man power idle.[15]

Eccles' first question in choosing appropriate government measures during economic crisis was not, "Who needs help the most?" or "Which action will provide the most needed social benefits?" but rather, "How can capital, raw materials, and labor be brought back into productive activity?" Though, as he was careful to point out, the first two questions are "pertinent," they are not the central questions upon which policy should be built.

Eccles' brusque manner was reinforced in Washington by a native distrust of all things eastern, especially of eastern dominance of the nation's capital markets. Eccles came to Washington with something of a chip on his shoulder. His memoir begins with a metaphor which places him a visionary Joseph against first his brothers and then against "the intellectual East," an "Egypt" of strange gods and strange customs. Complaining of Roosevelt's economy drive in 1933, he wrote his friend, Secretary of War George Dern, that "New York, as usual, seems to be in the saddle, dominating fiscal and monetary policy."[16] His Banking Act of 1935 was, in essence, an effort to wrest control of the Federal Reserve System from New York bankers and place it in the hands of the Reserve Board in Washington. He noted petulantly in his memoir that "there was no agitation for the creation of an RFC so long as it was the private creditor institutions of the West and South that were being crushed by the depression. Because eastern institutions were able to safeguard their protective layers of fat by calling in the obligations owed them in the West and South" there was little support for an RFC until the western situation had become irremediable. After western banks collapsed "and the Eastern institutions lay exposed to a fall against rock bottom, then they demanded the RFC, and it came into being."[17] Eccles clearly harbored a populist anti-eastern bias, no doubt a legacy of the frequent need to go into New York capital markets in order to develop a remote western area chronically running an unfavorable balance of payments in its dealings with the rest of the nation.

It is significant that Eccles' imagery casts Roosevelt as a "pharoah," under whom the westerner worked out his stewardship. Eccles apparently did not feel comfortable even with the President, regarding him as a person who, though kindly, remained nonetheless an alien master. Eccles, a provincial, did not fit comfortably into the conviviality of the President's inner circle. Roosevelt and his close advisors respected Eccles and often harkened to him, but they nonetheless did not seek him out as a social companion. Eccles' father's dislike of the pretentiousness of eastern manners and dress was widely remembered in his family, and perhaps helped form the attitude of the son as well. During his entire seventeen years in Washington, Eccles took vacations only to Utah. When he left the Reserve Board in 1951, he returned immediately to the West, dividing his time henceforth between San Francisco and Salt Lake City.

Eccles' provinciality may not have been entirely a disadvantage, however. If it diminished his effectiveness in transforming his ideas into policy, it nonetheless may have helped in their formulation and contributed in some measure to their eventual acceptance by official Washington. It is possible that the provincial character of Eccles' home environment helped him to escape the entrapment of old ideas and favored some aspects of his advocacy of the new. It has often been observed that the gifted provincial, when he becomes conscious of national affairs, finds himself attempting to mediate between the ideals and values of his home society and those of the center society, for it is by the standards of the center society that his ultimate success and recognition will be measured. One possible effect on the individual of the strains inherent in such a situation was described by John Clive and Bernard Bailyn in their attempt to account for the unusual achievement of provincial Americans and Scots in the English Enlightenment:

> The complexity of the provincial's image of the
> world and of himself made demands upon him unlike
> those felt by the equivalent Englishman. It tended
> to shake the mind from the roots of habit and tradi-
> tion. It led men to the interstices of common
> thought where were found new views and new
> approaches to the old.[18]

The Biblical metaphors in Eccles' memoirs cast him as a "Joseph," abused
by "His Brothers," thrown into "The Pit" of the Depression and brought
to serve in Washington as "Pharoah's Steward," where his ideas ultimately triumphed over those of "The Magi" from the East. The self-conscious
provinciality running through this chain of images is so obvious as to
require no further comment. It is likely that forces similar to those
Clive and Bailyn have described permitted Eccles to see New Deal
problems from perspectives less readily gained by those who had spent
most of their lives near the center of national affairs. For example,
Eccles' distance from the center of national events prevented his participating in the reform movement which counted the Reserve System among
its most sacrosanct monuments. He thus did not hesitate, as did many
Democratic supporters of Roosevelt, including Morgenthau, to propose
legislation altering the system originally set up under Woodrow Wilson.

Eccles' provincial background may have contributed to the dissemin-
ation as well as to the formulation of the ideas he promoted. Forward-
looking ideas assume an uncommon quality when voiced by a provincial
from whom such ideas are not expected. The fact that Eccles was from
Utah and a Mormon always was included in accounts of his views on
deficit spending. In drawing attention to the anomaly of such ideas
coming from such a man, commentators unavoidably emphasized the
uniqueness of the ideas themselves. Paradoxically, even Eccles'
impatience with the usages that serve in polite society to smooth the
edges of social and intellectual discourse may have given him some
advantage in Washington. In speeches, he employed a directness which
imparted an uncommon force to what he said. Eccles' provincial
background helped shape the distinctive quality of insights he gained in
seeking to come to terms with the Depression. In all probability it
reinforced unusual aspects of his particular regional and family
background, exerting a discernible influence upon the development of the
ideas which had brought him to testify before Harrison's Senate
Committee in 1933.

In Washington, before the Senate Finance Committee, Eccles was
almost alone in suggesting that a balanced budget be deferred in favor

of increasing the "purchasing power" of the people through government spending. "When this is accomplished," he maintained, "and not before, can the Government hope to balance its Budget and our people regain the standard of living to which the material wealth of this country entitles them."19 Eccles made five specific proposals before the committee, including immediate granting of relief funds to the states, federal loans for self-liquidating public works projects, domestic allotments in agriculture, refinancing of farm mortgages, and cancellation of war debts. He ended his testimony with the assertion that "when recovery is restored, I believe that in order to avoid future disastrous depressions and sustain a balanced prosperity, it will be necessary . . . for the Government to assume a greater control and regulation of our entire economic system."20

At the time, Eccles' comments, provocative though they were, caused little reaction. All eyes were upon Roosevelt, hoping to discern the direction of the President-elect's thinking as he prepared to assume office. Testimony before a committee of a lame duck Senate was not likely to offer clues to future policies, particularly testimony from an unknown Utah Republican banker.

There might have been more interest in Eccles' testimony had it been known that he boarded a train for New York after his appearance at the hearings to keep an appointment with Roosevelt's close adviser Rexford Tugwell at Columbia University. There, over lunch, Eccles repeated for Tugwell's benefit the essence of his Senate testimony. Tugwell was surprised to hear a banker espousing such ideas, but otherwise did not appear to Eccles to be especially impressed. Eccles left Tugwell to visit the Secretary of War-designate, a Utah banking colleague, George Dern, leaving a copy of his testimony with Dern as well. Then, as he put it, "With this final job of missionary work behind me, I sped back to Utah."21

From Utah, Eccles watched with increasing dismay as the New Deal fiscal policy began to unfold. Letters he wrote George Dern, criticizing the President's budget balancing message, were discussed with Secretary of the Treasury William Woodin. Dern reported back to Eccles that his arguments were of no effect. The administration, committed as it was to "the sound economic policy of a balanced budget," was apparently not interested in a rationale for increased spending. On April 19th, Eccles wrote again expressing his growing concern with events in Washington:

> It seems to me . . . that the government is
> attacking our economic problems in the usual
> orthodox manner and I see little fundamental change
> in the methods they are using and those pursued by

the Republican Administration.[22]

Again, he received no indication that his letters were being taken seriously in high administration circles.

That October, however, Eccles was surprised by a telegram from Tugwell suggesting that they meet in Washington and again exchange views, should Eccles be planning another trip East. Eccles accordingly agreed to visit Washington during a planned business trip to New York City towards the end of the month. There Tugwell, then in the Department of Agriculture, introduced Eccles to Mordecai Ezekial, a long-time Department employee, and Secretary Henry Wallace. Eccles invited the three to a dinner at the Shoreham Hotel, where they could have a relaxed discussion, and by the following night, Harry L. Hopkins, Jerome Frank, and George Dern had been added to the group. This meeting marked the beginning of Eccles' identification with a group of New Dealers which, except for Dern, later came to be known as the "spenders." Recalling his first impressions of the group, Eccles perceptively described their motives and objectives and suggested what his own contribution to their work might be. "I think it is important to say of these men," he wrote,

> that while they were all devoted to Roosevelt, they viewed him as an instrument through which they could serve the country as a whole. The New Deal belonged to them as much as it did to the President . . . The pressures of human distress to which their work exposed them bore home the painful lesson that the task of removing fear and want from the land could not be accomplished within the framework of a balanced budget. On the other hand, they needed more than the doctrine of Christian charity to advance what they wanted to do in the face of strong political resistance. They needed arguments on how a planned policy of adequate deficit financing could serve the humanitarian objective with which they were most directly concerned; and second, how the increased production and employment that the policy would create was the only way a depression could be ended and a budget balanced.[23]

Convinced that neither Christian charity nor undirected humanitarianism was sufficient as a guide to effective recovery policies, Eccles felt it was his task in Washington to supplement these qualities, possessed by New Dealers in abundance, with "needed arguments" on how deficit financing could serve New Deal humanitarian objectives, end the

Depression, and ultimately balance the budget. "I am not necessarily an altruist," he said of himself in 1936, "I think I am a realist."[24] In his judgment, the New Deal in 1933 needed more of the brand of realism he had to offer.

Eccles' guests at the Shoreham expressed general agreement with his proposals for increased government spending but doubted that with William Woodin as Secretary of the Treasury and Lewis Douglas as Director of the Budget they could be translated into official New Deal policy. Once again Eccles returned to Utah with a sense that he had accomplished little in the way of exerting an influence on official Washington. Shortly thereafter, however, Woodin was forced by ill health to give up this duties. Henry Morgenthau, Jr., recently appointed Acting Secretary of the Treasury, had not met Eccles at the time, but was apparently persuaded to invite the Utah banker to join his staff. In mid-December Eccles received a telegram from the Treasury Department asking him to come once more to Washington. He reluctantly complied, and after a series of conferences with Morgenthau and others, agreed to move with his family to Washington for one year, beginning February 1934, where he was to serve as special assistant to the Secretary of the Treasury in charge of monetary and credit matters.

Thus Eccles entered the New Deal on terms vastly different from those with which FDR had invited Morgenthau into the Treasury earlier that same month. Morgenthau's elevation to high public office was primarily the consequence of his long friendship with the President and his wish to be of service to Roosevelt. Eccles, self-confident and brusque in manner, secure in the knowledge of his success as banker and businessman, came to Washington not as servant of FDR, but of ideas which he believed the Administration must adopt, both as theoretical underpinning and as policy base for the future New Deal.

Coming to Washington in February 1934, Eccles spent that spring and summer representing the Treasury in dealings with a number of different New Deal agencies. He took special pride, however, in his contribution to the drafting of legislation leading to the Federal Housing Authority. "I felt that in a depression," Eccles explained later, "the proper role of the government should be that of generating a maximum degree of private spending through a minimum amount of public spending. This was the basic justification for deficit spending."[25] "At a cost of $50 million to the government . . . the bill succeeded in generating $1 billion of useful private expenditures."[26] Contributing substantially to whatever project engaged his attentions and exercising a wide range of practical knowledge in business and banking problems, Eccles soon gained the respect of a significant portion of the New Deal community.

Late that summer, on "a blistering day in August," Morgenthau leaned over to Eccles during a White House conference and announced that he had discussed with Roosevelt the possibility of Eccles being appointed Chairman of the Federal Reserve Board, a position recently vacated by Eugene Black. Newspaper speculation soon began to center upon Eccles as the likely candidate though Morgenthau was sounding out others as late as September 19. When the appointment was finally made, on November 10, however, Morgenthau was willing to take credit for the choice. Under a notation titled "Things accomplished by H.M., Jr. during the week of November 11th," Morgenthau tersely listed as number one: "Eccles made Governor of the Federal Reserve."[27]

Eccles, no doubt, would have insisted on sharing at least a part of the credit for his new appointment. As soon as Morgenthau had broached the idea to him in August, he began efforts to determine if he was seriously under consideration for the position. Tied by family and business obligations to Utah, and having come to Washington with the understanding that he would stay no longer than June of 1935, he was able to approach the prospect of the Reserve Board chairmanship with considerable independence. Receiving assurance that he was indeed being considered for the position, he prepared a memo entitled, "Desirable Changes in the Federal Reserve System" , which he offered to FDR as the sine qua non for his accepting the chairmanship. After a stormy legislative battle, the basic provisions of Eccles' memo were incorporated into the Banking Act of 1935, considered by Congress concurrently with Eccles' equally stormy nomination hearings.[28]

Thus fortified, Eccles superimposed upon the staid and comfortable bureaucracy of the Reserve System a small staff sympathetic to his own ideas. Over the next several years, observers of government economic policy were treated to the unusual experience of watching central bank officials take the initiative in the promulgation of unorthodox ideas on fiscal and monetary policy. Eccles remained Chairman of the Board of Governors until 1948 and continued as Vice-Chairman until 1951, always an outspoken and controversial figure. After leaving Washington, he returned to Utah, reassuming leadership of the varied enterprises controlled by the First Security Corporation and actively engaging himself in both corporate and civic affairs well into the ninth decade of his life. He was one of the first prominent businessmen to oppose the Vietnam war, he crusaded vigorously in pro-natalist Utah for population control, and was still involved in business affairs at the time of his death in December, 1977.

There is no reason to question the essential correctness of Eccles' later contention that the main lines of his economic analysis were "based on naked-eye observations and experience in the intermountain region."[29] Asked by a New York Times reporter to explain how he arrived at his unorthodox views, he revealed his anti-intellectual bias, commenting that "When affairs are going well, only the theorists philosophize, but when they go badly, practical people must do some thinking."[30] A close examination of the development of Eccles' economic thought as revealed in his speeches between 1928 and 1933 supports his contention that his exposure to other writers on economic problems of the 1930's was minimal, serving primarily to confirm and clarify an analysis he had already made independently. Eccles decided earlier than most observers that the Depression was not a cyclical downturn which, if allowed to run its course, automatically created the conditions for a subsequent recovery. Attempting to account for the catastrophe of a depression that would not go away, Eccles concluded that "underconsumption" was the fundamental problem, a condition which had been brought about by our world industrial machinery being thrown out of balance on account of the failure to stabilize the price level."[31] It was particularly important, he maintained, for policy makers to realize that "the end of production is consumption and not money, and whenever our capital accumulations reach a point where our production is beyond the ability of our great mass to consume goods, not because of lack of desire, but because of lack of purchasing power, you have a depression." Prospects for profits were so small that even record low-interest rates would not draw out investment. Abundant credit was being used only to refinance old debts, not to launch new enterprises. Industrialists would not begin activity "until you create employment giving buying power to the consumer." Only one agency could do this, Eccles concluded, "and that is the government." Five billion dollars used to create employment would raise price levels, start purchasing by people who will spend nearly all their income, and restore confidence throughout the nation. The cost could be more than repaid with taxes from the newly-generated income.

Eccles scoffed at the folly of attempting, in depression, to balance the budget. "Now [that the budget] is practically balanced," he wrote in 1932, taking Hoover at this word, "we should look for a period of prosperity, I suppose. Would it not be better to consider means of reviving business, and then we may find that the budget is already balanced, and that we have an excess. . . . The matter of economy is negative, the matter of spending is positive, and we have been doing the negative thing rather than the positive."[32] The crucial question, he maintained, was the level of national income, not the size of the deficit. Any hope for permanent adjustment must depend ultimately upon "fundamental economic plans," which will determine "the flow of money," and, once established, "will of necessity center in the distribution of purchasing power and in the allocation of income between investment and expenditure." To accomplish this Eccles recommended, in addition to greatly increased levels of government spending, an altered tax structure, with heavy taxes on upper income brackets and on undistributed corporate surpluses. He rejected the argument of many that everything possible to initiate useful, well-planned, and efficiently-run public spending projects had been done. Recommending the "expansion of social services of all kinds," he continued that

> No matter how luxurious the services this kind of spending money may provide for the people, it cannot justly be called extravagant. The more surplus income is spent, the more market there will be for business, the more men will be actively employed, the more wealth will be created, the larger will be the national income.

Finally, he held out a rhapsodic vision of the utopian world which government spending would make possible:

> If and when society shall again obtain to a state of high productivity it will be found that the educational and cultural activities of life occupy the central place. Slum districts will be eliminated; parks and playgrounds will be increased; public health service will be extended; our entire population will enjoy the benefits of modern housing; and we will have learned to treat criminal and mentally defectives more scientifically. We will have more and better schools; education for children and adults will grow in quality and extent; there will be a growing demand for the cultural things of life; the art of living, the art of using leisure time, will be developed beyond our capacity now to forsee.[33]

This set of ideas, with its focus upon national income and its suggestion that deficit spending would raise the national income to a point where the budget would automatically come into balance, was not common in 1932, when Eccles had completed the formulation of his analysis. There were a few economists and publicists developing theories grounded in views very similar to Eccles', including the English economist, Keynes, popular American economists William Trufant Foster and Waddill Catchings, Chicago's Paul Douglas, Jacob Viner, Eccles' colleague Lauchlin Currie, and journalist Stuart Chase. Eccles was not an economist, however. Indeed, he had no academic training beyond a rudimentary high school level. His work and life since the age of twenty-two had been devoted to the practical problems of making a success of his family's business enterprises. While there was a handful of economists following lines of thought similar to Eccles', the number of banker-businessmen moving in that direction was few indeed.

Eccles' achievement depended primarily upon his ability to break out of prevailing modes of analyzing the economic scene. His starting point was his realization that the Depression, unlike earlier depressions would not correct itself. He was making this point at the same time President Hoover's advisors were preparing budget estimates on the presumption that recovery would come in 1931. Hindsight suggested to subsequent observers that Hoover was being particularly obtuse, if not misleading (as Roosevelt charged) in projecting so early a recovery. But inference from past experience and widely-accepted economic doctrine supported Hoover's view fully. The most recent depression of 1920-21 had passed within a year. Business cycle theory, at which American economists excelled, assured businessmen and policy makers that a descent invariably created the conditions for a subsequent ascent. There was no reason to believe that this would not happen in 1931.

Eccles did not indicate why he came earlier than most to believe spontaneous recovery would not occur as usual, but two explanations seem plausible. First, the economy of Eccles' home state, based primarily upon livestock, agriculture, and mining, had not experienced the prosperity enjoyed by more industrialized areas after the depression of 1920-21.[34] This fact would tend to encourage a certain amount of skepticism concerning the prospects of an early recovery from the later depression. The inferences Eccles drew from the 1920-21 experience would not be the same as those most policy makers and economists, living in the more industrialized East, had drawn. Second, Eccles had not been exposed to the tide of opinion led by professional economists which emphasized the cyclical nature of economic fluctuations. Those who followed the latest doctrine of the experts knew that economic movements were cyclical in nature and that recovery could be expected soon.[35] Eccles was not as fully in touch with the teachings of economic theories as were bankers in the East. He accordingly began to search on his own for an effective means of stimulating the economy.

By 1932 Eccles was arguing that positive government intervention provided the only possible hope of recovery. "The government, if it is worthy of the support, the loyalty, and the patriotism of its citizens," he said, "must so regulate . . . the economic structure as to give men who are able and worthy and willing to work the opportunity to work and to guarantee them sustenance for their families and protection against want and destitution."[36] This proposal seems commonplace today. It seemed much less so at the time, however, even in the desperate conditions of 1932. Virtually everyone accepted the idea that government intervention of limited scope and duration was desirable. But once needed correctives were achieved, through cooperative efforts of business and government, through restructuring of price and income mechanism, or through monetary pump priming, it was assumed that the government could withdraw and that America could go back to business as usual. Rare was the banker-industrialist who would have proposed government "regulation" of the economy and federal "guarantees" against want. But Eccles represented a people still close to their nineteenth-century traditions, a group not sharing the normal American aversion to such proposals. If the word "church" were substituted for "government", the statement would easily have received the endorsement of the Mormon church hierarchy. Eccles was only transferring to secular government responsibilities which church government in Utah had under taken for decades as a matter of course.

Eccles rejected the idea that balancing the budget would promote recovery, arguing that fiscal accounts would balance only when the depression, the main cause for the imbalance, had been corrected. In the meantime, the drive to balance the budget could only prevent the government from taking action which could promote recovery. In taking this position, as in others, Eccles' ability to escape the entrapment of old ideas was as essential as his ability to come up with new ones. His escape on the budget balancing question was relatively easy, compared with the difficulties Hoover, Roosevelt or Morgenthau experienced in that regard. Eccles had been distant and uninvolved when the reform movement which had attached crucial importance to a balanced budget was instituted. Old dogmas tended less to obstruct him because he had never learned the catechism of the old faith. He could look away from the budget figures to what seemed to him more important indicators of national well-being.

The critical problem, in Eccles' estimation, was the drastic drop in national income. Eccles' explanation of this calamity centered upon a maldistribution of income, a circumstance which prevented consumption from keeping pace with production. His analysis of these problems was enhanced by a "macro-economic vision" of the workings of the economy. While other bankers were concerned with keeping their institutions solvent, Eccles was noticing that such actions had the aggregate effect of assuring that most banks would ultimately fail. "By forcing the liquidation of loans and securities to meet the demands of depositers", Eccles proposed, "were we not helping to drive prices down and making it increasingly difficult for our debtors to pay back what they had borrowed from us"? As an owner of lumber mills, Eccles was painfully aware that production could be resumed only when demand increased. As an owner of banks, he noticed that the drastic decline in values impeded repayment of debts contracted before the decline.[37] Eccles' business interests were notably diverse, and of commanding importance in a relatively undeveloped region. A sense of the need for an appropriate relationship between savings and investment comes readily to members of a growing provincial community, unhappily dependent upon capital from abroad. The effect of bank policies on the lumber industry and the effect of lumber on construction were all amplified as matters of personal concern, leading Eccles to the macroeconomic vision which permitted his insight into the workings of aggregate components of the wage and credit structure. He saw interrelatedness where many businessmen saw only the problems of the particular sector with which they were concerned.

How then did deficit spending come to occupy so important a place among Eccles' recommendations for stimulating recovery? Eccles' macroeconomic view made it evident that in its effect on the economy, government spending was no different from private spending. It was essential to keep the spending stream flowing and if private spending dried up under depression conditions, only government spending could supplant it.

"The assumption of spontaneous revival through new investment has always rested on the fallacious belief that people and banks will not indefinitely hold money in idleness," Eccles wrote in 1933. "The only escape from a depression must be by increased spending. In the absence of new fields for investment in a world already glutted with unsalable products, the only way to increase spending is for the Government to spend." The government, he maintained, could borrow idle funds and spend without concern for profits, a course that would spell disaster to a private firm.[38]

Eccles later saw his conversion to deficit spending as a rejection of his father's outmoded system of values, especially his father's devotion to thrift. "The difficulty," he said, "is that we were not sufficiently extravagant as a nation."[39] But if thrift can be properly seen as avoidance of waste, then Eccles did not depart as far as he thought from the important values of his father's life. The great crime of the Depression, from his point of view, was the waste caused by idle productive facilities. He would willingly encourage the vice of public extravagance if it would eliminate the enormously greater waste caused by idle resources. He was simply choosing the only apparent means of eliminating the greater waste. The thrift and industry commended to him by his father were still cardinal virtues.

When Eccles wrote his memoirs in 1950, he maintained that his father's career had "governed my own conduct from the time of his death in 1912 to a memorable day in 1930." At that time, distressed by the Depression, the younger Eccles "became disenchanted of . . . [his father's] simple faith," beginning, as he put it, "my search for a body of ideas and practices more suited to an economy that had outgrown the frontier."[40] It seems likely, however, that Marriner's eventual estrangement from the Mormon church caused him to underestimate the influence upon his own thought of his Mormon background. One suspects the ideas of the elder Eccles continued to be influential far longer than the son remembered, and indeed, that Eccles' most distinctive insights derived in part from his family's Mormon pioneer heritage. David Eccles' portrait long dominated the Salt Lake City office of his son, occupying a conspicuous place over the marbled mantlepiece. The small bronze bust of FDR was on the mantlepiece below.

Eccles nonetheless retained a profound respect for the enormous productive capabilities of the liberal capitalism which had been the source of his father's wealth, telling Frederic A. Delano that it was "the system we want to preserve." Other businessmen, not possessed of the alternative visions available to Eccles, felt there was no room for compromise, that government encroachment upon the prerogatives of private business might irreparably damage the productive capacity of that system. Eccles was acutely aware of "the difficulty of keeping the private economy going concurrently with the introduction of large elements of public control." But long before he discussed the problem with Gulick in 1937, he was sure he had found the means of overcoming that difficulty.

It is, of course, obvious that many persons not sharing Eccles' background came to similar conclusions and that many who shared his background came to different conclusions. No one would contend that only a Mormon industrialist could have been permitted access to Eccles' vision or that all Mormon industrialists would have shared it. Some writers have expressed wonderment, however, that a Mormon banker could have arrived independently at such insights. Basil Rauch, in reviewing Eccles' memoir was disappointed that the book "does little to help us understand how Saul became Paul. We are asked to believe that the forty-year-old Mormon banker was converted to compensatory economic theory by 'naked-eye observation and experience' without benefit of Keynes."[41] In fact, Eccles' background, far from inhibiting the development of his ideas, could easily have encouraged them. It must be remembered that the great variety of enterprises Eccles controlled in

58

the Mountain West made him very nearly _sui generis_ among westerners, among Mormons, and even among Mormon industrialists. Perhaps his singular position, plus his unusual sharing of the vantage points of all these group favored so distinctive an accomplishment in the development of economic thought.

Rauch's comment on Eccles' memoir raises another point. His implication that commitment to a compensatory fiscal policy is unlikely without exposure to Keynes is not uncommon among historians and economists who have written on the development of fiscal policy. The historian John Morton Blum spoke with obvious relief of a moment when "at last the insights of Keynesian theory . . . [penetrated] both the academic world and some councils of government."[42] In commenting on a set of papers by prominent economists which implied that the evolution of fiscal policy in America had been primarily the work of Keynes' disciples, Leon H. Keyserling contended that "the inbred insularity of the academicians first divorced them from much influence upon what was done . . . and later led them to do the wrong things when their influence increased." He concluded, "With all due respect to Keynes, I have been unable to discover much evidence that the New Deal would have been greatly different if he had never lived, and if a so-called school of economics had not taken on his name."[43]

Those familiar with Keynes will notice that he, like Eccles, concluded that aggregate supply and demand need not find an equilibrium at a level of full employment. The "multiplier" concept which Keynes borrowed from R.F. Kahn, the "propensity to consume," and the "liquidity preference" all are part of Eccles' system, sufficiently well-formulated to lead to similar policy conclusions. Keynes was important to New Dealers, but not as an influence upon policy. Nor was he of decisive importance in forming the new economic ideology New Dealers were moving towards in 1937-38. However, as we shall see, he was important in providing an external theoretical justification for that ideology after it was well on its way to becoming accepted by a preponderance of New Dealers.

ECCLES AND ROOSEVELT

The nature of Eccles' associations with his New Deal colleagues was to be of great importance during the Recession of 1937. He was hardly confirmed as chairman of the Board of Governors when tension began to arise between himself and Morgenthau. During the next several years their relationship flared at times into such acrimony that they deliberately avoided seeing one another for short periods. Their disagreements often arose from small misunderstandings, one feeling the other had betrayed a confidence or disregarded a common understanding.[44] The nature of their respective responsibilities, however, would have tried the patience of men far more compatible in personality than Eccles and Morgenthau. Eccles was convinced at the time he was appointed head of the Reserve System that monetary policies must be combined with appropriate fiscal policies to achieve stability. Morgenthau became head of the fiscal arm of government convinced that the main aim of fiscal policy was to finance government operations as economically as possible and to move towards a balanced budget. Eccles freely offered advice on matters Morgenthau felt were his own concern. When in 1936 the Treasury began sterilizing gold to prevent the potential inflationary effect of enormous incoming gold movements, Morgenthau gained for the treasury a powerful instrument of monetary control. Though responsibility in fiscal and monetary matters had been divided by Congress between two separate agencies, it was clear that the policies of one had important effects upon those of the other. In such circumstances, men as dissimilar in their convictions on economic matters as Eccles and Morgenthau would be certain to have difficulties.

Lauchlin Currie became concerned about the possible harmful effects of feelings between the two officials in 1936, reminding Eccles that monetary policy must be supplemented with proper tax policies and "a flexible public spending program in . . . which things the Treasury has a decisive voice." Cooperation with the Treasury, he suggested, "must be the cornerstone of our policy if it is to have any chance of success." Morgenthau, he pointed out, was "a person intensely loyal to the President and extremely jealous of the prerogatives of his office." Currie then offered insightful assessment of Eccles' role in Washington. "I know you to be one of the most disinterested people I have ever met," Currie wrote.

> I know that you put ideas and objectives above personalities. I know you are in Washington today not for the purpose of enhancing the authority of your office for its own sake, but because you feel that you can make a contribution to the most pressing problem of our day. Since the contribution you can make rests in the final analysis on the degree of cooperation you can obtain from the Secretary, I think you will be prepared to make real sacrifices for the sake of your wider objectives.[45]

There is evidence that the tension between the two men was increased by a competitive spirit which developed, at least from Morgenthau's viewpoint, over who exercised the greatest influence with the President on fiscal policy. Late in 1936, Eccles prepared a memo for Roosevelt urging caution in moving towards a balanced budget. Morgenthau apparently felt threatened, expressing his fears that if he did not "dynamite" Eccles' argument, he might "find that Eccles will become the President's fiscal advisor."[46]

Certainly in any such competition, Morgenthau held important strategic advantages over Eccles. Getting the attention of the President was much easier for Morgenthau than it was for Eccles. The Morgenthau's long friendship with the Roosevelts, the Hudson valley gentleman tradition in which both families were steeped, gave Morgenthau advantages which the westerner could not even approximate. Morgenthau had been brought into the Treasury with a jovial "We'll have fun doing it together."[47] He and FDR had a standing appointment for lunch each Monday. There were indeed times when, as Morgenthau told his staff in October 1937, the President was consulting him "on everything"--when he was with the President "almost constantly."[48]

Eccles very rarely was extended such privileges. There is a particularly striking anecdote in Eccles' memoirs which underscores the frustration of an advisor on important policy matters who did not enjoy the advantage of being included in the President's inner circle. In late 1939, Eccles arrived at the White House for a coveted luncheon appointment to discuss several matters of importance to the Federal Reserve. Upon arriving, the Federal Reserve Chairman was told that the President was behind in his appointment schedule. Eccles was asked to wait until a conference with Senator William G. McAdoo of California was ended. Twenty minutes later, Eccles was ushered in, but the senator refused to take the President's hint that he was about to sit down for lunch. McAdoo finally left, but as the luncheon ended, the President summoned his Scotty, Fala, throwing the ball for her to retrieve for several minutes. Finally, the relaxation over, he turned to Eccles to talk business. But just as the conversation began they were interrupted again when the President noted that Fala had committed an egregious social error on the carpet in the President's office. Then and there the dog was taught the error of her ways, as Eccles put it, "under the general supervision of the President of the United States." Finally, one and one-half hours after Eccles' arrival, the two turned again to business, only to be interrupted momentarily by the announcement that the President's next visitor had arrived. Eccles was ushered out without getting a chance to discuss the matter bringing him to the White House.

Eccles and the President

"A few minutes with Roosevelt was a prize sought by all," Eccles recalled. "To gain it and exploit it took as much advance planning as if the objective was a D-day landing. And when at last an appointment was set, a host of distractions often cut across what was discussed and what was to be decided."[46] The Morgenthau Diaries make it clear that Morgenthau seldom underwent the trials in gaining access to the President which were for others, by Eccles' account, a common experience. Certainly insofar as influence upon the President was a function of time spent with him, Eccles worked at a distinct disadvantage.

There were three reasons why Eccles was less successful than Morgenthau in gaining access to the President. His background, as we have seen, was markedly dissimilar, preventing him from achieving the relaxed familiarity which characterized the group closest to the President. His personality was brusque compared with the genteel style to which Roosevelt had been bred; at times, it was even abrasive. Eccles had little patience with small talk. He was a man who, when there was business to be done, resented anything that might distract from expeditious consideration of the matter at hand. He would have found it difficult to understand a suggestion from the President with regard to public office that they would "have fun doing it together." It was simply not his style. He wrote that he was infuriated by the Fala incident until his colleagues William Clayton and Elliot Thurston pointed out the humor in the situation.[50]

Eccles worked under another disadvantage as well, stemming from the particular governmental office which he held. Morgenthau, as Secretary of the Treasury, was a top-ranking administration official and thus could legitimately act as spokesman for government policy. Eccles, though appointed by the President, was chairman of an independent regulatory commission in which decisions and policy were, in theory at least, to be determined by the seven-man Board of Governors. After appointment to the Board chairmanship in 1934, Eccles felt the need to be circumspect in his public utterances. On the one hand, he had to avoid conveying the impression that his own opinions represented those of the entire Board of Governors. On the other hand, he found it necessary to prevent any suggestion that he was spokesman for the Administration—a role which might compromise the cherished independence of the Federal Reserve System. Though Eccles still managed to speak his mind when he felt circumstances warranted, his situation nonetheless imposed real constraints. In the spring of 1935, Presidential Secretary Steve Early complained of Eccles' reticence to speak out since his appointment to the Federal Reserve Board. "We are under attack with our best gun silenced," he told Marvin McIntyre.[51] Eccles rejected Frederic A. Delano's 1936 suggestion that he publish his Wharton School address in the Federal Reserve Bulletin with the explanation "that it would be inadvisable to print talks of this character in the Bulletin, since it would almost certainly be misunderstood and we would be accused of using the Bulletin for partisan political purposes which would, of course, do more harm than good."[52]

Eccles managed, despite such handicaps, to develop a following of persons with similar views on administration fiscal policies. His speeches were particularly effective in attracting the attention of like-minded New Dealers and New Deal partisans. In November 1935, he addressed a hostile convention of the American Banking Association in New Orleans, speaking extemporaneously from notes he had prepared after arriving in New Orleans. The speech prompted Stuart Chase to write, "I thought it was the most admirable summary of the Administration's policy and the actual results achieved which I have yet seen." The secretary of Aubrey Williams, assistant to Harry Hopkins, wrote that Williams was "very anxious to obtain a copy of Mr. Eccles' speech." Frederick A. Delano, of the National Resources Committee, requested twenty-five to fifty copies to send to friends, suggesting the speech be made into a pamphlet. George T. Ross, then an employee of the NRA, wrote that after rereading the speech several times, he had come to the conclusion that it

> represents a philosophy which alone can justify our governmental program. I have often thought that, whether or not Woodrow Wilson's governmental concepts were essentially correct, his strength was in his being guided definitely and usually consistently by a philosophy of government which itself was his greatest bulwark against attacks from those who called upon opportunism as their weapon in place of opposing political philosophy . . .. Frankly, your speech contains the only definite, logical, and comprehensive answer I have seen to three-fourths of the attacks on the Government's spending program-- and a clear explanation as to why it was necessary.

Among the many congratulatory letters were notes from Secretary Wallace, Attorney General Homer Cummings, W.I. Myers of the Farm Credit Administration, Paul Appleby of the Department of Agriculture, and representative T. Alan Goldsborough. Myers and Appleby requested extra copies to send to friends.

Speeches Eccles gave the next spring in Philadelphia and New York prompted similar responses. William I. Myers again requested copies for his friends. Herbert Gaston, Morgenthau's aide, wrote that Eccles' presentation was "a tough one for anybody to answer. This is the philosophy on which this election is going to be won." The eminent publicist Walter Lippmann added his own perceptive comments. "As you know," he wrote Eccles,

> I am in substantial agreement with your own philosophy in these matters. My one quarrel with your speech is that you treat this aspect of the administration's policy as if it exists separated from what in rough description we might call the collectivist measures. Surely they have greatly counteracted and neutralized and made more difficult the monetary and financial policy. In fact, there have been two contradictory philosophies at work and my impression is that if your philosophy had been applied consistently, leaving the other one aside, it would have worked twice as effectively. At that, it is pulling us out of the hole and overcoming the damage done by the other policy as well.[53]

These letters indicate that years before the Recession, Eccles had cultivated a small but significant group of friends and admirers both inside and outside of the Administration--persons who were predisposed to support Eccles' contention when recession struck, that a stepped-up spending program was a vital necessity.

Other Washington contacts were to be useful to Eccles in the recession crisis. Through his Reserve Board appointment, Eccles met the President's uncle, Frederick A. Delano, of the National Resources Committee, and Delano's colleagues on the committee, Ralph E. Flanders, Henry S. Denison, and Beardsley Ruml.[54] Delano had been a member of the Federal Reserve Board and vice-governor before he resigned in 1918 to enter the army. From 1921 to 1936 he was chairman of the board and federal reserve agent in the Richmond, Virginia Reserve Bank, while serving also from 1933 as vice-chairman of the National Resources Committee. Ruml, an executive of the Macy corporation, was appointed a director of the New York Reserve Bank by Eccles in the summer of 1937. These men met with Eccles frequently during the early New Deal, exchanging views on fiscal policy and coming to similar conclusions. They were to be helpful in promoting Eccles' ideas during the winter of 1937-38, when the Reserve Board chairman was locked with Morgenthau in a grim struggle over who would exercise decisive influence on the President in the formulation of a recovery program.

The Recession of 1937 raised anew the complex and difficult questions confronting policy makers throughout the decade. How can the government provide greater social benefits for its citizens, promote recovery, institute changes to minimize the extremes of future cyclical fluctuations, and yet not interfere with the fundamental workings of the system, nor frighten the business community? "The government," Eccles maintained,

> can spend money, because the government has the power of taxation and power to create money and does not have to depend on the profit motive. The only escape from a depression must be by increased spending. We must depend upon the government to save what we have of a price, profit, and credit system.

Eccles had arrived in Washington with arguments to justify New Deal deficit financing and to show "how the increased production and employment that the policy would create was the only way a depression could be ended and a budget balanced."[55] Though he had presented these arguments to New Deal Officials since 1933 and to the public on every justifiable occasion, it took a Roosevelt recession to move them into the mainstream of New Deal thought. By that time his ideas, supported by other practical men of like mind, and by a growing group of professional economists, provided the most convincing justification for a resumption of spending policies forced by circumstances upon a reluctant president. Strong justification was needed, for government spending as an anti-recessionary measure probably commanded less general acceptance in 1937 than it had at any time since Herbert Hoover had made it the foundation of his own anti-depression policy in 1929.

_____

CHAPTER FOUR

GOVERNMENT SPENDING IN DEPRESSION--"A NEW EXPERIMENT IN OUR ECONOMIC LIFE"

PUBLIC SPENDING AS AN ANTI-DEPRESSION POLICY

Many of the reformers who had advocated a budgeting system in the 1920's also supported the use of government spending as a "balance wheel" to mitigate economic fluctuations. Eccles was probably unaware that a variant of his spending proposals had enjoyed wide popularity in the East during the 1920's and had been applied under Hoover with unprecedented vigor. The doctrine was discredited because the rationale recommending it had limited government spending to levels well below those needed to combat the Great Depression. By the time Eccles arrived in Washington in 1934, little remained of the once optimistic hopes of reformers for combatting depressions through contra-cyclical timing of government expenditures.

The concept of "government spending" used as it now is, separately from any indiction of the nature or purpose of the spending, is a direct product of Eccles' point of view and an indication of how fully such views now permeate American thinking. Before the New Deal, it was as uncommon to speak of "government spending" as it would have been to speak of "family spending." There were few contexts in which the phrase, used without reference to the purpose of the spending (such as public works, or military), would have had any practical positive meaning.

During the nineteenth century the question of whether possible excess government revenues could properly be used for public works experienced a history very similar to the question of whether or not there should be a central budgeting authority. Constitutional scruples and the intrigues of congressional politics prevented the formulation of a consistent policy with regard to the acceptable amount of government involvement in public works or "internal improvement" projects.[1]

In addition, nineteenth century policy makers felt that public works spending bore only an indirect relationship to general economic activity. One of the main constitutional arguments politicians used to oppose public works was that they were not sufficiently general in their economic benefits, that they promoted particular, rather than the "general welfare."[2] They saw the economic benefit from such projects (the model being the spectacular success of the Erie Canal) to be more in terms of the benefits in expanded trading and job opportunities offered by the completed project than in terms of possible economic benefits of the construction itself. Workers, particularly recent immigrants, were attracted to construction sites, but the work offered them was by no means considered a charity and the wages paid were the same whether the projects were being undertaken with public or with private funds. The deliberate inauguration of public works as a device to create jobs for the unemployed was, with a few exceptions, a twentieth century innovation.

It was common in the nineteenth and early twentieth centuries, when referring to public works, to distinguish them from the occasional work offered to the indigent on poor farms or in workhouses in exchange for public assistance. The former consisted of the building of canals, dams, bridges, and highways—major projects of lasting utility requiring numbers of dependable skilled workers. The persistent problem of caring for the poor caused public officials in many communities to devise work projects so that the community might be recompensed in some measure for its charity. But because the poor were often in ill health and were generally lacking in skills needed for major construction projects, "relief work" projects were usually of the "make-work" type, offering little in the way of a lasting contribution to the community. There was no federal involvement in work relief in the nineteenth century, local government and private charities bearing the burden of providing for paupers.[3]

As the nineteenth century progressed, the increasing severity of industrial depressions caused periodic unemployment of such massive proportions as to overwhelm institutions traditionally caring for the poor. An innovative response to the problem, employing careful timing of government expenditures, began in France, where official bulletins issued at the turn of the century urged governmental agencies to hold public works in reserve to provide constructive employment for those losing their jobs during future industrial depressions. Under the stimulus of studies by the British social reformers, Sidney and Beatrice Webb, and the statistician, A.L. Bowley, the idea gained currency at about the same time in Britain. In 1911 Parliament established a permanent committee to aid the Minister of Labor in timing public works so they would correspond with cyclical downturns in business activity.[4]

Serious attention to the possibility of using public works to counter depression began in the United States under the stimulus of the Depression of 1920-21. At the instigation of Herbert Hoover, President Harding in 1921 convened a conference to conduct an extensive study of unemployment as it related to business cycles. Committees of this conference sponsored several studies over the next eight years, the most famous published in 1923, under the title of Business Cycles and Unemployment.[5]

The work of the President's Conference on Unemployment influenced the attitudes of public officials and business towards public works through most of the 1920's and 1930's. The analytical approach of studies sponsored by the President's Conference reflected the business cycle mentality common among economists, government policy makers, and many businessmen during the 1920's. "The modern view," Wesley C. Mitchell, the Columbia economist and student of business cycles wrote, "is that economic" crises are but one feature of recurrent 'business cycles.' Instead of a 'normal' state of business interrupted by occasional crises, men look for a continually changing state of business-- continually changing in a fairly regular way. A crisis is expected to be followed by a depression, the depression by a revival, the revival by prosperity, and prosperity by a new crisis." The widespread acceptance of the main lines of Mitchell's analysis as the latest in scientific research and opinion suggested that business crises did not signal fundamental change within the economy, but rather were incidental to a regularly-occurring phenomenon, the course of which was well-understood and predictable. "A period of depression produces after a time certain

69

conditions which favor an increase of business activity," Mitchell explained further. "Experience indicates that, once begun, a recovery . . . tends to grow cumulatively." Finally, "While the processes just sketched work cumulatively for a time to enhance prosperity, they also cause a slow accumulation of stresses within the balanced system of business--stresses which ultimately undermine the conditions upon which prosperity rests." Thus, "business cycles run an unceasing round, each cycle growing out of its predecessor and moving into its successor."[6]

Students of the role of public works in mitigating the extremes of the business cycle worked under the assumptions Mitchell had expressed. If change in economic activity is cyclical rather than secular, then public works can be timed to act as a "balance wheel" to stabilize the fluctuations by countering the tendencies prevailing in the private sector. The proposal threatened no long run change in the ordinary relationship between government and private enterprise, since from one cycle to the next the ratio of public spending to private spending would not change. The government would not be required to expand into new and controversial areas of activity, but was expected only to manage more systematically the functions already considered within its legitimate realm. The government would not compete with private industry for labor or materials, since its projects would be inaugurated at times when there was a surfeit of unemployed and excess plant capacity and cut back when the opposite conditions prevailed. Thus, the rationale for public works spending neither admitted nor threatened fundamental change in the functioning of the American economy.[7]

The argument for the efficacy of public works spending as a balance wheel rested upon the assumption that future fluctuations would be no more intense nor prolonged than past ones had been. A.L. Bowley had concluded in 1909 that a reserve of only three to four percent of "normal" public works expenditures would be sufficient to compensate for the loss of wages during depressions, thus effectively smoothing out the extremes of the cycle.[8] Bowley's statistics were gathered from the 1896-1906 decade in England, where public expenditures already occupied a larger place in the economy than in America, but his figures were taken as broadly indicative of what could be done with properly-timed public works expenditures in the United States.

The conclusion seemed justified by the American experience with the 1920-21 Depression. In 1921 the President's Conference on Unemployment had achieved some success in urging mayors of major cities to expand public works, "the greatest effort on record," Pennsylvania State Industrial Board member Otto T. Mallery recalled, "to expand public works during an unemployment period." He voiced a widely-held opinion concerning the lessons to be learned from that experience when he pointed out that:

> Successful execution of public works assisted the
> resumption of private construction on the large
> scale noted in 1922. The total probably shortened
> the depression, but is only a partial index to what
> may be accomplished in the next unemployment period
> if the states, counties, and towns incorporate their
> experience into administrative methods of long-range
> planning.[9]

While these references were to state and local projects, the experience
served as the basis for arguments used in behalf of federal projects.
The traditionally appropriate range of feasible projects for federal
spending was known to be significantly smaller than for state and local
governments (the public works projects for states and cities were about
five times those of the federal government in 1923), yet advocates of
federal action maintained that "the federal one-fifth is a convenient
key to unlock many doors."

Mallery advised consolidation of the various government agencies
involved in public works spending in order to assure that spending would
be used more effectively as a compensatory factor in the economy. He
recommended matching grants to induce the greatest amount of spending
from local agencies, particularly in road construction. Mallery's supporters proposed various means of financing the expenditures but most
felt a reserve should be saved during prosperous years to be freed when
depression threatened. Though policy makers were brought by political
considerations to stress the "pay-as-you-go" method of public financing,
they did not rule out the idea of borrowing to pay for such projects
during sharp business downturns. They further recognized that the
effect of public works spending would be amplified beyond the mere
provision of jobs on public projects, as "the purchasing power of
wages," creating a demand for basic necessities, "exerts a cumulative
effect upon general industry and employment."[10] Government officials
could see public works spending as an acceptable depression remedy
because past experience, especially the Depression of 1920-21, suggested
that a relatively small outlay could effectively mitigate business
cycles without damaging the long-range fiscal condition of the government or altering the relationship of government to private enterprise.

The reasoning favoring public works spending was also reinforced by
its happy conformity with the lingering progressive obsession with
efficiency and economy. Public works pursued during depression, when
interest rates, labor costs, and prices were low, would give the
taxpayer the maximum possible benefit for his tax dollar. Long range

planning would insure that a backlog of projects, adequately planned and researched, and tested for soundness and utility, would be on the shelf when needed. The ultimate effect, over the business cycle, would be to provide needed public services and facilities at the lowest possible cost, while at the same time minimizing the waste and inefficiency caused by unemployment in depression. Americans would enjoy the dual benefits of obtaining public facilities at bargain prices and gaining more stable incomes with which to pay for them.

Policy makers of the 1930's denounced "relief work," the alternative form of government spending in depression, because of the same considerations causing them to praise public works spending. The President's Conference on Unemployment expressed its opposition to relief work in terms which betrayed a sense that the proffering and accepting of relief work somehow corrupted both giver and receiver. While the roots of this distaste undoubtedly lay in the moral opprobrium associated with the workhouse method of poor relief in the nineteenth century, the main points of the committee's argument were couched in terms of economy and efficiency:

> Relief works are improvised to afford emergency employment and are performed by necessitous persons often without consideration of their fitness and usually at wages below the market rate. Quantity and quality of production are secondary matters.

Reformers of the 1920's rejected relief work because quantity and quality of production tended to become secondary considerations in such projects. Otto T. Mallery pointed out the ominous lessons highlighted by the experience of Massachusetts with relief work in 1895:

> Wages of from one to two dollars per day were paid; only simple kinds of work were undertaken; not enough work could be extemporized for the applicants; workers were rotated; the total expenditure was inadequate; from a business point of view the results were not economical . . .
> General experience in relief works shows their inadequacy to relieve national unemployment, the pitfalls to be avoided, and points towards long-range planning as a more economical and potent method.[11]

Relief work seemed to have no place in an age of scientific planning and administration, violating, as it did, the cherished efficiency ideal.

It is not surprising, then, that Herbert Hoover, the foremost champion of efficiency and economy in public affairs, lent his support during the 1920's to legislation proposing that public works be planned far in advance, and that the level of public works spending be keyed inversely to the level of economic activity. The automatic working of such a device, divorcing public works from political influence, carried great appeal to heirs of progressive reform, providing the ideal counterpart in federal fiscal policy to the Federal Reserve System in monetary policy. Hoover saw this rationale for public works spending as buttress to the prosperity he hoped as President to sustain well into the decade of the 1930's.[12]

PUBLIC WORKS EXPENDITURES UNDER HOOVER

Hoover's action during the Depression in promoting public works spending was entirely consistent with the philosophy recommended in the unemployment conference reports. Shortly after the Wall Street crash the President sent a telegram to the governors of the states explaining that "one of the largest facts of that can be brought to bear," in the effort to absorb unemployment caused by the "disturbed conditions" of 1929 "is that of the energetic yet prudent pursuit of public works by the Federal Government and state, municipal and county authorities."[13] Six months later, he took pride in announcing to the United States Chamber of Commerce that "the acceleration of construction programs has been successful beyond our hopes." This acceleration of public works, he concluded, has been a major factor in helping the economy attain "a state of recovery within this short period greater than that attained during a whole year or more following previous equally great storms."[14]

The next month, in thanking governors for their response to his request, the President called the use of public works to combat depression "a new experiment in our economic life of the first importance," representing "an advance in economic thought in government and in service to our people." No longer would it be necessary to regard depression "as an inevitable fever which must run its course," or to undertake public works "in the sense of semi-charity."

> This time the Nation has realized that as a sound
> economic policy, that prudent expedition of
> construction could be to an important degree used as

a balance wheel to maintain security of employment,
to maintain consumption of goods, to thus contribute
to economic stability, and above all to relieve
hardship. [15]

The President did not state how much the federal contribution to the
expansion of public works had been, but combined federal, state and
local expenditures for that purpose amounted to $1.7 billion, a figure
$200 million greater than had been spent during the same period in
1929. [16] In July 1930, Hoover announced that total federal expenditures
for fiscal 1931 would be $209 million more than for the previous year,
the increase to be used for "the speeding up of buildings, inland waterways and public works generally, in order to assist in unemployment." [17]
These figures were modest compared with later expenditures under
Roosevelt, but did represent, as Hoover maintained, a pioneering effort
on the part of the federal government and as such were substantial.

The President, however, while urging expanded use of the new anti-
depression device, seldom failed to stress the built-in limiting principles which were to choke off its effective use as the crisis deepened.
He frequently specified when recommending increased public works, that
only "prudent" projects, "for which the necessary technical preparation
has been or can be completed," should be pursued. [18]

Pressure to expand works projects beyond limits permitted by the
President's standards of proper planning and need moved him to an increasingly defensive posture as the Depression deepened. By the end of
1930, his reservations seemed almost to dominate his advocacy. "The
Congress," Hoover warned in his second annual address, "will . . . have
presented to it numbers of projects, some of them under the guise of,
rather than the reality of, their usefulness in the increase of employment during the depression." Any expansion of construction work, the
President maintained, must be subject to "certain common-sense limitations." New projects would have to be "of sound economic purpose," as
determined by "searching technical investigation." Finally, the
President asserted that:

> The volume of construction work in the Government is
> already at the maximum limit warranted by financial
> prudence as a continuing policy. . . . Our
> immediate problem is the increase of employment for
> the next six months, and new plans which do not
> produce such immediate results or which extend
> commitments beyond this period are not warranted. [19]

A canvas of government departments had shown that few projects remained which could meet the President's standards of planning and need—only enough to absorb a maximum of $1.5 million. Hoover accordingly requested appropriations in that amount.

Over the next two years President Hoover found himself increasingly concerned with the need to resist congressional efforts to expand government spending and relief. Convinced that in difficult times economy and efficiency in government were even more important than they normally would be, he found himself in the awkward position of opposing the very proposals that in 1929 had been his first line of defense—"a new experiment in our economic life of the first importance." Not only would ill-planned spending programs be wasteful, the President maintained, they would cause either an increase in taxes, thus reducing purchasing power, or if financed by borrowing, would deprive industry and agriculture of needed capital. In either case, the proposed spending programs would defeat their own purpose. By 1932, the Hoover administration's unprecedented acceleration of public works projects had largely depleted the roster of works which could be pursued without violating Hoover's standards of public need and proper planning. Little additional money could be spent because it was felt there remained few useful projects upon which to spend it. The only remaining outlets for spending lay in the areas of relief work, direct relief, or extension of social services, and the prevailing philosophy of government spending in the 1920's had already ruled against these alternatives.

Still another factor constricting further expansion of public works became significant as in fiscal 1931 and 1932 the budgetary surpluses of the 1920's melted into deficits of alarming proportions. The shock of these deficits, the first since the federal budgeting system had been inaugurated in 1921, led the President to a reordering of the arguments upon which his growing opposition to increased spending had been based. Whereas in 1930 he had emphasized the dearth of useful projects as the limiting factors, he now placed greater stress on the argument that a balanced budget was more essential to recovery than the expansion of public works. Concern for economy had replaced concern for efficiency on the President's list of weapons to be used against increased spending.[20]

Hedged about by these constraints, the effect of government spending on the Depression during the Hoover administration was negligible. In the President's budget message for 1933 (delivered December 1932), the early enthusiastic endorsement of public works to counter depression was gone. In its place was a terse statement which might well have served as the obituary for Hoover's "new experiment," had not Roosevelt succeeded him:

Speaking generally of public works, this program is
well in advance of the country's immediate need by
virtue of the vast appropriations made for this
purpose as a means of increasing employment. The
authorization of self-liquidating works . . . provides aid to employment upon an even larger scale
without burden upon the taxpayers. For this reason
the estimates for public works generally for 1934
show a marked reduction below the appropriations for
1933.[21]

The concept of using public works as a balance wheel had been an
eminently progressive and promising innovation, as worked out under
Hoover's guidance in the 1920's. It had been all but discarded by the
end of 1932. It had failed because the limitations built into the
rationale commending it did not permit expansion sufficient to have
telling effects upon a depression of unprecedented severity and duration. Though Hoover knew that spending had value in its general effect
upon the economy as well as in is specific product, he could not, in the
final analysis, take his attention from the final product. To continue
spending when everything useful had been bought already, and when there
was no money left in any case, seemed to Hoover to be an exercise in
folly.

In the heat of the 1932 campaign, Hoover's opponent, Franklin D.
Roosevelt proposed, as if it were a new idea, that a "nest egg" be set
up in prosperous times to provide for public works in hard times.
Hoover must have smiled wryly when he heard of the speech. "It will
doubtless surprise him," the President responded, "to learn that the
eggs have not only been laid but have hatched."[22] Certainly the product
of Hoover's endeavors in this regard had not been all he had hoped for.

EARLY NEW DEAL SPENDING PROGRAMS

Roosevelt assumed the presidency at a time when the popularity of
public works spending among policy makers was at a low ebb. It was a
tool which, in Hoover's hands, had been worn to a nub without visible
effect. Nonetheless Roosevelt, seriously lacking in alternatives, took
it for his own. He did so reluctantly, however, in accord with an
ordering of concerns different from those of Hoover. "The urgent

76

question today," Hoover had announced in May 1932, "is the prompt balancing of the budget. When that is accomplished I propose to support adequate measures for relief of distress and unemployment."[23] "If starvation and dire need on the part of any of our citizens make necessary the appropriations of additional funds which would keep the budget out of balance," Roosevelt responded, "I shall not hesitate to tell the American people the full truth and ask them to authorize the expenditure of that additional amount."[24]

The early approaches of Roosevelt to the problem of relief illustrate the differences in viewpoint of the two leaders. Hoover, consistent to his belief that relief work was wasteful and inefficient, did very little as president to promote federal relief work projects, relying almost entirely on public works.[25] Roosevelt was more flexible. He began in March 1933 to expand government spending to include a much broader range and variety of projects, particularly adding projects which would have been classified by Hoover as "relief work" and hence unacceptable on grounds of inefficiency. Roosevelt's impulsive humanitarianism led him eventually to break down the old distinction between public works--employing skilled men at standard wages to build needed enduring structures--and relief work--providing jobs for the poor and inept on makeshift projects of dubious value. The distinction had once served to set the poor apart as persons deserving of the stigma endowed by public wardship. The Great Depression underscored the absurdity of the old belief that paupers somehow deserved privation and public calumny. Respectable self-reliant, able-bodied people found themselves poor, through no fault of their own, and with no independent means of altering their situation. Roosevelt understood more clearly than did Hoover the importance and dimension of this change, seeking through his disregard of the traditional distinction between public works and work relief to provide employment that would preserve a maximum of self respect and pay at a living wage.

Nevertheless, Roosevelt's public discussion of New Deal work programs shows a marked degree of ambiguity and uncertainty. Through most of the decade, the President remained as uncomfortable with the apparent success of his spending programs as with the failure of his efforts to balance the budget. The reason, in retrospect, seems obvious. Unprecedented circumstances were forcing the President into unfamiliar and uncharted waters. Yet he could not bring himself to abandon use of those charts that he possessed, however remote their relationship to the new situation. Confronted with widespread deprivation and unemployment, the President had to take action that would relieve the situation. "Direct relief," or the dole was clearly, according to conventional belief, damaging to initiative and self-respect. The best way to put money into the hands of the people, it was widely known, was through public employment in useful, enduring projects--public works.

Yet the previous administration had exhausted the roster of such public works, at least according to the limits and standards which had governed their planning and use during the period when the attitudes of both Hoover and Roosevelt were being formed. Roosevelt could significantly expand levels of government spending only by departing from Hoover's standards in one or more of three directions. He could lower previous standards of care in choosing needed projects and giving them adequate planning and technical preparation. He could resort to hitherto disreputable "relief works." He could employ persons in useful areas hitherto considered inappropriate for government activity on ideological grounds.

Neither Roosevelt nor his chief advisors had any expectation that government spending could help combat the Depression, except on a short term basis, a fact which greatly complicated their decision making. Throughout most of the decade Roosevelt could not bring himself to depart substantially from the position he had taken in April 1932:

> It is the habit of the unthinking to turn in times like this to the illusions of economic magic. People suggest that a huge expenditure of public funds by the Federal Government and by State and local governments will completely solve the unemployment problem. But it is clear that even if we could raise many billions of dollars and find definitely useful public works to spend these billions on, even all that money would not give employment to the seven million or ten million people who are out of work. Let us admit frankly that this would be only a stopgap. A real economic cure must go to the killing of the bacteria in the system rather than to the treatment of external symptoms.[26]

This skepticism entered into Roosevelt's attitude towards the various relief and public works programs he inaugurated on an emergency basis in 1933 and 1934. The cumbersome names chosen for the various spending programs of Roosevelt's first term are evidence of a tentative and uncertain attitude towards spending as the President groped towards a viable works program while attempting to cling to older standards of economy and efficiency.

The Civilian Conservation Corps initiated in early April 1933 offered the low wages and unskilled jobs usually associated with relief work. The program had the redeeming virtue, however, of employing young men on useful permament projects yet untouched by Hoover's programs because the federal government had not previously involved itself in massive land and forest management activities. Happily combining Roosevelt's devotion to the conservation of natural resources with the need to provide jobs for youth, it was to be perhaps the most popular and enduring of the early New Deal spending programs. The President did not expect, however, that the program would provide a substantial stimulus to the economy.[27]

Roosevelt set up the Federal Emergency Relief Administration a month later as an agency for disbursing relief funds to state governments which then determined their specific application. The $500 million appropriated for the program was to be used insofar as possible "to encourage real public works," but a number of projects, the President later noted, were "too hastily planned or of the 'leaf-raking' type." Despite federal guidelines, direct relief to the unemployable accounted for a large portion of FERA disbursements. Though the President remained uncomfortable with the direct relief and work relief features of the FERA, he allowed the agency to continue until August 1936, primarily because it met human needs that apparently could be met in no other way.[28]

Under Title II of the National Industrial Recovery Act, Congress established the Public Works Administration in mid-June 1933. Initial funding for this agency was $3.3 billion. The PWA was administered by Harold L. Ickes in the classic public works tradition, carrying out carefully-planned enduring public projects of unquestioned utility. By the standards of the 1920's, the PWA under Ickes was a model of careful and efficient use of public funds. But by the standard which was to become of first importance in measuring he efficiency of depression spending programs--the speed with which money was put into the spending stream--the PWA was a plodding failure. Ickes had awarded only $900 million in contracts by the beginning of 1934. Of this amount he had actually spent but $110 million.[29] In any case, public interest was quickly drawn from PWA activities towards the novel and controversial National Recovery Administration established under Title I of the same act. Though these two agencies, so different in conception, have been seen as strange bedfellows, it was originally expected that the PWA would provide an immediate lift to the spending stream, which the NRA, with its dramatic restructuring of the traditional determinants of production and distribution, would then sustain. Neither expectation was realized, and the summer rally was followed by an autumn slump, leading the President to improvise hastily the Civil Works Administration in November to help the unemployed through the winter of 1933-34.[30]

The Civil Works Administration was the first major attempt by the Administration to combine the newly found advantages of work relief (putting money quickly into the spending stream) and the traditional advantages of public works (efficient use of public funds). The President explained that the Public Works Administration had accomplished little "because of the unavoidable time-consuming process of planning". The Federal Emergency Relief Administration, on the other hand, had been "too often concerned with projects of little or no value . . . almost exclusively undertaken by unskilled manual labor and . . . generally of low efficiency." The CWA under Harry L. Hopkins did not approach the middle ground the President had hoped for. Roosevelt intended it to be similar to the FERA, but administered by the federal, rather than local government, to achieve better control over projects in the interest of both speed and usefulness. But he abandoned it the next spring, partly out of alarm over a cost disproportionate to the number of useful projects completed. Hopkins had spent nearly a billion dollars during the short duration of the agency. The President's summary of CWA accomplishments in the notes to his papers seemed to emphasize that its success lay as much in the demonstration of speed as in efficiency. "It provided definite proof that an extensive work program could be quickly and profitably undertaken with benefit to the communities and to the unemployed."[31]

After dissolution of the CWA, the burden of work relief again fell upon the FERA, which increased its rolls to a January 1935 peak of $2.5 million. During this period, the FERA retained essentially the same organizational structure as before, its major departure being in stepped-up efforts to diversify the kinds of employment offered so that work appropriate to the skills and aptitudes of those needing employment might be found.[32] Despite these efforts, FERA remained primarily an agency providing direct relief. Though the dole was much cheaper to administer than work relief, Roosevelt was anxious to terminate the program. In December 1934, grants to the states were drastically curtailed, with the expectation that local governments could and must reassume responsibility for the unemployable still in need of direct relief.

In his annual message (January 4, 1935) the President underlined in terms reminiscent of Hoover his commitment to the reduction of relief rolls. History, he maintained, taught that continued relief "induces a spiritual and moral disintegration fundamentally destructive to the national fibre." Though attempting to hold to a distinction between "relief" and "work," condemning the first while recommending the second, the President clearly included "cutting grass, raking leaves, or picking up papers in the public parks," under the heading of "relief." "The Federal Government must and shall quit this business of relief," he promised. Of five million on relief rolls, the President concluded, one and one-half were unemployable and must henceforth be cared for on the local level. The other three and one-half million were to be provided employment by the government, "pending their absorption in a rising tide of private employment." A new agency was to be created, "charged with the orderly liquidation of our present relief activities and the substitution of a national chart for the giving of work." This agency, which became operative in May 1935, became known as the Works Progress Administration.[33]

The plan for the WPA was the culmination of the Administration's haphazard experience with works programs. The words "relief" and "public" were avoided in favor of "progress," which carried a dual meaning. It promised greater care in assuring constant attention to the usefulness and successful pursuit of projects undertaken—"Of progress on all projects"—and also indicated that the WPA was to help the unemployed to "progress" from the relief rolls to project employment to private employment, "in the shortest time possible." All work was to be "useful in the sense that it affords permanent improvement in living conditions or that it creates future new wealth for the nation," a principle clearly deriving from the older conception of public works. Projects should be "self-liquidating," insofar as possible and should not compete with private enterprise. Thus, in conception the WPA honored ideals of both public works and relief work projects. The WPA was closest to relief work, however, in that it was to offer the maximum possible "direct labor," (resulting in low administrative costs), and its wages were not to be competitive with those of private employers. Employees would receive a "security wage," larger than a dole, but kept below prevailing private pay scales either by limiting pay rates or the number of weekly hours employed. Finally, projects were to be chosen so they could readily be tapered off as workers moved into private employment.

In essence, the President borrowed from the older conceptions of both public works and work relief to create a program possessing the dignity of the former and providing jobs with the efficiency and flexibility of the latter. But through the scope of activities to be undertaken and the limiting of projects in both time and character, the WPA was to lean more towards relief work than public works. Roosevelt planned for the older CCC and PWA ultimately to be absorbed into the new agency. It would eventually coordinate the work of over forty newer programs, including the Resettlement Administration, the Rural Electrification Administration, and the National Youth Administration and others employing historians, painters, writers, librarians, and actors in a remarkable variety of projects.[34] By 1936, when the WPA reached its zenith, most government programs offering work to those unemployed because of the Depression fell under its jurisdiction.

Marriner S. Eccles firmly supported the WPA as administered by Harry Hopkins. If public works spending, in its narrow definition, had been discredited as an antidote for depression, it did not follow, in Eccles' view, that "spending" in a more general sense would be equally ineffective. In spite of the President's admonition to engage only in useful works, Hopkins developed an enormous variety of outlets for government funds, many of them highly unorthodox by previous standards of utility. The WPA became an institutional embodiment of the abstract "government spending" which Eccles had been advocating since 1931. The divorcing of "government spending" from its hitherto necessary attachment to a particular object or class of objects representing goods delivered for public dollars spent (a dam, a building, or public works) required a significant alteration in popular conceptions of how the government should use public funds. To speak of the "pump-priming deficit" as Eccles did in the Treasury in 1934 was to begin to suggest that there were positive effects resulting from the mere act of creating deficits, irrespective of what the object of expenditure is. This bold proposition had to make its way against a generation taught to believe that economy and efficiency were the cardinal principles of public administration.[35]

Roosevelt and Morgenthau remained attached to the idea that useful works should be produced as tangible products of monies spent. But Hopkins broadened the term "useful works" to include production of plays, writing tour guide books, and copying and classifying historical records, activities which by the practical standards of most Americans, hardly fit into the "useful works" category and which drew forth a storm of protest from Roosevelt's opposition. The term, "spending," possessed the virtue of being sufficiently ambiguous to describe what Hopkins did with public funds, and his reputation as a "spender," used first as an epithet, and later--by some--with considerable respect. grew until it overshadowed all his other accomplishments. If Eccles was the resident Aquinas of government spending, Hopkins was its Loyola, putting into vigorous practice the principles Eccles sought to rationalize.

Roosevelt's choice of Hopkins to head the WPA meant that the Ickes ideal of efficiency--providing the finest possible public monuments at the minimum cost--was being supplanted. The Hopkins ideal of efficiency--providing a maximum of employment and spending in a minimum amount of time--was gaining dominance. The economic arguments for the transition were as yet vague, caught up for the most part in the widely-used and rarely-defined metaphor urging the government further to "prime the pump" of economic activity. But the social arguments, in which Hopkins had always excelled, were clear and unmistakable. It was at this point that the arguments of Eccles on how a planned policy of adequate deficit financing could serve the humanitarian objectives of

New Dealers were provided with a practical instrument sufficiently flexible to make them effective.

THE END OF PUMP PRIMING

While Hopkins was expanding WPA activities, Eccles was putting his Federal Reserve economists to the twin tasks of perfecting the needed economic arguments for further spending and finding a means of measuring and describing precisely the effects of government spending on general economic activity. Through the knowledge thus gained, Eccles and his aides hope to eliminate the enormous waste caused by idle human and material resources. The problem, as they saw it, was more technical than social. In a sense they were efficiency experts, half-knowingly experimenting with new concepts of efficiency on a scale much grander than that of those concerned with efficiency in the 1920's. Whereas earlier experts meticulously analyzed a single factory to assure efficiency, Eccles and his aides were attempting to grasp the essentials of the vast economic mechanism of America so they might pull the appropriate levers and put the aggregate of men, materials, and machines into productive activity. To Eccles and his staff, the traditional "public works" standards of thorough planning and efficiency still championed by many were inhibiting the process of reactivating the nation's producing plant.

In February 1935 Eccles confided to a group of Boston businessmen his belief in the ultimate significance of the cause he espoused. "I do not wish to preserve capitalism for its own sake," he explained, but rather because it offered a better guarantee of "the good life" than did "capitalistic dictatorship, or socialism, or communism." Any defense of or attack upon capitalism, he maintained, "must be directed towards its efficiency--its ability to satisfy in an adequate and equitable fashion the material needs of mankind. If it cannot be defended on these grounds it is doomed." Eccles was convinced that his policies could forestall any such doom.

> I hope ['and I believe', Eccles had pencilled in the
> text] that the inherent instability of capitalism
> may be corrected by conscious and deliberate use of
> three compensatory instruments, taxation, varying
> governmental expenditures, and monetary con-

trol . . . If they are not established or if they are not successful in achieving economic stability then, as surely as I am standing here, you will not have _compensatory_ but direct controls in every important sphere of economic activity.[36]

Support of Eccles' position on compensatory spending declined as the Depression continued because of concern over the succession of budgetary deficits which began in 1931. Eccles was confronted not only with the task of converting those who had consistently opposed compensatory government spending, but also of reconverting those who had initially supported the policy, only to witness its apparent failure when employed by the Hoover Administration. In his attempt to turn New Deal policy around, Eccles framed both a definition a compensatory spending and a justification for the policy more comprehensive and sophisticated than that of policy makers of the 1920's.

Eccles' early conclusion that this depression "will not correct itself" helped him to overcome the prevailing cyclical view of economic activity and to begin a search for secular changes in the functioning of the economy. Even "pump-priming" theory (a rubric which became current about 1931 for various rationalizations of government spending) did not go so far as Eccles in this regard. While the metaphor suggested that this depression might not right itself without government intervention, it suggested further that the pump, once primed, would continue flowing without further aid or intervention.

Eccles' analysis went much further in that it opened the possibility that the pump, once flowing, might require continuous government monitoring and regulation to assure a full and steady stream. One of the more remarkable aspects of Eccles' analysis was his calm assurance, from the very beginning of his Washington tenure, that this unprecedented expansion of governmental power could be effected without intolerable consequences for the government, the business community, or for the people. As long as there were idle productive resources, Eccles maintained, "the more surplus income is spent . . . the larger will be the national income." The expenditures would create the needed extra income to repay the debt and more.[37] Here Eccles' gift for macroeconomic vision was particularly evident, for while most persons saw deficits only as barriers to a balanced budget, Eccles saw them in relationship to what he called "national income," a concept close to our gross national product. Even if debt continued to mount, it made no difference, so long as national income grew even faster. The insight is especially important, because it made it possible in 1937 and 1938 for New Dealers to tolerate the prospect that federal indebtedness might continue to mount for an unforeseeable period.

Roosevelt in 1937 had by no means settled upon Eccles' formula as the last hope for avoiding the imposition of "direct controls" over the American economy. In fact, he continued to find Eccles' spending proposals disturbing. Unable to shake himself from progressive ideals of what constituted appropriate government relief and works activities, the President smarted under continuing charges that his spending programs had been poorly planned, inefficient, and political in motive and use. Even in 1938, when the notes to items printed in Roosevelt's _Public Papers_ were written, nearly every reference to his meandering succession of spending programs was accompanied by an apology for their various weaknesses.

The spending programs were embarrassing to Roosevelt for several reasons. Like unbalanced budgets, government spending, as Roosevelt rationalized it, had become a symbol of hard times. The recommendations which led to the establishment of the WPA repeatedly referred to the temporary nature of the employment to be offered. The use of the term, "emergency public work," in designating proposed WPA projects suggested that as opposed to "normal public building operations," the WPA was a necessary response to an extraordinary situation, certain to end when the emergency which had required its creation was over. Thus the "absorption" of WPA workers into "a rising tide of private employment" would indicate, as would a balanced budget, that recovery had been achieved. In addition, it was, of course, obvious to all that a major obstacle to a balanced budget was relief spending. Eliminating "emergency public works" and balancing the budget would be twin achievements signaling that New Deal reforms had been vindicated through a prosperous recovery. Spending projects, like budgetary deficits, so long as they continued, were an affront to the President's claim to have vanquished Old Man Depression.

Equally important was the fact that there had been steady progress toward recovery since 1934. The setback in the fall of 1933 had been followed by a continuous rise in almost every index of economic activity. Recovery was coming much later and much more slowly than anyone would have dreamed in 1929 but the significant fact, which Roosevelt reminded Americans on every possible occasion, was that the New Deal was bringing a return to prosperity. "We are justified in our present confidence," the President said in his January 1936 annual message:

Restoration of national income, which shows continuing gains for the third successive year, supports
the normal and logical policies under which agriculture and industry are returning to full activity.
Under these policies we approach a balance of the
national budget . . . National income increases;
employment increases. Therefore, we can look forward to a reduction in the number of those citizens
who are in need. Therefore, also, we can anticipate
a reduction in our appropriations for relief.

With a self-assurance bordering on smugness, the President quoted from
"a wise philosopher at whose feet I sat many, many years ago."

This world in its crisis called for volunteers, for
men of faith in life, of patience in service, of
charity and of insight. I responded to the call
however I could. I volunteered to give myself to my
Master--the cause of humane and brave living. I
studied, I loved, I labored, unsparingly and hope-
fully, to be worthy of my generation.[38]

Such sentiments, however justified they may have seemed to
Roosevelt's admirers, did not encourage introspection. New Dealers
found it possible to shrug off the criticism of those claiming
Roosevelt's policies were devoid of design and clear direction so long
as progress towards recovery continued. There was no need to harmonize
policies with ideals so long as recovery clothed the New Deal with
apparent coherence and substance. It did not matter that the present
run of deficits threatened to go far beyond the worst of previous
peacetime years. The coming recovery would remove the deficits and
repay the debt. It did not matter that workers in unprecedented
numbers had long been on federal payrolls performing service of dubious
permanent value. The coming recovery would put them back into private
employment. Certainly permanent New Deal changes affecting the
structure of the economy would remain to reduce the magnitude of future
contractions. Social security and unemployment insurance would help
sustain purchasing in recessionary periods. The invigorated labor union
movement would exact from industry a better portion for the workers.
Farmers would be encouraged to continue their efforts to adjust
production to reasonable market needs. Stock market investors would be
protected by government regulation of the security and investment
industry. But in contrast to these enduring structural reforms, relief
spending and continuing deficits were considered temporary expedients,

to diminish with the rise in national income. And as long as they were so explained, it was difficult to regard them as permanent positive instruments of economic stabilization.

The administration could argue, as it did, that the spending program had played an important role in the overall recovery plan. But that argument was accompanied, as the year 1936 drew to a close, with the promise that the time for such policies was nearly past. "Business conditions have shown each year since 1933 a marked improvement over the preceding year," the President pointed out in his January 1937 Budget Message.

> These gains make it possible to reduce for the fiscal year 1938 many expenditures of the Federal Government which the general depression made necessary. Although we must continue to spend substantial sums to provide work for those whom industry has not yet absorbed, the 1938 budget is in balance; . . . We expect, moreover, if improvement in economic conditions continues at the present rate, to be able to attain in 1939 a completely balanced budget, with full provision for meeting the statutory requirements for debt reduction.

The "balanced budget" which the President presented for fiscal 1938 did not include debt retirement and it presumed that relief needs would not be over one and one-half billion dollars, a projection, as the President explained, "based on the assumption that industry will cooperate in employing more men and women from the relief rolls than during the past year." Roosevelt expressed his hope that all employers would attempt during the next six months to give employment to those presently receiving government help. If they did not, he warned, the question of a balanced budget for 1938 must remain an open one." The President put part of the burden for achieving a balanced budget upon industry, but he took upon himself part of the burden as well, in laying down guidelines for future administration and congressional spending proposals:

> Expenditures must be planned with a view to the national needs; and no expansion of Government activities should be authorized unless the necessity for such expansion has been definitely determined and funds are available to defray the cost.[39]

The previous four years of experience, painfully evolving a spending program sufficiently flexible to make of it a useful instrument in pursuing a compensatory fiscal policy, was momentarily put aside. The new standards of government spending might have been those Herbert Hoover had espoused in 1930. In Roosevelt's view "national needs" still meant specific structures--highways, bridges, or dams. Spending had been primarily a humane response on the part of the Government to help citizens in distress. With full recovery on the doorstep there was little likelihood it would be resumed.

The 1937 budget message relieved Morgenthau of a nagging fear that Eccles might supplant him as chief fiscal advisor to the President. Through the spring of that year, Morgenthau worked closely with the President as the two made determined efforts to bring the budget back into balance. "I wish you'd hear the President talk about balancing the budget to Eccles," Morgenthau jubilantly told his staff on April 5. "If he'd only say publicly what he told him, it would be marvelous."[40] The ambiguity in Morgenthau's prounouns was shortly to be resolved. Just five days later Eccles issued a public statement announcing a change in Reserve policy:

> Under present conditions of an accelerating recovery, a continued easy money policy to be successful in achieving and maintaining a balanced recovery must be accompanied by a prompt balancing of the Federal budget and the subsequent retirement of public debt by the Government in relationship to the expansion of private credit.[41]

Eccles had decided that inflationary pressures on prices and wages must be eased. The need to encourage investment through a continued easy money policy prevented the Federal Reserve from taking action by raising interest rates. The Treasury, therefore, should reduce the federal contribution to the spending stream. It was time to move toward a balanced budget. A fortnight later the President himself responded to Morgenthau's wish. In a message to Congress to hold the line on expenditures, Roosevelt publicly avowed that:

> while I recognize many opportunities to improve social and economic conditions through Federal action, I am convinced that the success of our whole program and the permanent security of our people demand that we adjust all expenditures within the limits of my Budget estimate.

The passage, perhaps the strongest statement the President ever made on the importance of balancing the budget, had been drafted by Morgenthau's assistant, Herbert Gaston, and inserted in the speech at Morgenthau's urging. "The President," Morgenthau exulted, "gave me . . . everything that I asked for . . . It was a long hard trying fight but certainly at some time during the weeks that I argued with him he must have come to the conclusion that if he wants his Administration to go forward with his reform program he must have a sound financial foundation."[42] Thus, optimistically did Morgenthau expect the year 1937 to bring a consummation of the President's fiscal program and of New Deal reform. He remained steadfast in the progressive faith of his youth--that fiscal integrity is the foundation of enduring reform.

CHAPTER FIVE

MORGENTHAU'S SEARCH FOR A PROGRAM
"A QUESTION OF THE WHOLE POLICY BEING AT STAKE"

RECOVERY PROMISES A BALANCED BUDGET

During the summer of 1937, the Secretary of the Treasury responded dutifully to voices calling him to take up the burden of leading the New Deal into the Promised Land. Morgenthau was delighted when, in spite of disappointing tax revenues, the President reaffirmed his intention to have at least a cash balance in fiscal 1938 and a full balance with a provision for debt retirement in 1939, even if this meant cutting back programs for which funds had already been appropriated.[1] Not content with a campaign simply to hold the line on expenditures, Morgenthau openly expressed his wish to dismantle the spending agencies themselves.

The Bureau of the Budget, he told Daniel Bell, had "just scraped the barrel clean. Now, what I want to do is take the barrel apart, see? . . . I want to take the barrel apart so they can't fill it up again."[2]

Confident that he had become principal shaper of New Deal fiscal policy, Morgenthau accepted an invitation during the summer of 1937 to speak on the expenditures of the federal government at a November meeting of the Academy of Political Science. The name of the organization was misleading. Founded in 1880, the Academy had traditionally used its annual meetings as forums on important public issues, including in its proceedings businessmen and political figures as much as academicians. The New York City conference Morgenthau would address was entirely devoted to the theme "Expenditures of the Federal Government." Attracting the elite of the city's banking and financial community, the gathering provided the perfect occasion for Morgenthau formally to announce, as Secretary of the Treasury, how the President's promised balanced budget was now to be achieved.

Morgenthau attached great importance to the planned address. Treasury staff members were to work on it for a nine-week period, from September 13 through November 9. During the second week in October, the speech preparations became a major preoccupation of top members of the Treasury staff, and remained so for over a month, until the speech was given. Fifteen major meetings, lasting from one to three hours, were devoted exclusively to the address, in addition to countless hours spent writing and revising successive drafts and gathering needed data.

In August, however, the speech seemed far in the future, and Morgenthau's confidence in the direction of Administration fiscal policy permitted him to escape the Capitol for a late summer respite in Hawaii. After his return in mid-September, he set his staff to the task of preparing the address. The Secretary called his Director of Research and Statistics, George C. Haas, and an Assistant Director of the Research Divison, Harry Dexter White, to an initial planning session on the thirteenth of the month. He had chosen them, he explained, because he wanted men who were familiar with the budget. Haas and White were to gather data which would help the Secretary explain how the Administration

> can . . . balance the budget and plan our program through June 30, '41; . . . where are we going to go the next three years on spending and on revenue . . . in order to really balance the budget and pay off some of the debt.

Morgenthau laid considerable stress on his wish "to be just as frank as

I can about the whole thing." If the speech went well, he would hope in the future "to do three or four of these a year. I think it is very, very important that this be done. And . . . it's a good time to do it before Congress is here—let it sink in."[3] With these sketchy instructions, Haas and White began work on the November 10 speech.

There was no clear indication in mid-September that a significant break in the progress towards recovery was imminent. Haas had prepared a memo in August suggesting the possibility of "a slackening in business activity, and perhaps even a temporary decline." "The longer term outlook, however," he hastened to add, "continues to favor a general upward trend in business."[4] A tightness in the New York money market had been observed in early September, leading Eccles to telephone from Utah his assent to joint Treasury Federal Reserve action to ease the situation.[5] But discussion inside both the Treasury and the Federal Reserve continued through September to give no indication that officials of the two agencies expected anything more significant than a late-summer slump. Thus, from mid-September to mid-October, Morgenthau built his speech upon the assumption that recovery would continue without significant interruption and that a balanced budget for the next fiscal year (1938-39) at least was assured. The emphasis at this stage of the speech preparation was not upon committing the Administration to make strides towards balancing the budget. Such a commitment was assumed. The more important objective was to plan a long-range fiscal program appropriate to a situation in which the budget would be in balance. The program was to show how orderly progress towards repayment of the New Deal debt would be undertaken during the four remaining fiscal years for which the Roosevelt administration would be responsible. Morgenthau looked forward to explaining publicly how the wisdom of past New Deal policies, including government spending programs, would shortly be vindicated by four years of carefully planned fiscal "integrity" and debt retirement. The Secretary felt the speech preparation and delivery would provide him the perfect opportunity to set the fiscal direction of the Administration for the remainder of Roosevelt's tenure as President. It was to be a critically important address.

It was September 30 when Morgenthau met a second time with research staff members to work on the speech, this time with Haas and another assistant, Lawrence H. Seltzer. In this meeting, Morgenthau elaborated the address.[6] One aspect was to be retrospective. It was to explain the role of past fiscal policies in bringing recovery. "We had to spend money," Morgenthau explained to Haas and Seltzer, "we had to lift ourselves up by our bootstraps; we've done it."[7] Putting money into recovery agencies had been good business for the government just as it was "for the fellow who borrows ten thousand to help a four thousand a year business move to a seven thousand business."[8]

The President in 1933 could have pursued more radical policies with the emergency powers that were granted him, Morgenthau pointed out, but he did not. "The President can be trusted' he had his six-shooter and he never fired a single shot. Now, the only thing we did was we borrowed . . . I think we ought to paint a pretty good picture for what we did; I don't want to apologize."[9] In looking back to 1933, Morgenthau's aides were to prepare an explanation for the efficacy of past New Deal spending programs in bringing recovery and to explain that these programs had been more moderate than many the President might have chosen.

The prospective aspect of the speech, however, was to have an entirely different goal. "My objective," Morgenthau stated, "is to try and get a public interest and backing to really balance this budget in an intelligent manner . . . to show them that I, as Secretary of the Treasury, first, know what I am talking about, and second, that I've got an objective that I'm shooting at."[10] Morgenthau's aides, as they looked to the future, were to present statistics suggesting that the main cause of the deficits of the past four years had been public works and relief expenditures. It followed, in Morgenthau's view, that to eliminate the deficits permanently it was necessary to eliminate the spending agencies. If the agencies remained, Morgenthau explained to Haas and Seltzer, people would be tempted to continue using them. Reverting to the molasses barrel metaphor he had used with Bell, Morgenthau wanted his speech to explain why it was now necessary to "take the barrel apart."[11]

Morgenthau's staff was prepared for the seemingly contradictory task of explaining that even though past New Deal fiscal policy had been beneficial, future policy, to be equally beneficial, would have to move in the opposite direction. Until October 1937, most members of the Treasury staff, including the Secretary, would willingly have subscribed to the proposition that it is not necessary to have a balanced budget at all times and under all circumstances. Tax revision studies prepared that summer under the supervision of Haas had led to the conclusion that:

> In general, a tax structure which, over a period of years, perhaps a decade or more, yields sufficient revenues to meet all the expenditures of the period, including the retirement of debt created to meet temporary deficiencies, would appear to satisfy any reasonable and realistic test of adequacy.[12]

The economic benefit of government spending in depression would be complemented by adding advantages to be gained from repaying debt during periods of prosperity. Clearly, the use of fiscal policy as a contra-cyclical device was both understood and advocated by important Treasury officials in the summer of 1937.

Haas and Seltzer drew upon these ideas in early drafts of Morgenthau's speech to explain why the administration had once embraced deficits but must now abandon them. "We have deliberately used an unbalanced Federal Budget during the last four years," they wrote in early October, "to restore balance in the budgets of the American people. That policy has succeeded. We have licked the great depression." Such deficits had not been harmful earlier, they reasoned, because most of the funds spent came from bank credit expansion and absorbed neither funds needed for capital investment nor taxpayers' dollars. By 1937, however, recovery had advanced sufficiently that the opposite fiscal policy would be needed to maintain orderly progress. "Any deficit-spending that takes place form now on must be financed in large part by capital funds that would otherwise be available for business purposes." With words Eccles, no doubt, would have endorsed at the time, Morgenthau's aides gave the heart of their argument:

> The basic philosophy of our deficit spending of the last few years requires that a program of substantial debt retirement be undertaken shortly.
>   We wish to preserve the power of the Federal Government to act as a balance wheel in restoring economic order in the future if the need again arises. To preserve this power, we must liquidate during prosperity the debts incurred during periods of depression.

The government had had no difficulty borrowing funds in the past, they argued, because it was well known that one day the President, Congress, and the public could be trusted to join in a determination to balance the budget and reduce the public debt. "That time has now arrived," they announced.

> It was the strong support of the American public that made it possible for us to bring this country out of the depression and to carry through many important reforms. With this same support we shall accomplish the much simpler task of balancing the Federal Budget.[13]

The "philosophy" prepared for Morgenthau was built upon the doctrine that the government should take action to mitigate the extremes of the business cycle by borrowing to spend in depression and taxing to repay the debts so incurred in prosperous times. But the usefulness of that "philosophy" in the fall of 1937 as apology for past spending and justification for curtailing present spending rested on the assumption that the Depression was indeed past. By October 14, when the Treasury staff met again to discuss the draft, two events had significantly altered the situation. The fist caused Morgenthau momentarily to fear that a balanced budget, even though still desirable might not be possible to achieve--certainly not in fiscal 1938, perhaps not even in 1939. The second, by the logic of the "philosophy" Morgenthau's staff was preparing, suggested that a balanced budget under the new conditions, even if possible, might not be desirable.

RECESSION THREATENS

Morgenthau was greatly disturbed when, in an October 4 address, the President hinted strongly that he might soon call a special session of Congress to consider several needed reform measures, including wages-and-hours legislation, executive reorganization, placing the Agricultural Adjustment Administration on a continuing basis, and several TVA-type projects. The Secretary wrote Roosevelt a letter the next morning to express his reservation. "I believe that you and I," he wrote the President,

> are equally determined to balance the Budget for 1938-39, including a reasonable amount for Debt Retirement. In order to accomplish this, it seems to me extremely important that before you obligate yourself to spend anything at all in addition to the commitments already made for 1938-39, you give Mr. Bell and me an opportunity to go into this situation with you fully and examine it yourself with the utmost care.[14]

Morgenthau discussed the special session at length with his staff on October 8, making the point clearly that he was not so much against reform as against any unanticipated increase in government expenses. Reform, he felt, must at that point be judged not in terms of the social benefits to be derived from the proposed measures, but rather in terms of its possible effect on the Treasury. Especially threatening, in

Morgenthau's view, would be the additional costs of programs under new farm legislation proposed by Secretary of Agriculture Henry A. Wallace.

Morgenthau was unsuccessful in his attempts to dissuade the President from going ahead with plans for the special session but was mollified when, on October 12, Wallace expressed his desire to assist in encouraging private business enterprise "so that they can go ahead and take up the slack which would be left due to government ceasing spending."[15]

The Secretary's fears were further allayed when FDR arranged for him to be present at a meeting with Congressmen Robert L. Doughton (Democrat of North Carolina) and Carl Vinson (Democrat of Georgia) in which the President told them "with a real 'burr' in his voice" that "if any committee passes an appropriation over and above his estimates he would immediately serve notice on that Committee that they must find the additional revenue . . . From my standpoint," Morgenthau concluded, "the interview was 100% perfect."[16] The balanced budget did not seem threatened for the moment, at least by the President's reform program. With that front secure, Morgenthau could turn his attentions to a potentially more serious assault from another quarter.

Economic data had been received which suggested that the expected summer slump might be far more serious than anticipated. The picture appeared so dark by October 11 that some members of the Treasury staff were already speaking of "the present recession in business". Morgenthau's first response to the bad economic news was to call his staff together and ask them to determine how much ground there was left to stand on. He wanted an irreducible minimum figure on what tax yields might be in the light of the apparent recession. Fearful that a slump might cause the President to temporize in his commitments, Morgenthau sought reassurance that a balanced budget, at least for 1938-39, was yet possible.[17]

The Secretary became more concerned when, on the morning of October 12, he received a call from Earle Bailie, a friend and former Morgenthau Treasury appointee, who had resigned amidst protest over his Wall Street connections. Bailie reported that all signs pointed to a recession so severe that "taxes are going to be seriously affected." The "whole movement," he maintained, is "man-made." The Recession was not a product of excesses in the business situation as in 1929, but rather was caused by a "lack of confidence bordering almost on disorder," a "sort of utter discouragement."[18]

Though shaken by such reports, Morgenthau sought to maintain a brave front during his regular 9:30 staff meeting the morning of October 14. He drew comfort from two aspects of the situation as he interpreted it. First, he concluded that things were not quite as bad as Bailie and his colleagues maintained. Morgenthau felt that New York bankers, in spreading talk of imminent disaster, were attempting to steer Roosevelt away from his proposed reform measures. Regrettably such prophecies by the respected elite of Wall Street tended to be self-fulfilling. The financial titans had "come pretty near to a sitdown strike," Morgenthau maintained, and under such circumstances "there's nothing we can do . . . but let it burn itself out like a forest fire."[19]

Herman Oliphant, the general counsel to the Treasury, concurred in the Secretary's judgment. "They wouldn't be satisfied with anything short of just turning the whole thing back to them and letting them do as they please with it," he complained. Morgenthau, convinced that Roosevelt's proposed reforms "are not very radical," had little sympathy for the bankers' complaints. The situation did not yet appear so serious that a change in economic policy would be necessary to meet what was essentially a political problem. The Secretary concluded with Oliphant that "you can't satisfy them." For the moment, at least, the Treasury would "just have to operate and disregard them."[20]

Two members of Morgenthau's staff, Assistant Secretary Wayne C. Taylor and economic advisor Jacob Viner. offered dissenting opinions. Viner especially made the point that the President should not let the hostility of his critics cause him to disregard their complaints. The Chicago economist supported, by implication, Bailie's view that the President's reforms were frightening business and that the fears of businessmen, whether justified or not, were the major cause of the downturn. "You either want . . . them to put their money to work," Viner advised, "or want to take their money away from them and put it to work yourselves. Those are the two alternatives." The interpretation of Viner and Taylor suggested that the most effective ameliorative action would be for Roosevelt to move away from the reform measures frightening potential investors. Morgenthau was not yet ready to countenance such a proposal.

The Secretary took heart from the President's response to the crisis. "I've lived with that man now day in and day out for the last week", he told his staff. "and I come out reassured . . . The man couldn't have been more natural, more frank . . . Everybody you talk to—the one person they're worrying about is Roosevelt, and I come out reassured."[21] The importance Morgenthau attached to the unusual adjectives he chose became clearer as the discussion progressed. Responding to a comment from Viner, the Secretary indicated what the President's "frankness" might mean in policy terms:

> Roosevelt's come through this . . . and what's his
> reaction? Is it 'Should I call together Ickes and
> Hopkins and Wallace and say that we've got to spend
> some more money?' No . . . his reaction is 'I'm

going to call together the biggest contractors in
America, a number of labor unions, and I'm going to
sit down and talk to them; how can they go to work
and build houses over two or three years?' Now,
what more do you want?[22]

Throughout the meeting, Morgenthau seemed to equate the President's
frankness with his apparent determination not to resume spending. This
curious association was not accidental or trivial, for the crucial need,
as Morgenthau saw it, was that the President affirm the integrity of the
Administration by going ahead with a balancing of the budget, as he had
so long promised. In Morgenthau's idiosyncratic use of the word, to be
frank was apparently to deliver on one's promises.

The nature of the personal relationship which existed between the
Secretary and the President reinforced Morgenthau's view. He found the
President's frankness and determination to avoid further spending reas-
suring because, so long as the President remained in this present frame
of mind, the way was open for the Secretary to perform a critically
important service for "the boss." It was Morgenthau's earnest wish, as
he told his staff, that,

> out of all this . . . will come a statement that I
> can make committing the Government on fiscal policy
> as far as we can see it reasonably; no further;
> calling a spade a spade; not trying to hedge; not
> trying to cover up something in innuendo or any way
> else; in other words, take the public in our confi-
> dence as far as we know our mind . . . I can't do
> any more than to be completely honest and
> frank . . . [23]

An even more intimate aspect of the relationship between the two
men reinforced Morgenthau's determination to hold his ground against any
compromise. Morgenthau was acutely sensitive to the fact that
Roosevelt's credibility on the budget-balancing issue had been badly
compromised since 1933. Given his idealized view of FDR as a benevolent
father, it seems entirely possible that the Secretary, at this juncture,
felt the necessity of taking action to make certain that Roosevelt's
crown had not slipped--that the "two of a kind" would remain two of a
kind in their moral stature as in other aspects of their lives. It
seemed as important to Morgenthau that he be able to retain his esteem
for Roosevelt as it was that he retain Roosevelt's esteem. Morgenthau
could not permit a situation to develop which might tarnish his personal
vision of Franklin D. Roosevelt. So long as the President remained

"frank" in dealing with the Recession, Morgenthau was comforted and reassured. His speech could still serve the Administration as a guide to future fiscal policy.

Nevertheless, the Secretary sought to forestall any last-minute wavering on the part of the President by asking his staff for the first time to write an explicit commitment to a balanced budget prominently into his Academy address. He opened the speech-planning meeting on the afternoon of October 14 by telling his staff "Right at the beginning of my discussion I wish to say that I believe that it is imperative that, without any 'ifs,' 'ands,' or 'buts,' the Federal budget for the year 1939 be balanced." He objected that the draft Haas and Seltzer had prepared did not make this point strongly enough.[24] As he continued, Morgenthau revealed that unnamed others were putting pressure on him to back away from his prime objective. "I won't stay and knowingly and consciously have an unbalanced budget in order to correct the mistakes made by other people." he insisted.

> We have come to a cross road. The cross road is when private business needed the money which the Government has been taking up to this time, and we are at that cross road now . . . It's not balancing the budget which is putting the stock market down. Then why the hell should we unbalance the budget to cover up the mistakes of other people? . . . Today, up to now, I have seen no signs of anybody of responsibility who wants to unbalance the budget in order to stop this drop in the stock market.[25]

With the economic picture so uncertain, Haas and Gaston expressed their concern over the advisability of making a strong statement. Morgenthau should not burn his bridges behind him. Haas warned. "We crossed it Sunday night," Morgenthau replied, "when the President signed this thing." (The President had apparently approved the preliminary draft.) "We are all in the clear. I have made my fight for the last three weeks and I figure we have won."[26] Through October 14, the growing possibility of recession, far from temporizing Morgenthau's position, made him even more determined than he had been two weeks before to commit the President in his speech to a specific date for achieving a balanced budget.

The logic of the speech draft prepared by Haas and Seltzer implied that a balanced budget under the new circumstances might do positive harm to the economy. But Morgenthau, for reasons of his own, steadfastly refused to follow that logic to its obvious conclusion. He could not admit that he might be forced to choose between a balanced budget and recovery. During the next weeks, as the economic crisis deepened, he sought desperately for a resolution which would assure both. As he did so, his position began more and more to resemble that of Lewis Douglas in 1934, as described (many years later) by Morgenthau himself: "Budget balancing was all right but Lew had wanted to balance the budget immediately--at the expense of almost everything else, including the Administration's relief and recovery programs. Life was not that simple. A great deal was at stake."[27]

A BALANCED BUDGET TO FIGHT RECESSION

During the three-week period from October 14 to November 3, Morgenthau held conferences concerning the speech with members of his staff almost every working day. The most significant external event of the period was the dramatic stock market decline on October 19--"Black Tuesday." The decline had repercussions within the Treasury which, by November 3, were to necessitate a significant change in the reasoning used in support of an early balanced budget.

The day after the drop in the market, members of Daniel Bell's staff from the Bureau of the Budget were invited to join Treasury staff members in considering a critique of the speech draft prepared by Jacob Viner. The economist chose to concentrate on passages in which the writers claimed that the deficit had "played an important part" in raising our national income from less than forty billion dollars in 1932 to approximately seventy billion in 1937. "Your fourteen billion dollar investment in America," the draft read, "is currently yielding us a return of more than two hundred percent a year." Viner's comments went to the heart of the problem that was developing for New Dealers. "You must argue as you do," he said,

> that the federal deficit was a contributing factor
> to the recovery, but the claim that all the recovery
> was attributable to it . . . would be difficult to
> support by reasoned argument, especially before an
> audience most of whom are convinced that the contin-
> uance year after year of the deficit has been a
> hindrance to recovery. I would certainly eliminate
> the statement that the 14 billions of deficit is
> yielding 28 billions per annum in national income.

On that basis, why not have had a 30 billion deficit? . . . If all the recovery is claimed for the
deficit, what about the rest of the New Deal
program?

Viner objected further to optimistic views of the current
economic situation expressed in the October draft. "I would advise,"
he said,

that you take the line that what could be done by
deficit financing towards bringing recovery,
relieving distress, and substitution for temporarily
idle private capital, has been done, and that the
remainder of the task, still a sizeable one, must,
in the interest of the security of federal finances,
be done strictly within the limits of a balanced
budget, and of no increased tax burdens.[28]

Here Viner began to change the rationale upon which the speech had been
built. Since recovery now appeared to be uncertain, Viner suggested
that the earlier positive reason for balancing the budget be replaced
with a negative one. Haas and Seltzer had argued in early drafts that
the budget should be balanced to prevent a precarious inflationary boom.
Viner wanted to replace this argument with the simple assertion that
since 1933, budget deficits had been drained of their stimulating power
and would no longer be effective. The budget should be balanced because
there was no longer a reason to have it unbalanced.

Morgenthau did not pursue Viner's comment, but as the meeting drew
to a close, the Secretary expressed his delight with the progress that
had been made. When Lawrence Seltzer proposed that if "we are going
into a tailspin I would chuck the speech," the Secretary responded
evasively, "All right. I have time to think this over," and went on to
work out further details with other staff members.[29]

When Morgenthau met with his staff on the morning of October 22, a
significant new turn was taken, as the need to recast the speech in the
light of changing events became more pressing. Winfield Riefler, a
professor at the School of Economics and Politics of the Institute for
Advanced Study and occasional advisor to the Treasury, directly
confronted the issue Morgenthau had bypassed when raised by Jacob Viner
and Lawrence Seltzer two days before. What is to be done with the
speech if by November 11 a major recession is clearly underway?

Riefler rejected the essentially negative and defensive posture of
both Viner and Seltzer. He suggested that Morgenthau direct himself to
the fears of the moment, discuss them forthrightly, and offer the con-

clusion that under the present circumstances, "we have decided that the most constructive action which the national government can take . . . is to proceed to an immediate balancing of the national budget."[30] The moment was significant, for it marked a major change in Morgenthau's rationale for balancing the budget, a departure from the attitude which had characterized his budget-balancing efforts since he had become Secretary of the Treasury in 1934. A balanced budget, in Morgenthau's view, was no longer to be just a desirable by-product of recovery. It was to be the major instrument through which recovery was to be achieved. Morgenthau and Gaston expressed their satisfaction with the new course upon which Riefler so deftly had launched them. "Under these circumstances," Riefler continued, "the task of the Administration is to clear the tracks for the expansion of private business, not supplant it with increased Federal spending."[31]

It was clear the following Monday that the implications of the new direction were not lost upon Morgenthau. He explained to his staff that he had been trying "to think out a succession of steps which will pull this country out of deficit spending and put it on a balanced budget and still keep the country going along." The speech intended to accomplish these tasks was "forming layer by layer." The Secretary avowed that he was taking upon himself an enormous responsibility in affirming "that, . . . we are moving fast enough . . . to keep this country from going into a tailspin and, at the same time, keep this government solid." He wanted "business to do the spending in place of the Government."[32]

During the last weeks of October the Academy of Political Science speech became more important than even Morgenthau had originally dreamed. Morgenthau, through his speech, would begin the task of shoring up the fading confidence of businessmen. The big financiers trusted him. Morgenthau assured his staff, because he had always been frank and honest with them. Would the speech, he asked his administrative assistant, Cyrus Upham, "in any way satisfy the New York Times?" "Yes," was the reply, "I think it would probably inspire a good deal of hope in the New York Times and me." "The Secretary of the Treasury or the President should say it," Morgenthau concluded. "I don't think anybody is going to laugh at it when I get up and say it. I think they definitely want to know are we headed towards State socialism or continue capitalistic?"[33]

November 3 was a particularly trying day for Morgenthau. For reasons he did not specify, the Secretary at last came to the conclusion that the nation was "headed into another depression", and that the President "had to do something about it." He phoned the White House that evening to communicate this message to the President. In a heated discussion Roosevelt indicated his belief that a small group of opponents were deliberately depressing business so they might make certain demands on the Administration. "Mr. President," Morgenthau responded, "I do not see that kind of people. The only person I talk to is you . . . This question that I am raising is one that has to be settled just between you and me."

Roosevelt's reply must have cut to the quick. "Have you talked to Eccles?" he asked. "Eccles has a program and I asked him why he did not show it to you." Morgenthau no doubt saw an ominous connection between the President's reference to Eccles' program and a comment concerning the Academy address with which FDR ended the conversation. The Secretary asked if the President might be able to go over the final draft of the speech the next Saturday. "Yes," Roosevelt replied, "I want to talk to you about that very much because I think in several places you make too categorical statements and I do not want to be saying things now that we will have to withdraw two months later."[34] Apparently, the question was not to be settled between just the two of them.

THE INTERVENTION OF ECCLES

Morgenthau was backing quickly away from his earlier opinion that the situation be allowed to "burn itself out like a forest fire." "Last night," he explained to his staff on the afternoon of November 4, "was the first time I got these feelings in my bones and I got this thing in my mind that the President has to do something now; this week. I had not got that feeling until yesterday."[35] In spite of his newfound urge to encourage action, the Secretary, unlike Eccles, had little prepared in the way of specific proposals. FDR, in high dudgeon at the cabinet meeting earlier that day had complained that he was "sick and tired of being told by the Cabinet, by Henry and by everybody else . . . what's the matter with the country and nobody suggests what I should do."

Morgenthau broke the startled silence by asserting that something could be done about public utilities, railroads, and housing but did not indicate precisely what that "something" might be. "You just name the problem," he offered lamely, "and I will take it up." The only specific proposal the Secretary was prepared to make at that time, however, came in the form of a suggestion that FDR, in a planned November 15 address, reassure business that the Administration was not antagonistic. "What business wants to know," Morgenthau asserted, in words he had used earlier with his staff, "is are we headed toward State socialism or are

we going to continue on a capitalistic basis?" When the President complained that he had "told them again and again," Morgenthau maintained
that the President should, nevertheless, "tell them for the fifteenth
time on November 15, because . . . that's what they want to know."

"What about telling them that you are going to reduce the cost of
government?" Postmaster General James Farley added, "That's what people
are interested in." Morgenthau left the meeting pleased with himself
and elated that he had led the Cabinet in standing up to Roosevelt. "I
suppose the President thought he could down me in front of the whole
cabinet," he wrote that day in his diary, "but instead of that his
Cabinet handed it to him."[36]

The offerings of the Cabinet to the President seem in retrospect to
have been meager indeed. The gist of their proposals, as Morgenthau
remembered them, was that the President again should reassure business
of his belief in capitalism and renew his pledge to balance the budget.
Whatever action might be taken later in the matters of utilities, railroads, and housing would be subsidiary to these needed reassurances.
The President was being urged to give his own version of the speech
Morgenthau had been preparing for over a month.

Meanwhile, Morgenthau had begun to follow up on the President's
suggestion of the night before that he should talk to Eccles. On the
morning of November 4, he had spoken to Eccles on the phone, explaining
that he wanted "to talk business," at a luncheon meeting the two had
previously arranged. During the uncomfortable telephone conversation,
Eccles overcame his apparent reluctance to unveil his anti-recession
program, and the two agreed to exchange memos on how to deal with the
crisis at their afternoon meeting. "Nothing is more important than this
situation," the chairman said, "I don't think we could possibly spend
our time to any better advantage, no matter how much it takes, than
considering immediately just what the present problem is."[37]

That afternoon, after the cabinet meeting and the scheduled meeting
with Eccles, Morgenthau met with eleven top members of the Treasury
staff, including Daniel Bell from the Bureau of the Budget to report the
day's events. "This thing has gotten so important," Morgenthau announced
dramatically, "it isn't a question of getting down to words; it's a
question of the whole policy being at stake now." Morgenthau reported
that he and Eccles had found points of agreement during their luncheon
discussion. Both felt the high costs of building were retarding an
expected building boom which Administration officials had hoped would
sustain the economy when government spending was cut back. "For once,"
he told his staff, "we had two hours without [Wayne C.] Taylor having to
pull us apart. We both kept our good humor." But finally Eccles had
come to the point upon which they fundamentally disagreed. Eccles, as
Morgenthau explained,

> says that at this stage we must speed up our expen-
> ditures and that we must spend through Hopkins and
> through Agriculture fast, to stop this deflation.
> And that's where we go apart. He read my speech
> carefully and said my speech is deflationary; that
> it would have been very nice a month ago, but I just
> can't give it; shouldn't. That this is a problem
> that only one person can handle and . . . why should
> I go out on the end of a limb; this is the
> President's problem . . . I am a fool to do this;
> this is the President's party.[38]

In Morgenthau's view, Eccles' disturbing questions could not have been raised at a worse moment. "The ground is slipping from under our feet as fast as I have seen it slip since I have been in Washington," he told the staff. He reminded them that the speech "is [to be given] the 10th of November and the stakes is the United States. That's what we are talking about and I am willing to do anything to get results."[39]

As the meeting continued, Morgenthau asked each staff member if the speech should be given as planned. Only White and Haas opposed it. The rest were still convinced that the address would have a favorable psychological impact. Morgenthau's administrative assistant, William McReynolds, and Under-Secretary of the Treasury Roswell Magill agreed that a promise to balance the budget would be "ten times better in effect" than the announcement of another round of pump-priming. There was "enough reassurance in the speech as is to turn the economic tide." As Morgenthau put it, "Now if I go up there as Secretary of the Treasury and make a wobbly speech and say I don't know whether we are going to spend any more money or not, I just add to the fear . . . I think what people want to know is this: have we a policy down here and what is it?"[40]

The imponderable which might have prevented Morgenthau from delivering the speech as planned was, of course, the President's attitude. The President had agreed to the speech the previous Saturday (October 30), Morgenthau reported, but in the meantime Eccles had "gotten to him." The Secretary's November 3 phone conversation with Roosevelt revealed growing presidential doubts about the advisability of Morgenthau's delivering the speech as planned. In view of these developments, White suggested, it might be best to make a speech that was less forceful and effective, but would not leave the Secretary on a limb in case others were to win the President over. Morgenthau seemed disturbed but unpersuaded by White's argument. He was determined to push the Administration as far in the direction of balancing the budget as the President would permit.

Roosevelt's problem was how to take action when there seemed no unobstructed direction in which to move. "My reaction," Morgenthau wrote of an interview on November 8,

> was that he [the President] is fighting like a cornered lion; that he does not want to be tamed and still. on the other hand he does not know where he can put his strength at this particular juncture to bring about recovery.
>
> Of course, the Fascist governments are going ahead and it is most vitally important that this country shouldn't have an industrial slump because it gives the enemy of true liberalism an opportunity to crack down on us as the most important Democracy and point with pride to our failure.[41]

On Saturday November 6, the President went over the draft of Morgenthau's address and penciled in several additions. The changes the President made were not drastic, but their spirit and intent was clear. Where Morgenthau was to avow that "I strongly favor a vigorous program for the progressive reduction of federal expenditures to the minimum demanded by the government's responsibilities," Roosevelt compromised the position by adding a paragraph of his own in which he maintained that:

> Obviously, however, one reaches a point in reducing government expenditures at which no further reductions can be made, unless it is decided to cripple many essential governmental activities--in other words unless it is decided to make drastic changes in national policy . . . Such a course, I believe, would not have the approval of either the American people or their elected representatives in Congress.[42]

Where the draft proposed that tax laws "should be so written and administered that the taxpayer can continue to make a reasonable profit with a minimum of interference from his own federal government," Roosevelt added, "provided that the taxpayer cooperates with his government in carrying out the purpose and spirit of the tax laws."[43] Where Morgenthau was to express his opinion that the balanced budget "should be sought by a reduction in expenditures without an increase in the total of the tax burden," Roosevelt intimated further that any failure would be partly the fault of industry. "But I have also shown that there is a limit of reductions; and that balancing of budgets needs the help of industry to keep up total tax receipts unless we are again to resort to deficit financing."[44] The President also altered Morgenthau's concluding statement. Where Morgenthau was to promise that the Administration would do "everything possible" to balance the budget, but "in no event . . . will allow anyone to starve," the President inserted, "nor will it abandon its broad purpose to protect the weak, to give human security and to seek a wider distribution of our national income."

The President thus inserted a muted, but clear note of defiance in a speech intended to be conciliatory, and maintained loopholes permitting further spending, should this be needed. Lawrence Seltzer objected to some of the President's changes, but Morgenthau was reluctant to push for further alterations. "If you want to go over and see the President, go ahead and let him tear you limb from limb," he told Seltzer.[45] In discussions with his staff the day before the speech was to be delivered, Morgenthau was obviously pleased with the draft. "If the President . . . should say to me, 'What does Danny Bell think of this speech?' what should I tell him?" Morgenthau asked the Budget Director.

"I think it's a good speech," Bell responded.

"That's what I told him," answered Morgenthau.[46] In high spirits, the Secretary put the final touches on the speech he would deliver before the Academy of Political Science meeting the next day.

MORGENTHAU BEFORE THE ACADEMY

There is no reason to believe that the program or the session of the American Academy of Political Science meeting Morgenthau was address had been deliberately planned to embarrass the Administration. But clearly Morgenthau found himself in alien territory. Of the twenty-two members of the program committee. nine were executives of major New York banks, four were executives of giant corporations, two were heads of major insurance companies, two were former government officials hostile to the Administration (Lewis Douglas, former Director of the Bureau of the Budget, and Ogden Mills, Secretary of the Treasury under Hoover), and two were well-known economists. Over a thousand members of the New York academic, financial, industrial, and commercial community attended the gathering, the largest attendance in the previous fifty-two year history of the American Academy.[47]

Morgenthau was to be preceded on the program by Senator Harry F. Byrd, Democrat of Virginia, a notoriously outspoken critic of Administration spending programs. S. Parker Gilbert, chairman of the meeting and executive of the J.P. Morgan Company, though not a formal participant, editorialized freely in introducing the speakers. Morgenthau's legal advisor, Herman Oliphant later commented indignantly the "the whole set-up there, including Parker Gilbert's speech was an attempt to take you into camp and give an Al Smith Liberty League dinner." During the meeting, George L. Harrison, President of the Federal Reserve Bank of New York, leaned over to Thomas S. Lamont, another Morgan executive and whispered, "You've certainly got the Secretary of the Treasury boxed in here tonight, haven't you."[48]

Senator Byrd's speech was directed squarely at Administration fiscal policies, accusing government officials of "devious and misleading" methods of reporting expenditures in order to make the enormous size of the deficits less apparent. His calculations of the growth in public debt per capita compared a pre-war figure of $59.00 to a 1936 figure of $460.00. "Today," he summarized, "about one-third of every person's income would be required to meet government expenditures, if we paid as we spend." The audience responded with enthusiastic applause when he asked rhetorically what should be done about the situation and answered, "The only constructive thing to do is to stop writing checks."[49]

S. Parker Gilbert praised Morgenthau in introducing him for "giving his best efforts to re-establishing effective control over government expenditures.[50] Now, under his leadership," Gilbert continued, "plans are under consideration for revision of the revenues which will be of great importance to the country." The token applause greeting Morgenthau contrasted sharply with the warm reception given to Senator Byrd. The audience listened attentively, clearly approving Morgenthau's assertion that "the basic need today is to foster the full application of the driving force of private capital." But when the Secretary arrived at a carefully-phrased avowal that "we are definitely in a transition period between unbalanced and balanced federal budgets," several audible guffaws rang out from the audience. There was laughter again when he assured them that the Treasury intended "that the collection of taxes shall be as little burdensome to the taxpayer as possible." The Secretary left the meeting feeling he had been betrayed by those who should have been his friends, "I didn't know what I was going up against;" he told his staff the next Monday. "Maybe it's just as well." Herman Oliphant was incensed at the treatment Morgenthau had received at the hands of the New York crowd. It was, he said, "a disgraceful and disrespectful performance."

"There's no bitterness here," Morgenthau answered, "because it's just as well. Herman, for me to know how these people feel."

"I think we sit here and lose the feel of what the typical leadership of American business and finance is," Oliphant responded, "and it's very illuminating to realize the hopelessness of trying to work with them."[51]

The press response would not seem to have justified Oliphant's anger at the disrespectful attitude of the audience. _Time_ magazine called the speech "the most satisfying public words business has heard from Washington since the inception of its 'Breathing Spell' two years ago."[52] Editorials in the _New York Times_ praised the Secretary of the Treasury for "holding out the olive branch" to business.[53] On November 12, a full page of the _Times_ was devoted to the excerpting of favorable editorial commentary in newspapers from New York to San Francisco. American Bankers' Association President Orvill W. Adams and Senate Finance Chairman Byron P. "Pat" Harrison were reported to have publicly praised the speech.[54]

The reaction of Morgenthau's "boss" to the speech was somewhat less enthusiastic. The President brought up the speech in a meeting with his Cabinet on November 12. The President said (as noted by Roswell Magill who attended the meeting in Morgenthau's absence), "that the address had been well received by the newspapers, as a very constructive statement. He thought it was 'possibly too constructive'." "As the Cabinet knows," Magill continued, "the Administration is doing all it can to balance the budget but he [FDR] does not regard that as the most important question before the country."[55]

The ultimate test of the efficacy of Morgenthau's speech was, of course, the response of the economic indices. And by no index could the speech be said to have been a spectacular success. The stock market, a sensitive, if capricious barometer of business confidence, experienced a one-day rally following Morgenthau's speech, reaching its highest point of the month, nearly 96 on the _New York Times_ Index. The rally was undoubtedly buoyed by Eccles' announcement the same day (which shared the first page _New York Times_ headline with Morgenthau's speech) of a major administration housing drive designed to elicit the investment of private capital. The following day, however, the market leveled out, and by November 20 it had dropped nearly ten points. At no time during the rest of the month did the index rise above 90, and after a rally early in December the year ended with a descent into the mid-eighties.

Morgenthau's speech had less effect on other indices. The Federal Reserve Index of Industrial Production moved relentlessly downward from its highest point since 1929 (119 in May 1937) to 102 in October, 88 in November, 84 in December, 80 in January 1938, and finally to 76 by May 1938.[56] The same general pattern prevailed with indices of construction contracts awarded, factory employment, factory payrolls, and freight car loadings.

On November 5, Eccles had offered Morgenthau has opinion that "a statement by anybody . . . except the President himself," would have no effect. Even a presidential statement to be effective would have to be one in which FDR "shows a recognition of the trend and undertakes to correct it by having some positive program . . . He should go before Congress with a message that not only recognized exactly what the situation is, as he sees it, the causes for it, but what ought to be done about it."[57] Morgenthau must have had occasion, during the rest of the winter of 1937-38, as business conditions continued to worsen to reflect upon Eccles' prediction and wonder what had been accomplished by a speech which he had thought in October might "keep this country from going into a tail-spin and, at the same time, keep this Government solid."[58]

The Secretary later displayed a touch of sensitivity on the question of whether the talents of his staff might not have been put to better use during a period when there was a critical need for practical policies to counter a developing recession. Early in December, fearing that he might find himself in a position similar to Hoover's, making promises of an upturn without solid evidence to support them, Morgenthau asked why he had not received memos on data his staff had prepared. Haas, Director of Research and Statistics, replied that he would have received them except for all the time they had spent on the speech. "Whatever energy was put into that", Morgenthau tartly responded, "it was most fruitful."[59] Morgenthau did not suggest what the specific fruits of the endeavor might have been, but it would seem, since the speech had no lasting effect upon either the economy or the economic philosophy of New Dealers, that it was important to Morgenthau because of its effect upon his own thinking concerning the general achievement of FDR and the New Deal.

John Morton Blum, a historian who worked closely with Morgenthau in his later years, noted that the former Secretary of the Treasury "to the day he died . . . argued that a balanced budget had never been tried and might have worked."[60] Blum's account is significant, for it indicates that Morgenthau continued to think of a balanced budget not as a consequence of recovery but rather as a potential instrument promoting recovery, an instrument which, had FDR chosen to employ it, might have "worked." Since the only situation in which New Dealers found themselves asking if a balanced budget might "work" (a very different concept from their very common hope that a balanced budget might be achieved) was that created by the recession crisis, one suspects that Morgenthau's whole subsequent interpretation of New Deal fiscal policy was crystallized by the pressures and anxieties of the weeks during which he prepared his Academy of Political Science Address.

It is important in this context then, that Morgenthau continued to regret the new direction Roosevelt's fiscal policy would take in 1938. Obviously, in Morgenthau's view, when Roosevelt missed the chance to balance the budget in 1938, he lost one of the great opportunities of the New Deal. At the same time--and this caused the deepest hurt-- Roosevelt determined in the wake of the Recession that the prize Morgenthau had fought to bring home as a tribute to "the boss" was not so important after all. Roosevelt maintained in a written address sent to Congress the week after Morgenthau's speech that he expected to bring the budget for fiscal 1939 "within a definite balance."[61] It was the last time he would publicly make such a commitment. In his Annual Message the next January he expressed his intention to balance the budget but placed as a condition necessary to such an achievement the need "to raise the purchasing power of the Nation to the point that . . . taxes . . . will be sufficient to meet the necessary expenditures of the National government."[62] In the Annual Budget Message, made public the same day, the President took pride in "declining deficits" but made no commitments to balance the budget at a specified future time.

Roosevelt's growing reluctance to push for a balanced budget as a specified policy objective was paralleled by a growing indifference to Morgenthau's advice on matters of fiscal policy, an indifference which had begun to make its appearance as Morgenthau worked on his Academy of Political Science Address. On this occasion, Morgenthau did not demon- strate the pliancy of opinion which had previously kept him at the President's side in spite of initial disagreement. The fact is most telling evidence of the severity of the crisis created for Morgenthau by the Recession. The good will of Roosevelt was of tremendous importance to Morgenthau, but he was willing to risk even that for a principle which by that time had assumed in his mind an overwhelming importance. Morgenthau had readily backed away on previous occasions from his urgings that the President commit himself to balancing the budget. Why was he not able to do so in 1937?

One answer must be sought in the high value Morgenthau placed upon the importance of moral integrity in government. Morgenthau saw the budget-balancing issue in these terms in 1937 for two reasons. First, he retained from his exposure to the budgetary reform movement of 1910 to 1920 a sense that morality in government was intimately related to the balancing of governmental accounts. A government which balanced the budget would be an honest and trustworthy government and would be seen by its citizens as such. The second point followed from the first. Morgenthau interpreted the New Deal as primarily engaged in bringing a spirit of humanitarian reform to the institutions of government. The essential quality of the reformer, in Morgenthau's view, was that he be pure himself. The viability of the New Deal as a reform movement depended upon how firmly in this crisis Roosevelt held to his promise to balance the budget. Only through a balanced budget could the moral credibility of the New Deal be maintained.

Another cause of Morgenthau's intransigence on the budget-balancing issue was his growing complaint, accentuated by the onset of the Recession, that the various New Deal measures did not rest upon a coherent underlying philosophy. Is a sense, he secretly feared what Eccles had long maintained; that a generous humanitarian impulse did not provide adequate guidelines for choosing the most effective public policies. In planning his speech, he was setting out to provide a more concrete philosophy for FDR, but he could not get beyond the assertion that a specific policy act, the balancing of the federal budget, would somehow give coherence to the whole range of New Deal programs. When this policy objective, the importance of which FDR had repeatedly affirmed, was abandoned by the President himself, Morgenthau could not bring himself to follow. He had no doubt that this time he must continue his mission even if he had to do it alone. "It took me six weeks to work out the philosophy in my speech," he told Harry White in December, "and I certainly couldn't in two minutes get a new philosophy. And when I worked it out, I worked it out with the President. I mean, when I did that, it was as much his philosophy as it was mine."[63] Not in two minutes, nor in two decades, would Morgenthau depart from the philosophy he "worked out" in six weeks in the fall of 1937.

CHAPTER SIX

INTERREGNUM--"GROPING IN THE DARK"

THE STRUGGLE FOR INFLUENCE WITH FDR

On November 10, the day Morgenthau delivered his Academy of Political Science speech, Roosevelt's close friend, Felix Frankfurter wrote him an urgent letter which expressed the thoughts of many New Dealers. "The people," Frankfurter wrote, want to hear

> from your own lips, that <u>you</u> are not panicky, that
> you know better than any of the croakers that there
> are difficulties and what they are. that nobody is
> more concerned to do what can be done towards

remedying difficulties, that you have a well-defined
direction toward objectives to which you will adhere
because they are the objectives of national well
being.[1]

Neither the President's message to the extra session of Congress on
November 15, nor his speech recommending legislation to stimulate
housing on November 27 were likely to still Frankfurter's anxieties.
Two days after the housing speech, Morgenthau confided to his staff that
he was

> terrifically shocked that the President . . . can't
> call for Plan A or Plan B or Plan C, the way the
> Army or Navy is supposed to do if we are attacked on
> the Atlantic Coast . . . Well, we're being attacked
> now in a certain way, and the President should have
> certain plans. He's got nothing. And there is
> nothing in the Administration.[2]

In the following months the Recession deepened with no signs that the
President was responding to the advice Frankfurter had offered him.
Late in December, an economist, "high in the councils of the New Deal,"
anonymously pointed out to reporters that the previous three months had
wiped out two years of recovery. Sometime in 1938, he predicted, a
crisis as acute as that prevailing when Roosevelt took office would grip
the country. In January, the editors of Common Sense, a left-leaning
periodical, commented ominously that "If the present rate of decline
should by any chance keep up, March 4, 1938 would find business as it
was on March 4, 1933 . . . It seems likely that we are in another
profound depression, even before fully getting out of the last one. And
this time with eight million unemployed and a national debt of over 35
billion to start with."[3] Among New dealers, this sense of impending
calamity continued into the early spring of 1938. In a mid-February
conference to prepare a presidential statement on price levels,
Secretary of Agriculture Wallace told Morgenthau that he hoped the
statement would leave the public with the impression, "that we know
which way we're going and that we have a policy, and that the whole
Administration is headed in the same direction." A clear statement of
New Deal policy. Wallace felt, would ease public fears and lead to
increased buying. Above all, Wallace hoped they could prevent the
President from coming out "with another statement about a reform of some
kind . . . I think it would be unfortunate to come out with a statement
of that sort at this time."

"Don't you feel," replied Morgenthau grimly "that you're groping in the dark?"[4]

The deep, almost desperate anxiety evoked by the 1937 Recession made an indelible impression upon most New Dealers. Alarmed to find themselves in a conceptual cul-de-sac, men such as Morgenthau and Wallace searched anxiously for a philosophy which would permit them to regain their bearings. They wished to set a firm direction for the New Deal--to articulate a set of fundamental propositions which all New Dealers could subscribe to, and which would establish a policy framework capable of meeting future crises. Such anxieties weighed also upon the President, and with similar effect. In late November 1937, FDR escaped Washington for a short vacation cruise, accompanied by Harold Ickes, Robert H. Jackson, and the ailing Harry Hopkins. After a quiet week of relaxation, affording ample time to reflect upon the situation, the President returned to the Capitol, convinced, as he told Morgenthau, "that it is very important that he restate the New Deal philosophy." It was such a "restatement" of the New Deal philosophy which Morgenthau and other New Dealers waited upon during the bleak months of early 1938.[5]

Shortly before Morgenthau was to deliver his Academy of Political Science address, Eccles sent the President a memo which undoubtedly influenced Roosevelt to qualify his support of the speech as Morgenthau had planned it. Eccles' arguments were well calculated to impress the President with the gravity of the situation. Raising up the ghost of Hoover's presidency, the Reserve Board Chairman warned the President that,

> The Republican Party was wrecked by relying on wishful thinking that business would turn up, while at the same time pursuing policies that intensified the depression. The Democratic Party can likewise be wrecked if it makes the same mistake. The situation today is too serious for us to rely on wishful thinking. A drastic and long-continued recession at this time would discredit the whole New Deal . . . If effective action is again delayed at this time [as it was last winter on cost and price advances], the repercussions on our whole social, political and economic structure may be disastrous.

Eccles then recommended specific action on three different fronts. First the Administration "should seek to dispel present pessimism and to create a favorable psychological background for the prosecution of its specific measures." On this general objective Eccles and Morgenthau were agreed, though Eccles thought business confidence would best be helped by a tougher government policy towards excessive labor demands

117

and by other measures promising better profits, while Morgenthau thought business confidence would best respond to a balancing of the budget.

Eccles' second proposal brought him and Morgenthau into open disagreement. It was this portion of the memo which had caused the Secretary to lament on October 4 that suddenly his whole policy was "at stake." Eccles suggested that the Administration should handle its fiscal accounts so as to "maintain current consumer incomes and buying." Specifically, he recommended that "In order to maintain consumer buying power and to make possible a technically-balanced budget in the fiscal year 1939, it is imperative that Government expenditures be maintained and, if possible, increased in the next six months." Eccles explained further that social security taxes were creating an "excess of cash receipts" in the Treasury. The significant factor in the present situation was not the bookkeeping deficit, but the decline in national buying power resulting from an excess of cash collections." Rendering his priorities in a sequence characteristic of his approach to national economic problems, Eccles added, "the business need for government expenditures is far greater now than in the past year. The human need may also be greater." Spending, he maintained, should be channeled through WPA and crop loans, both of which "would go almost 100 percent into consumer buying."

Eccles' third proposal consisted of a set of measures designed to stimulate private capital expenditures. He had concluded that "apart from a great interest in Government expenditures, private expenditure on residential building is the one great source we can rely on to increase consumer income and buying power." To accelerate new housing construction, he recommended that the government lower the cost of mortgage money and provide subsidies for builders, but not suppliers. In Eccles' opinion, construction workers and building materials manufacturers were already getting too much--pricing new housing beyond the reach of most Americans. As a further stimulus to private investment, Eccles suggested a temporary change in the undistributed profits tax to permit plant and equipment expenditures in excess of depreciation allowances to be credited against undistributed profits for a limited period of time. Corporations with earnings under $15,000 should be totally exempted from the excess profits tax, he suggested. "It would be a cheap price to pay for the removal of the bulk of the opposition to the tax, much of which, in the case of the small corporations with no access to the capital markets, is legitimate."

The memo, despite sharp warnings that the 1929 Depression could be repeating itself, was on the whole balanced and judicious. It did not propose that all eggs be put into the spending basket. It supported the widespread argument that a better psychological climate for investment was needed and it recognized the need to stimulate private investment

through positive action. Moreover, it recognized the President's concern for a balanced budget, suggesting, in fact, that one of the most
important objectives of the proposals, especially the spending proposal,
was to assure that the planned 1939 balance would not be lost. Certainly, when one considers that the Treasury at the time was offering the
President little more than successive drafts of Morgenthau's speech, the
document was relevant and useful.[6]

Nevertheless, it would seem that at this stage of the Recession the
primary effect of Eccles' proposals was to forestall full implementation
of alternate policies, rather than to precipitate the implementation of
his own. Eccles' memo was no doubt a factor in the President's decision
to retreat from his earlier endorsement of Morgenthau's address. It may
have led the President to temper his promises to balance the budget but
it by no means caused him to rush headlong into a new spending program.
For several months, as the Recession deepened, FDR would wander in a
no-man's-land out of which emerged at times ghosts from the New Deal
past--hints that a new NRA-type plan was under consideration, whispers
of further monetary gimcrackery--but never solid signs that the
President had a program clearly in mind.

The period was particularly distressing for Morgenthau and Eccles.
Morgenthau was afraid that Roosevelt would ruin all chances for a
balanced budget by starting a massive spending program. Eccles feared
the President would spend too little, too late. As the winter wore on,
Eccles and Morgenthau kept the President's incoming file well stocked
with memos and suggestions for combatting the crisis. The proposals of
first one, then the other. came to the President's attention, offering,
if taken collectively, a muddle of confusing, contradictory advice.
Morgenthau's proposals had but one common denominator--all were intended
to obviate the need of renewed spending. Eccles insisted repeatedly
that if spending were not resumed soon all would be lost. Morgenthau
and Eccles both admitted New Dealers were "groping" to find constructive
solutions to the nation's economic problems.

STRATEGIES OF ECCLES AND THE SPENDERS

Ironically. Eccles' provincial background, which may have favored
the achievement of his insights into the economic problem, was in part
responsible for his difficulties in gaining personal access to the
President. The degree to which Morgenthau was steeped in the rhetoric

119

and attitudes of early twentieth-century eastern reformers inhibited him from gaining newer perspectives during the Depression. Yet it facilitated easy and comfortable access to a President who shared that rhetoric and those attitudes. Eccles' Utah background permitted him to accept ideas which those in the Roosevelt-Morgenthau tradition found difficult to countenance and to treat lightly ideas which had become dogmas of their faith. But it also stamped him as an exotic bird, brilliant and fascinating, but not among those regularly invited to a fireside gathering at Hyde Park. Morgenthau had influence, but the circumstances bringing him to so powerful a position tended to discourage fresh insights. Eccles had the insights, but the conditions favoring those insights inhibited his possible influence.

While most administration leaders were still searching for answers to the haunting questions of the causes and cure of the Recession, Eccles and a number of well-placed allies were faced with a quite different set of concerns. Convinced that they had the answers to the economic problems besetting the President, they applied themselves to the task of persuading him to adopt their policy recommendations. Eccles' effectiveness as advocate of the policy was hampered, however, by the constraints built into his position as head of an independent regulatory agency as well as by his relatively restricted access to Roosevelt.

The Reserve Board Chairman felt the restraining effects of his office especially keenly in speeches and congressional testimony during the recession period. His first major speech after the onset of the Recession was in December 1937 at an annual meeting of the American Farm Bureau Federation in Chicago. Though complemented by Leon Henderson, assistant to Harry Hopkins, Benjamin V. Cohen, then of the National Power Policy Committee. and others, Eccles, was not satisfied with the address. "I personally do not feel," he wrote Chester C. Davis of the Board of Governors, "that I got over very well to the farm group my economic thesis as to what had happened and as to what might be done about it. The principal reason being that I felt too restrained. I was afraid I might say something which the newspapers would pick up to the embarrassment of the Administration or the Board, and, therefore, I do not believe I proved to be much of a salesman."[7]

On Wednesday December 8, Eccles testified before Senator Robert Wagner's Committee on Banking and Currency, an obviously delicate task for the Reserve Chairman, as Senator Wagner had long been one of the most persistent Congressional advocates of large-scale spending programs. Eccles' remarks were carefully planned to avoid giving the impression that he was openly advocating a resumption of spending. When asked how much subsidy should be given to the housing industry he insisted that in offering his opinion, he was "not advocating. I do not want to be put in that position at this time." During the course of the hearings, he was brought by the Senators' questions to offer a suggestive opinion that the Government is "not quite flexible enough. We are too slow stopping our spending and we may be too slow in starting it." When asked what effect the Recession would have on the effort to balance the budget, he replied that it "will make it extremely difficult, if not impossible, should the depression continue." Though Senator Townsend tried to push the matter further. Eccles changed the subject back to a discussion of housing problems. His comments were picked up by the press and treated as signs of dissent within the Administration from the Morgenthau position on budget balancing, but the press reaction was neither dramatic nor prolonged.[8]

A much greater play was given to Eccles' testimony in January 1938 before a special Senate Committee on Unemployment and Relief chaired by Senator James F. Byrnes. At the commencement of his testimony, Senator Byrnes stressed the point, presumably at Eccles' request, that Eccles "did not want to come and is a reluctant witness." Eccles opened his testimony with the clear warning that "I am expressing my own views, and not necessarily those of the Board or the Reserve System or the Administration. I am not here representing anyone except myself." During the testimony, however, he boldly stated, "A billion dollars of increased spending, if it worked quickly enough, and went into consumer-buying power, would act as a very great stimulus, in my opinion, and would tend, I think, to stop the Recession."[9] When questioned further about the statement, he tried to mute its tone by explaining that "I made no recommendation. I am not recommending. I am merely attempting to outline these things." Despite his protestations, the billion-dollar proposal was widely reported in the press, without emphasis, of course, upon Eccles' insistence that it represented only his personal views. It is possible that Eccles was perfectly aware of the play his comments would receive in the press and intended the caveats he offered to cover him if criticized. In any case, many reporters saw the statement as a harbinger of an impending official reversal of the policy Morgenthau had announced in November. Morgenthau was obviously displeased with the tenor of Eccles' remarks, commenting "snappishly" to reporters "that he was the only proper man to talk of such matters."[10] Eccles suffered as did the President from a sense that circumstances prevented him from taking effective action to counter the crisis. The President's inaction, however, was caused by uncertainty as to what should be done. Eccles was convinced his proposals would be effective, but was inhibited in his efforts to persuade Roosevelt. If the President, like a "cornered lion," did not know where to put his strength, Eccles, knowing exactly where the President's strength must be put, lacked the means of insuring its timely application.

Eccles was resourceful, however, and though his public pronouncements were limited in their effect upon administration policy, he had other assets which he used skillfully. First, Eccles, with the aid of Lauchlin Currie, was a master of the art of writing pithy, persuasive memos. Beginning in October 1937, a sequence of carefully-timed memos made their way from his office to the White House, urging upon the President a wide-ranging anti-recession program with immediate resumption of government spending at its base. Those presenting general recovery programs were prepared October 31, 1937; March 8, 1938; April 27, 1938; and June 6, 1938. In all of them Eccles stressed the need to supplement private spending with stepped-up government spending. He also sought to minimize the amount of further borrowing needed to finance programs and to innovate programs, particularly in the housing construction and railroad industries, which would entice private investment at the smallest possible government expense. Eccles proposed low-interest loans, guarantees for private lending, and broadening of RFC activities, all as possible means of achieving this end. In addition, he felt that where government funds would be needed in large quantities, such as for increased WPA spending and for farm programs, the maximum amount possible should be secured from the "stabilization fund" remaining from the gold devaluation of 1933-34. Eccles also urged that the President consider changing the Social Security law, beginning payments for old age insurance immediately rather than waiting until 1941, so as to reduce the deflationary effect of social security taxes.

The nature of these programs indicates that Eccles recognized Roosevelt's continuing desire to balance the budget as soon as possible. "The only possibility of achieving a balanced budget within the life of this administration", he argued in June, "rests on stopping deflation this year". A second theme, which in some memos loomed at least as large as the need to balance the budget, was the necessity of meeting the challenge of totalitarianism, a concern Eccles knew Roosevelt had been preoccupied with for several months.[11]

It is difficult, of course, to measure the impact of these memos upon the President. Certainly they, along with advice the President was getting from other advocates of spending within the Administration, at least served to keep him aware that spending must be kept open as a possible option in case spontaneous recovery did not occur. To post-New Deal eyes the memos contain a far broader approach to the economic problem than for example, the suggestion of an anti-monopoly campaign spearheaded by Assistant Attorney-General Robert H. Jackson, or Morgenthau's continuing confidence that a single symbolic gesture, the balancing of the budget, or even (as he hoped in March) a strong presidential statement, might bring recovery.

Eccles was to be singularly effective, however, in exploiting indirect means of bringing his ideas before Roosevelt. As the Recession began, several informal gatherings of New Dealers took place in Washington. Such conferences, often attended by men of different departments and including second or third rank officials, shared a common goal, to help prepare an anti-recession program and thus rescue the New Deal. Eccles was actively involved in at least one of these groups. During the fall and winter, a series of meetings were held at the homes of various Washington officials. Those attending included Eccles, Currie, Harry L. Hopkins and Leon Henderson of the WPA, Jim LeCron, Harry Dexter White, Aubrey Williams, Isadore Lubin of the Department of Commerce, Mordecai Ezekial, Paul Appleby, Senator Robert LaFollette, Jr., and Henry A. Wallace.

The informal discussions of this group led to the conclusion that everything possible should be done to bring about "abandonment of the deflationary policy being followed by the Administration and adoption of a new spending program." This initial objective was to be achieved through "use as far as possible of the financial resources of the Administration in the way of sterilized gold, gold profits, etc., so as to make the resulting increase in the national debt as small as possible." It was also desirable to include in the program "such forms of spending as to get a much larger volume of private funds into investment, which would facilitate the eventual withdrawal of government support while activity based on private financing continues to expand."[12]

One aim of the gatherings was to develop a common approach to a spending program which would be all the more convincing to FDR because it came in similar form from various departments of the Administration. Those close to cabinet members were specifically urged to get word to the President that strong action was needed. Obviously, Eccles participated in the discussions of this group as one of several like-minded New Dealers. But it is interesting to note that almost every one of the group had been among Eccles' admirers since he had begun his Washington career in 1934 and had written letters complimenting him on his speeches and requesting copies for friends. Three of the group, Hopkins, Wallace, and Ezekial, were among those who had been Eccles' guests at the Shoreham Hotel meeting in the fall of 1933. It would not be an exaggeration to suggest that by 1938 Eccles had become generally recognized as the ideologue of the New Deal spenders, offering, as he wrote, the "needed arguments on how a planned policy of adequate deficit financing could serve the humanitarian objective with which they were most directly concerned."[13] In the spring of 1938, Eccles was in some measure reaping the rewards of capital he had invested over the previous four years in the form of speeches and persuasive arguments to officials in all departments. Though his personal access to the

President was limited, his ideas found their way to the White House through a multitude of channels. In mid-April, after Roosevelt had announced his recovery program, a member of the group modestly proposed that their discussions "may have served in some light degree to help provide a basis of action which has [now] been taken."[14]

Members of the National Resources Committee were also Eccles' allies in urging a spending program upon the President. Roosevelt's uncle, Frederic A. Delano, enjoyed frequent access to the White House and had long been an admirer of Eccles. The two often exchanged opinions on economic problems and were to work closely together in the fall of 1938 on the President's Fiscal and Monetary Advisory Board. Another member of the Resources Committee, Beardsley Ruml, exercised influence, through Harry Hopkins, in promoting Eccles' ideas. He was to participate with Hopkins in the top-level conferences which finally led Roosevelt to his policy decisions in late March and early April.

The President's son, James, became a figure of considerable importance during the Recession crisis. In the fall of 1937, he was appointed personal secretary to the President. Paul Appleby remembered that Jimmy had become "a sort of intelligence agent for FDR--he had succeeded . . . Louis Howe."[15] Apparently he was to act as liason for the President with various administration officials, thus relieving his father of a portion of his heavy schedule of appointments. The younger Roosevelt was sympathetic to Eccles' ideas, and no doubt helped bring them to the President's ear. He and Eccles began having weekly conferences each Monday, beginning November 1, 1937, and continued to see one another regularly into the summer of 1938. James Roosevelt served as a link, during this period, not only between Eccles and his father, but also between Eccles and other advocates of spending within the Administration. His tenure as Presidential Secretary was short and attended by occasional ill-will and even rancor form those who resented his control over access to FDR, but for Eccles, at least, it no doubt permitted a degree of influence he might not otherwise have had.[16]

Particularly important was the strong tie which existed during this period between advisors (both offical and unofficial) surrounding Eccles and WPA Administrator Hopkins--those engaged in building a rationale for spending and those who had mastered the arts of spending. Certain members of the two groups worked closely during the winter of 1937-38. On November 8, two days before Morgenthau's speech to the American Academy and just a week after Eccles' first recession memo, Lauchlin Currie, Leon Henderson of the WPA, and Isadore Lubin left a memo of their own with the President very similar in tone and analysis to that which Eccles had delivered the week before. They pointed out that a maladjustment of costs and prices, not the undistributed earnings tax, the capital gains tax, "or various regulatory activities of government," had been the chief cause of the Recession. Though they stressed the point that the Recession "could be severe and prolonged if the government does not intervene," their program was perhaps even more moderate than Eccles' on the issue of spending, proposing primarily that the government transfer items from the 1939 to the 1938 budget, meet the winter's WPA needs, start PWA projects immediately, and attempt to stimulate residential building. "The objective of a balanced budget for 1939," they stated explicitly, "should be retained."[17]

Henderson continued throughout the Recession to direct trenchant memos and letters to Hopkins and to other members of Hopkins' staff. Deputy WPA Administrator, Aubrey Williams was one of the key advocates within the WPA of the spending rationale, a man of great sensitivity to human values and keen historical perspective. Beardsley Ruml became a close associate of the group during the winter of 1937-38, supplying the offices of both Eccles and Hopkins with a series of memos analyzing the social and political implications of the Recession, should it be allowed to continue, and offering his opinion that a spending program would have to come eventually and should be begun early rather than late. He had been appointed a director of the Federal Reserve Bank of New York by Eccles in the summer of 1937, thus securing an official position within the Reserve System. It is significant that all of these men had exchanged ideas on economic problems with Eccles in the past and that Williams, Lubin, and Henderson had taken the time to write Eccles letters congratulating him on past addresses. Moreover, Appleby recalled that all but Ruml were participants in the informal discussions held in Washington that winter.

The approaches and insights gained by Currie, Ruml, Henderson, and Williams as they exchanged ideas on the Recession quite naturally found a focus in the common attitudes of their respective chiefs, Eccles and Hopkins. Eccles and Hopkins shared the notoriety of being the two most avid "spenders" in Washington, Eccles providing the rationale and Hopkins the execution. It is not surprising that they developed a certain affinity, especially as they matched forces to undercut the various drives for budget-balancing of Morgenthau and Daniel Bell. The relationship offered great promise to Eccles in this effort to get his ideas before the President as often and convincingly as possible. If there was one person in official Washington who approached Morgenthau in his freedom of access to FDR, it was Harry Hopkins. Indeed, the Roosevelts had taken Hopkins' daughter into their home upon the death of his wife that fall. During this period, the President demonstrated a paternal interest in Hopkins' well-being, and particularly a concern for his precarious health. There were hints that FDR had placed Hopkins high on his list of possible successors to the Presidency.[18] Hopkins had been one of the New Dealers present at Eccles' Shoreham dinner in the fall of 1933. He had followed Eccles' work in Washington with interest and shared Eccles' ideas on appropriate fiscal policy in depression. Moreover, he is reported to have attended some of the meetings held by the informal discussion group that fall.

However, a set of personal calamities was to diminish the extent of Hopkins' participation in the anti-Recession discussions of that winter, clouding for a time the prospect that he could insure timely access to FDR of the proposal of the spending faction. That fall his wife died of cancer. Shortly thereafter, Hopkins found that a persistent stomach ailment was also caused by cancer. On December 9, he left Washington for the Mayo Clinic in Rochester, Minnesota, to undergo surgical removal of the malignancy. The massive operation necessitated a long convalescence, and after leaving the clinic, he went in mid-January to Florida, where he was the guest of Joseph P. Kennedy. While in Florida, his assistants Aubrey Williams and Corrington Gill kept in frequent touch and consulted with him on events at the Capitol. Though Hopkins was physically removed for a time from the Washington scene, it is clear from the Eccles-Hopkins correspondence that neither of them had ruled out the possibility that his special relationship with the President might be of great use in the spring. On December 18, while Hopkins was still at the Rochester, Minnesota clinic, Eccles wrote a note expressing his satisfaction that Hopkins was at last getting the medical treatment he had long needed. "I do not know of anyone," he wrote,

> who has been under such heavy pressures as you have or who has drawn so heavily on nervous energy, so that I am not surprised that you are being laid up for repairs . . . My own free advice is that you rest and recuperate now so that you may be the quicker restored to this scene, which is going to need your presence more urgently a few months hence than at present, in my judgement.

On January 10, Hopkins wrote Eccles that he was leaving shortly for the South, "and will look forward to seeing you as soon as I get back, about the first of March."[19]

It is significant that advocates of balancing the budget as an anti-recession measure did not demonstrate the cohesiveness and commitment characteristic of the spending group.   There are no accounts of quiet meetings to plan common strategies among the budget balancers--nor is there evidence that anything that could be called a program was ever produced by them.   Morgenthau was alarmed to find that Eccles had given the President a program in early November partly because he had no such program himself.   There are suggestions in his diaries that he was aware of anti-recession discussion groups and resentful of not being included, but no indiction that he thought of organizing such himself.

During the spring Morgenthau continued to work within the pale of official Treasury contacts and procedures, devoting his time to the development of four anti-recession measures.   In late January the Secretary, with William O. Douglas and Jerome Frank of the Securities and Exchange Commission, began to plan the reorganization of a small utility company in New York state.   It was their hope that such a project might in some way serve as a model for larger projects which could stabilize the ailing utilities industry in the United States, and thus promote recovery. As an additional anti-recession measure, he proposed early in February that the Treasury stop sterilizing gold coming into the United States, hoping that the consequent expansion of credit reserves might impede the downward trend in commodity prices. Eccles argued that the proposed action would have no effect, but enticed by Morgenthau's accompanying proposal to increase WPA expenditures by $250 million, was persuaded to give his consent.   The joint Treasury-Federal Reserve announcement was made on February 14.[20]

Fear that monopolistic practices in the vital building supplies industry were holding prices to an artificially high level led to Morgenthau's next anti-recession measure.   Working with Agriculture and Labor Department staff members, he helped draft a statement explaining that while the Administration wished to raise prices in general, it would take action to lower prices in the building supplies industries which had been artificially kept at pre-1929 levels.   The President released the statement on February 18, taking pains to attribute it to the agencies drafting it.   This statement cleared the way for more concrete anti-monopoly activities. Under Morgenthau's sponsorship, an interdepartmental committee reviewed the pricing practices of the building materials industry, concluding that prices of iron and steel products, cement, and gypsum were being kept at inappropriately high levels through price-fixing practices of trade associations.   The high price of these products was impeding the new residential construction badly needed by the ailing economy. Morgenthau helped draft a proposal requiring that all government cement purchases be made through the Division of Procurement, that successful bidders for government contracts make cement available to all government contractors at the same price and that confusing price statements be cleared up. The President approved the proposal and announced the action on March 21. The next day FDR left Washington for Warm Springs, Georgia, where he had planned to enjoy a brief respite from the White House regimen. In Washington, Morgenthau examined various plans to stimulate housing and added to his concerns a consideration of what could be done to help the ailing railroad industry.

Two aspects of Morgenthau's efforts that spring to find an effective anti-recession policy are particularly striking. First is the piecemeal nature of his approach to the problem. The reorganization of a bankrupt utility company was somehow to revivify the entire industry. It was hoped that a presidential statement on the price structure if followed up with "a couple more clarifying . . . statements," might "change the whole psychology."[21] Cessation of the sterilization of gold would "give the President a chance to think clearly and take the pressure off him . . . If the President did have some of the pressure eased, he would find a solution to the present-day problems."[22] Lowering the cost of cement might start a building boom and pace recovery.

Morgenthau called officials from other government agencies to help in planning some of his proposals. Several of them, whether advocates of spending or not, expressed their discomfort at the obvious lack of a coherent administration program. Secretary of Agriculture Wallace hoped that the price statement would leave the public with the impression that "we know which way we're going and that we have a policy, and that the whole Administration is headed in the same direction." Mordecai Ezekial desired that any statement will be broad enough to not merely harmonize these recent statements, but to set forth a broad statement of policy which subsequent action for the next several months would all presumably fit into; to enunciate a program".[23] A memo prepared by Treasury staff members was to "evidence that the Administration has embarked upon a program rather than the adoption of unrelated and sporadic measures."[24] Yet, despite this urgent hope, the Secretary of the Treasury continued to take up first one idea, then another, never sitting down to plan a comprehensive program which might clearly be instrumental in the economy as a whole.

The second noteworthy aspect of Morgenthau's springtime recession policies is that with one exception they demonstrated a preoccupation with institutional reform. There is clearly evident the hope, lingering from an early New Deal, that by rearranging the structure of a power company. by creating a new institution to lend to home builders or to railroads, or by preventing the collusion of construction materials suppliers, permanent changes could be effected which would then automatically exert general healing powers. Except for the cessation of sterilization, which was a measure directed towards general, not specific problems, each of the measures was a response to a particular problem dividing recession from recovery. There was no macroeconomic vision among these men--no model which might give a clue to the interrelationship of investment, interest rates, employment and national income.

DECISION AT WARM SPRINGS

While Morgenthau moved from project to project, Eccles continued his efforts in behalf of a resumption of major government expenditures. On February 1 he sent to James Roosevelt, then planning a trip to the south which was to include conferences with Harry L. Hopkins, "a tentative program to combat the recession." "I hope it will assist you in discussing matters with Harry Hopkins," Eccles wrote. In the program Eccles reiterated his opinion that "The longer a spending program is delayed, the more eventually will have to be spent." The first item included the suggestion that "the quickest outlet for increased expenditures of a maximum activity-creating nature is W.P.A." But the program which had by this time become standard for Eccles as well as for other members of the informal discussion group, included specific proposals to stimulate housing, rural rehabilitation, railroad equipment building, highway construction loans to small business, and to accelerate old age pensions.[25]

The next day, Wednesday, February 2, Eccles spoke to a gathering of officials of the Federal Reserve System. It was precisely the sort of platform Eccles enjoyed most, an occasion offering him an opportunity to speak frankly to his colleagues on important national issues without the fear that reporters might misinterpret his statements to the embarrassment of the Administration. Obviously in a philosophical mood, he offered his opinion that

> We are in an interim period in our economy--in
> somewhat of a no-man's land--in which we are some-

what groping in order to find formulas that will so modify the conditions under which we operate, and which have failed in the past, as to give us some assurance that we can go forward in the future . . . I would like to see as little regimentation--as little direct regulation of the activity of the individual as possible. I would like to see the Government's function to be that of the compensating factor in the economy through functional methods.[26]

The next week he sent yet another memo to the President, offering essentially the same program he had sent with James Roosevelt to Harry Hopkins' Florida retreat. He began the memo by calling the President's attention to his prophecy of last October that no natural upturn could be expected. Events, he suggested, had confirmed the truth of the earlier statement. Again he used sharp words to warn the President of the gravity of the crisis. "The Federal Government is making a negligible contribution to community buying power in comparison with 1934-35," he wrote. "We appear to be launched upon a severe depression of considerable duration." The Reserve Board Chairman warned that big business was using the opportunity "to drive for repeal and inaction". The President's own "recent policy of inaction . . . has given a new lease on life to the reactionaries. They see both you and the New Deal discredited."

Eccles then tied the theme of conservative domestic opposition to world fascism, precisely as the President had done during the final stages of Morgenthau's speech preparations on the previous November. Roosevelt's concern, expressed to Morgenthau on November 8, "that Fascism is winning out in this world and that Democracies are gradually becoming weaker" had become a growing theme in writings and speeches of New Dealers as the Recession deepened. Roosevelt, Morgenthau, Eccles, and Hopkins were among those who spoke of the growing threat of fascism to liberal democracy. The takeover of Brazil by Getulio Vargas on the day Morgenthau gave his Academy address underlined the ominous possibility that fascism might be gaining a foothold even on the American continent. Hitler's demand for the union of Austria with Germany was approaching its fulfillment as Eccles wrote this memo to the President. "The greatest threat to democracy today," he maintained,

lies in the growing conviction that it cannot work. The growing Democracy must likewise have strong leadership if it is to meet the challenge of Fascism. I urge that you provide the democratic

leadership that will make our system function. Only
in that way can the growing threat of Fascism be
overcome.[27]

In these passages, Eccles expressed the fears of all those who wished
FDR well. The policy thus far appeared all too much like that of Hoover
in 1929-33. If allowed to continue it would discredit the whole New
Deal. Should this be allowed to happen liberalism would suffer a blow
which, given the apparent strength of fascism, might well be fatal.

Shortly after sending this memo to the President, Eccles, at the
urging of his physicians, took a short vacation in Utah. On March 22,
the President left Washington as well. Three days later, Morgenthau took
advantage of the President's absence to retire to Sea Island for a short
rest. It would have seemed that upon their return the three would be
fresh and fit to rejoin battle. The President resolved the issue,
however, before Eccles and Morgenthau could face off again.

Events moved rapidly after Roosevelt reached Warm Springs. On
March 12 Germany invaded Austria--an event which was ominous in itself
and had a depressing effect upon the American stock market. Shortly
after Morgenthau's arrival at Sea Island, he called Roosevelt. The
President joked that "common stocks will soon be cheap enough for us to
buy some." Apparently Morgenthau saw it as no laughing matter. "We
must get our house in order," he wrote that day, "if we are going to
continue our leadership for liberalism."[28]

Morgenthau was unaware that Hopkins had been busily setting in
motion a chain of events designed to achieve that very end. Hopkins had
recently asked Leon Henderson to review to economic scene in Washington
and then join him on the way to see Roosevelt at Warm Springs. Aubrey
Williams and Beardsley Ruml in the meantime had taken quarters at Pine
Mountain Valley, a short distance from the President's retreat.
Henderson joined them there and the three spent their time preparing
various memos designed to convince the President that the time was right
for the resumption of government spending. While Hopkins pleaded his
case to the President, his crew of experts supplied him with an arsenal
of arguments intended to set the Administration on a new course.[29]

An unsigned telegram sent to Beardsley Ruml at Warm Springs
April 1, offers insight into the nature of the discussions taking place.
The author of the telegram proposed that the present "socio-financial"
policy be replaced with a "socio-economic" policy. The present policy
is "to balance expenditures with income, subject to (1) Relief of the
unemployed . . . (2) Armament necessities, (3) Maintenance of necessary
administrative services on an economy basis, (4) no new taxes." The
second, it was emphasized, would have similar social objective, but it
would be oriented towards, "the increase in production of goods and

services and the elimination of physical and human waste." The balancing of income and expenditure should be a secondary consideration. The primary objective of fiscal policy should be increased production. This would follow in the wake of growing demand stimulated by increased purchasing power. The government could increase purchasing power by deliberately creating budget deficits.

Planners of a "socio-economic" fiscal policy would first ask how much additional purchasing power is needed. They would then compute what additions could be expected from private sources. Finally they could adjust the budget deficit according to the expected need for increased purchasing power. This could be done through a spending program or through tax cuts. Then planners could decide which social needs any desired expenditures should be applied towards. "The present 'social-financial' policy forces adaptation of economic and production operations to prevailing financial necessities," the author maintained. the consequences were "economic strain and deficiency in production and on the financial side, no corresponding increase in confidence or stability."[30]

Henderson and Ruml incorporated this compelling analysis into their own memo, pointing out that "within recent months and more particularly within recent weeks, a number of observers in reflecting on the recent crisis in production have drawn together certain lines of thought which have not ordinarily been associated. As a result, there appears in broad outline an interpretation of the system which, if correct in the main should have a profound effect on current public policy." The memo offered a sample computation of the amount of government investment which would be needed to bring national income to a level of 80 billion dollars, a figure which, according to the National Resources Committee, would approach full employment. Concluding that a net government contribution of no more than $3 billion would be possible (though as much as $6 billion might be desirable), Ruml and Henderson estimated that $200 billion had been lost through idle men and machines since 1929, a figure which obviously dwarfed the recommended expenditure.

They then went on to rationalize increased government spending by suggesting that, contrary to popular belief, there had been enormous federal contributions to investment before 1933. This had gone unrecognized, however. because it took a form that kept us from recognizing it for what it was. That form was alienation of the national domain. The effect was the creation of purchasing power." Singling out precious minerals, land, and the use of tariffs and franchises as aspects of the public domain which had been alienated in the past without accounts being kept of the loss, the two maintained that "relative to the then national income, these contributions were of the first magnitude."

Henderson and Ruml's argument, if correct, made it "inconceivable that there can be natural recovery along 'orthodox' lines. Purchasing power must again be created by the federal government." They pointedly contrasted "national intervention to stimulate production," the method of totalitarian states, with "national intervention to stimulate consumption," the democratic method. The advantage of the latter was that "the form of industrial pattern . . . is determined not by the judgment or caprice of a few, but by the whole culture expressing itself through actions of individual consumers." The fundamental difficulty, they concluded, "lies in the ability of technology to produce goods faster than it can produce purchasing power and higher standard of life too absorb its product. The national state therefore has been forced to provide purchasing power concurrently with increased productive capacity." Even were the eighty to ninety billion figure of national income achieved, millions would fail to receive a share adequate to maintain a decent standard of living. "Therefore, out of the national income each year must go benefits, given in a dignified manner to these millions. The result will not only be the maintenance of purchasing power, but in the long run shall lead to the abolition of poverty in America."[31]

There were doubtless other memos prepared and presented to the President on that occasion and long discussions, all designed to convince him that it was time to act and that a resumption of spending was the only viable alternative. The arguments were reinforced by another discouraging dip in the stock market on March 25. In addition, the fall elections, which the President hoped would bring him gains in Congress, were a constant preoccupation. Congressional leaders in the absence of presidential action were threatening to initiate a "Business Recovery Act" of their own. Senator Harrison of Mississippi proposed legislation built upon the "philosophy . . . contained in the wise words expressed by the Hon. Henry Morgenthau . . . in an address before the Academy of Political Science in New York City on November 10th last year."[32] The growing Nazi threat provided the backdrop against which Roosevelt saw the ailing stock market, the forthcoming elections, and a feared loss of presidential initiative in shaping economic policy. Something had to be done before congress recessed for the summer. The memos prepared at Warm Springs, backed by the persuasive influence of Harry Hopkins, did their work. Before the President left Georgia, he had decided to recommend the resumption of spending. He would reveal the concerns which impelled him finally to act when he announced the program in mid-April.

Though anti-monopoly action became a part of the program made public in April, it was not a part of the discussions at Warm Springs. Robert H. Jackson and Benjamin V. Cohen, who had been working on the problem, met the Presidential party in Atlanta and accompanied them on the return trip to Washington. The decision to prepare an anti-monopoly message was made on the train en route to the Capitol.[33]

THE RESUMPTION OF SPENDING

Morgenthau's contact with the President during this time was limited to occasional brief phone calls, during which the planning of a recovery program was not discussed. His first indication that the President had decided on a new program came April 6 from his assistant Wayne C. Taylor, who had heard the news from Secretary Wallace. The next day, Morgenthau sat down to outline in longhand upon hotel stationary, a program of his own. He proposed emphatically that the President's spending and lending program be re-examined and that FDR should then "re-state the whole spending program to the country." In addition, there should be a re-examination of the results of all the new legislation of the past five years to find out "which parts are not working efficiently." He recommended that a small, highly-trusted group of officials meet twice a week with the President to get the various agencies "straightened out." It would be wise to "Announce to [the] public at once what [the] President considers necessary in additional reform. Keep this down to a minimum." The whole was to be presented through a careful publicity campaign designed to control statements by Washington officials and to sell the federal program in the various states.[34]

In the meantime, Treasury officials prepared memos for Morgenthau arguing both sides of the spending issue. George C. Haas titled his April 8 memo, "Is Increased Government spending necessary for business recovery?" His answer was an unmistakeable, "no." The same day, White prepared three memos, all taking in carefully guarded language the opposite position.[35] Morgenthau prepared another memo of his own on the train April 10. as he was returning to Washington, arguing somewhat belatedly that "the time seems most propitious for presentation to the people of a comprehensive statement of administration policy and of a program essentially the same as in his April 7 Sea Island memo," to be announced in a series of speeches by the President "The bullish effect of three speeches," he wrote,

culminating in a broad recovery program of immediate

134

action as announced in advance should be tremendous.
It would serve, I believe, to eliminate existing
confusion which is working to hold business down; it
would give the people such needed reorientation and
assurance and should greatly strengthen the administration's position . . . Presentation of this part
of the program should include an estimate of the
total cost of the program. a statement on the amount
you propose to ask Congress for and how you propose
to finance the expenditures.[36]

Such last-ditch efforts to derail the Warm Springs program were to
be of no effect. Morgenthau rushed to the White House shortly after his
train had arrive in Washington. Jimmy Roosevelt and Harry Hopkins were
with the President as the Secretary entered the room at 6:45 p.m. He
arrived just in time to hear the President say, "Well, then have we
agreed on a billion four hundred fifty?" The entire party sat down and
the President turned to Morgenthau. "We have been travelling fast this
last week," he said, "and we have covered a lot of ground and you will
have to hurry to catch up." When Morgenthau responded that, "Maybe I
never can catch up," FDR cajoled, "Oh, yes, you can--in a couple of
hours."

"He then took half an hour," Morgenthau wrote in his diary,

to outline the various schemes that he had in mind
for spending money . . . It seems to me that he has
lost all sense of proportion. I stressed the fact
very strongly that if we started a spending program
now and overlook the difficult things such as railroads and public utilities that we would be right
back where we were within six to nine months--only
worse off . . .

The most interesting thing is that he has
worked out his whole spending program without
consulting a single person at the Treasury, including his Director of the Budget, Bell. He has
absolutely no idea how much the thing is going to
cost and doesn't seem to worry or care . . .

I went away with the impression that he wants
to shoot the whole works as far as spending is
concerned and that he is really scared to death.[37]

Morgenthau opened his staff meeting the next morning by bemoaning
the fact that "for three weeks neither Magill [acting in his absence]

nor I have had any advice from the President . . . In three weeks
there's been no advice as to what he does or doesn't want."[38]
Morgenthau explained further that the programs as put to him last night
"just scared me to death--worse than I've been scared--and the thing
hasn't been thought through. And fear begets fear . . . The
President's attitude . . . in 1933 was, "Let's be calm and do things,
and overcome fear,' but fear begets fear."[39] Morgenthau complained that
the program contained "everything that Jimmy Roosevelt's been trying to
do . . . every single thing they've been advocating over there, they've
done, plus a few things we haven't heard." The new program was taken by
Morgenthau and his staff as a sign of the increasing influence of Harry
Hopkins through Jimmy Roosevelt. The President, Morgenthau told his
staff, has "lost control now, there's no question . . . I'm awful
afraid that the cards are all stacked against us. I don't think we've
got much chance."[40]

The next day Morgenthau, Eccles, and Hopkins met with Wallace and
staff members from several departments for lunch. Hopkins outlined for
Morgenthau a program "involving 'heavy 'public works to combine loans
and grants and to involve grants of about $450 million; a doubling of
the power of the U.S. Housing Authority to incur obligations; increases
in appropriations for highways and flood control and enlarged appropriations for Works Progress, National Youth Administration and CCC."
Expenditures were to be increased by the program to nearly two billion
dollars above the budget figures of January. Morgenthau would not give
his assent to the insistence of Eccles and Hopkins that the Treasury
would have no difficulty managing the program. He noted after the
meeting.

> The last thing I said to Jimmy Roosevelt . . . was
> 'Now, Jimmy, at last I have heard the program' . . .
> I wish you would take the following message to your
> father. After giving the matter further considera-
> tion I will let him know whether I can or cannot
> finance it.[41]

Morgenthau's assistant, Wayne C. Taylor, who had attended the luncheon,
wrote a brief critique of the program for Morgenthau. It captured
admirably the attitude prevailing in the Treasury at the time. Moreover, in its judgment of the efficacy of a possible spending program, it
offered a perfect reprise of the attitude of FDR and most prominent New
Dealers in 1933. Taylor wrote,

> Frankly I do not think that the program . . . shows
> originality or holds sufficient appeal to guarantee

its success. It is merely doing over again on a big
scale what we have tried to do before . . . It is
slow in taking effect and cannot be cut off when,
as, and if private expenditures have been resumed.
Above all it lacks originality at a time when the
country is expecting a great deal in the form of a
new approach to pressing problems. Even assuming
that it serves as a satisfactory stop-gap and it
gives the Administration a chance to reform its
lines, it must of necessity be followed by a new
program which will face the added handicap on
financing which will have been imposed by the proposed public works program.

Taylor emphasized further that the present proposals could be financed
with Federal Reserve and Treasury cooperation, but not this, "plus the
additional new programs which would inevitably follow."[42]

By the morning of April 13, Morgenthau had decided to tell the
President that he was "seriously thinking of resigning." Encouraged in
this course by Jacob Viner, who had decided to tender his own resignation, the Secretary saw Roosevelt at 10:30. Making clear his
disappointment that no one in the Treasury had been consulted in planning the new program. he announced his intentions. The President
consented to meet with Morgenthau and Bell to re-examine the program
that afternoon. "I left", Morgenthau wrote. "leaving him with the
distinct impression that unless he did change his program I would
resign."[43]

A special Treasury staff meeting was called at noon to help plan a
strategy for Morgenthau's meeting with the President later in the day.
Though the Treasury people were themselves in considerable disagreement,
it was concluded that Morgenthau should try to minimize long-range
spending programs under Ickes. Since the President seemed set on spending, it would be better to channel most of it through Hopkins. "We can
control Hopkins", Morgenthau said. "You can start him quick and he will
stop quick of his own accord. You can control him. These other things,
the experience we have had is, in the first place they don't spend the
money when you want them to do it. They spend it when it is
unnecessary. And you can never stop it and nobody can work with Ickes.
You just can't work with him."[44]

Morgenthau met with his staff again immediately after his two-hour
conference with the President. "To be brief", he reported, "the program
is just about the way it was. There is no change." Morgenthau had a
draft of Roosevelt's forthcoming message with him. Oliphant and Taylor
examined it and pronounced it the work of Leon Henderson. When

Morgenthau responded that the President said Aubrey Williams had written it, they remained unconvinced. Taylor concluded that Henderson must have written it for Williams.[45] Apparently Roosevelt had successfully convinced Morgenthau to give up his resignation threat.

The next day the President announced his program in a message to congress. That evening he explained it to the people in his first Fireside Chat since the previous October. In these speeches, he emphasized that the Recession had been caused both by a failure of the purchasing power of the people to keep pace with production and by an undue rise in the prices of many commodities. The President then outlined three categories of recommended action. Under "maintenance of relief" he recommended that $2.062 million be channeled through WPA, the Farm Security Administration, the National Youth Administration, the CCC, and other agencies. He recommended further an "expansion of credit", through the desterilization of $1,400 million dollars of Treasury gold and through a reduction in reserve requirements, the latter reluctantly consented to by Eccles. Finally, he recommended "definite additions to the purchasing power of the Nation" by renewing public works projects in the amount of $950 million to be spent through the FSA, PWA, and United States Housing Authority. "let us unanimously recognize", the President said, "that the federal debt whether it be twenty-five billions or forty billions, can only be paid if the Nation obtains a vastly increased citizen income."[46] Clearly, the President was deferring the balanced budget until some future time when national income would have increased sufficiently to permit a balance.

The Fireside Chat that evening relied heavily on the Henderson-Ruml memo presented to the President at Warm Springs. Outlining the program he had presented to Congress, with emphasis upon his determination not "to weaken or destroy great reforms which, during the past five years, have been effected on behalf of the American people", he explained that in the proposed new program he was thinking "not only of the immediate economic need of the people of the Nation, but also of their personal liberties--the most precious possession of all Americans." He then pointed to the disappearance of democracy in several other great nations "not because the people of those nations dislike democracy, but because they had grown tired of unemployment and insecurity." Finally, the people of these nations "in desperation . . . chose to sacrifice liberty in the hope of getting something to eat." The President maintained that the spending program of the last five years had "acted as a trigger to set off private activity. That is why the total addition to our national production and additional income has been so much greater than the contribution of the Government itself."

"History proves that dictatorships do not grow out of strong and successful governments, but out of weak and helpless ones", he continued. "Therefore, the only sure bulwark of continuing liberty is a government strong enough to protect the interests of the people, and a people strong enough and well enough informed to maintain its sovereign control over its government." The President justified his spending program by pointing out, as did the Henderson-Ruml memo, that the federal government, since the early days of the republic, has "rightly assumed the duty of promoting business and relieving depression by giving subsidies of land and other resources." Having depleted such resources, it must now use the resource of idle capital to achieve the same end. The cost of his program, he maintained was small in proportion to the enormous loss in national income caused by the Recession. "I propose to sail ahead", he concluded. "I feel sure that your hopes and your help are with me. For to reach a port, we must sail--sail, not tie at anchor--sail, not drift."[47]

Two weeks later, the President delivered his speech on the concentration of economic power, an outgrowth of arguments presented to him on the train returning from Warm Springs. With this address and the enactment of legislation needed to implement it, the recovery program of 1938 was complete. Time would tell what had been achieved.

CHAPTER SEVEN

**FROM NEW DEAL TO NEW ECONOMICS—
"WE MUST TAKE OUR CASE TO THE COUNTRY"**

AN ECONOMIC PROGRAM FOR AMERICA

The arguments Hopkins presented to the President at Warm Springs were to become increasingly significant as the year 1938 progressed. Henderson, Ruml, and Williams, of course, had designed them to overcome the President's resistance to renewed spending. Their memo interpreted spending as a legitimate and traditional government activity. The line of argument was well-calculated to appeal to the President in the spring of 1938. He needed assurance, both for himself and others, of the thoroughly American character of any new direction in economic policy. The arguments given him at Warm Springs provided that assurance.

The Warm Springs rationale contained implications for social policy as well. implied, rather than expressed, and hence not so immediately apparent. The "socio-economic" policy recommended in the telegram sent to Ruml and employed in the Ruml-Henderson memo proposed a reversal of the earlier New Deal approach to social problems. It began with an attempt to compute what level of national income would bring the nation near to full employment. Only after the desirable level of national income was decided upon and the amount of government investment needed to achieve that level of income were determined could policy makers begin to decide what forms the expenditures should take--whether for health care, education, housing, utilities, or the fulfillment of some other public need. The change was subtle, but offered profound long-range implications.

Equally significant for long-term policy was the implication that the economy had moved into a period of secular stagnation, requiring a continuous, or at least recurrent. government stimulus to insure full utilization of manpower and other resources. This was important to the spending rationale, preparing the way for New Dealers grudgingly to accept by that fall the possibility that spending might be needed for an indefinite period. Such an eventuality was as yet too disturbing to be openly discussed, but it was nevertheless implied in the arguments used at Warm Springs. The memos offered to the President departed little in content from memos Eccles had been sending to the White House since the previous October. The one clear innovation was the argument tying spending to a long tradition of government support for the economy. But the style and tone of the Warm Springs memos were markedly different from those of Eccles. Reflecting the same concerns and containing the same arguments, there was nevertheless, at least in the Henderson-Ruml memo, an evident enrichment of the rationale, a sensitive interweaving of historical and social awareness. Their memo was altogether more literate and humane than those the President had received from Eccles, expressing almost precisely the same ideas, but in a form more likely to appeal to a man of FDR's background.[1]

Roosevelt employed these ideas himself in his Fireside Chat of April 14.[2] They became standard fare for Americans following New Deal speeches on the new economic program during the early summer of 1938. Hopkins made public use of the rationale even before the President in a statement he prepared for an April 8 hearing of a special committee of the Congress to investigate unemployment. "The well-being of all our people," he told the congressmen, "can be approximated only with a rising national income which in and by itself will effectively lessen the burden of unemployment. I think we ought to face the fact," he said further, "that the productive system has always had what is in effect a subsidy of purchasing power ever since the early days of the nation."[3]

He addressed the Chautauqua Institution on July 16, telling the group that "In the past we cashed in our assets without recording their dissipation on our books." The debt incurred through new government investment should be watched, he maintained, "But it is something to be kept track of in relation to the credit of the nation." Deficit spending since 1933 had helped in "the restoration of the confidence of our people in their form of government, the conservation of the physical and spiritual welfare of our people, [and] the enrichment of social environment." But in addition to these "imponderables" it had "very materially helped in raising the level of our national income from 40 billion dollars to close to 70 billion dollars."

These achievements were of vital world significance, Hopkins maintained, because, "In many respects this country is holding the fort for democracy. All over the world, men and women who love human freedom are looking to the United States to find the answer--the proper economic and social balance that will make democracy safe." Upon reading the speech, Eccles wrote Hopkins that it was "one of the best defenses of the administration program I have seen." These themes were reiterated in six major addresses which Hopkins delivered during the summer in various cities form Boston to Memphis.[4]

Shortly after FDR's announcement of the spending program. Eccles was persuaded to speak at a May 13 gathering of the New Jersey Bankers' Association. The occasion, he concluded, "would afford me a very timely opportunity to say some things which I felt needed saying at this juncture." At the bankers' convention he offered his opinion that "The recently announced spending and lending program of the government is modest, if anything, too modest when measured by the need and gravity of the problem." In responding to a congratulatory letter from Gerard Swope, he intimated that it might be necessary in the future to provide a continuing stimulus to the economy through government spending. He wrote Swope that he had "been driven inevitably" to the conclusion that there is no alternative "for one who wishes to see capitalistic democracy preserved, other than the maintenance of a far larger volume of public expenditures for socially beneficial purposes than has been called for under past conditions."

He had stressed the same point the week before to a group of Richmond, Virginia Reserve officials suggesting that "there may be times when national income is at a high and rapidly advancing rate when it would be desirable from every standpoint to . . . maintain a flow of funds to impoverished elements of the population . . . whose purchasing power is necessary to sustain production and thus . . . make possible further profitable expansion of facilities."[5] Though he had not been present at the Warm Springs decision-making conferences, and though he felt that the level of spending must be increased further. Eccles none-

143

theless was active in publicly supporting the new direction that had been taken.

Despite his discreet distance from Georgia in 1938, Eccles was a major architect of the Warm Springs decisions, having been widely recognized, since 1934, as the most persistent and effective advocate of the various Administration spending programs. Particularly in the crisis attending the Recession of 1937, he used all the means at his disposal to encourage the immediate resumption of a spending program. Through his memos and through a deliberate diffusion of his ideas among those in the Administration sympathetic to his views, he exerted an important, if indirect influence upon the final decision-making process. It is interesting, however, that he did not participate directly in that process and did not take a major part in the heated discussions in Washington immediately prior to the President's announcement of the program. It may be that he deliberately maintained a low profile even after returning from his vacation to ease the necessary task of persuading Morgenthau to accept the new program. He undoubtedly knew that Hopkins was planning an offensive in behalf of renewed spending at Warm Springs, and immediately upon his return would have been fully informed as to what had been decided. But he may have kept himself aloof because he knew Morgenthau could be more easily reconciled to a Hopkins spending program than to an Eccles one.

Eccles' concerns extended beyond just the immediate policy decision, however, to a much broader problem. With Morgenthau, he shared the feeling that New Dealers were "groping" in a "no-man's land," improvising economic policies without reference to a clearly formulated set of underlying principles. The most crucial question was not whether the President would choose to spend his way out of the present crisis. It was far more important that progress be made towards the acceptance of an economic philosophy which might "give us some assurance that we can go forward in the future." This meant, of course, that Eccles' struggle was by no means over when the President announced a resumption of spending on April 14.

With these considerations in mind, Eccles continued his barrage of memos to the President into the summer of 1938. On April 27, he advised the President that "every effort should be made to increase the total volume of public and private expenditures in the next six months to prevent a further deterioration in the business situation." On June 6 he warned that "The thoroughly sound principles of a compensatory fiscal policy are being discredited through faulty execution. We are adding to purchasing power in a year of major depression far less than we did in 1936, a year of rapidly advancing production."[6]

Morgenthau and his staff were equally aware that the more far-reaching issue to be settled was one of philosophy rather than policy.

In fact, a major complaint against resumption of spending as Wayne Taylor had pointed out, was that it did not, in his view, move the Administration towards a final determination of governing philosophy. At best, it could provide a stop-gap, giving the Administration "a chance to reform its lines," but it would necessarily "be followed by a new program which will face the added handicap on financing which will have been imposed by the proposed public works program."[7]

It was the President himself who had told Morgenthau in December 1937 that "it is very important that he restate the New Deal philosophy."[8] But the policy decisions of April, 1938, were made not in the confident spirit that a new philosophical framework for administration policy had been forged, but rather in the familiar tone of another improvised response to a worsening crisis. That the recovery program betrayed a continuing ambivalence is obvious from even a superficial comparison of the two measures of which it was comprised. The first—a renewal of government spending was known to be effective in stimulating the economy, at least in the short run. The second—the plan to set up a Temporary National Economic Committee to study problems of monopoly— was an admission of lack of confidence in the long-run efficacy of the first. The spending program was to buy time while the Temporary National Economic committee was to review laboriously once more the structure of the economy to see if dislocations, particularly monopolistic trading practices, might yet be remedied and so make it unnecessary to resort to spending in the future. There remained, as Walter Lippmann had suggested of the earlier New Deal, "two contradictory philosophies at work," one attempting in classic progressive style to rearrange the structure of the American economy so as to obviate the need of further government intervention; the other pointing towards continuous government intervention, but at a level which would not be directly perceived by individual businessmen. Eccles' hope was to "see as little regimentation—as little direct regulation of the activity of the individual as possible." He wanted to avoid the disturbing alternative of having "not . . . compensatory but direct controls in every important sphere of economic activity."[9]

The President's announcement of the new program, together with the early summer speeches of Eccles and Hopkins, helped set the background against which the economic recovery, which became evident in mid-summer 1938, was interpreted. The Federal Reserve Index of Industrial Production, which reached a low of 76 in May, leveled out in June, and then began a steady ascent of five or six points for each month from July through November. By December 1 it had climbed to 93, still wide of the March 1937 mark of 117, but nonetheless showing a remarkable rally in so short a time.[10]

Among New Dealers the recovery was widely attributed, of course, to the President's spending program. By August, Adolph Berle, then in the State Department, and in close contact with Eccles, assured the President without qualification that "We are getting our recovery."[11] By October, Eccles had dropped his earlier warnings that still more government spending was needed. In that month he provided Senator Robert J. Bulkley with a set of statistics and memos showing "that the program and the so-called pump-priming, far from failing, are working. There is no other way to account for the reversal of the sharp deflation that threatened and probably would have produced another major depression but for vigorous government intervention."[12]

Even Morgenthau was brought momentarily to question the position he had taken in the crisis. That summer, as he prepared for a European trip to rest from his exhausting labors of the previous six months, he explained to his staff that "We distinctly need a fresh viewpoint on this thing. . . . We've taken this defeatist attitude right along, that it's something to be terribly ashamed of. Maybe it isn't. I don't know."[13] When the Temporary National Economic Committee began its hearings in early December, Leon Henderson was chosen executive secretary. Isadore Lubin provided an economic prologue for the hearings. Alvin Hansen, a recently converted advocate of Keynesian economic theory, and Lauchlin Currie became major witnesses. The hearings, as long-time government economist Herbert Stein later judged, became "a showcase for Keynesian economics."[14]

In mid-December, Eccles became embroiled in a public debate with Senator Harry F. Byrd on the Administration's spending programs which lasted well into January, involving exchanges both in public letters and in radio addresses. During this controversy, Eccles offered the public a thorough airing of the merits of his economic philosophy, warning pointedly that if Byrd's recommendations for drastic retrenchment were followed, "we would witness another sharp reversal and renewed deflation." The President called Eccles at the conclusion of one of the bouts to offer his congratulations. "You made the problem so simple that even I was able to understand it," he told the Chairman.[15] By January, the President himself, who earlier had been notably circumspect in making claims for the spending program was willing to affirm that it had "contributed materially. I believe, to the existing upward movement of business and employment."[16]

Other observers, sympathetic to Roosevelt, but not in the official New Deal family, were reaching similar conclusions about the recovery. During the previous winter, a group of young economists at Harvard and Tufts began a series of informal meetings. The purpose of their gatherings was essentially no different from that which prompted the informal discussions held by Morgenthau, Eccles, and Hopkins within the Administration at the same time. These economists shared the feeling that a loss of confidence in the New Deal at this critical time could have disastrous consequences for America and for the cause of liberal democracy in the world. Accordingly, they set to work devising a rationale which would affirm the validity of past New Deal policies and serve as the basis for a very specific set of present policy recommendations.

The ultimate result of the discussions was a tract published November 29, 1938, under the title, An. Economic Program for American Democracy, signed by Richard V. Gilbert, George H. Hildebrand, Jr., Arthur W. Stuart, Maxine Y. Sweezy, Paul M. Sweezy, Lorrie Tarshis, and John D. Wilson. Its success was immediate and significant. The book moved quickly into the best seller list for Washington, D.C. and remained there until mid-February, 1939. A second printing was made on January 27.[17] The press shortly began to interpret it as a key document for those wishing to understand the new direction in the Administration's economic philosophy. Henry Paynter, of the Washington, D. C. Star, reported the widely-held belief that An Economic Program for American Democracy "represents the first authentic attempt to tell compactly and in simple language the complete economic and social ideology of the 'New Deal'."[18] Jay Franklin of the Boston Globe reported January 12. 1939 that "In New Deal circles, credit for finally committing the Roosevelt Administration to the theory of public spending, both for national investment and to build up national incomes, goes to a group of seven economists at Harvard University and Tufts College . . . In their book for the first time the effects of haphazard spending and investment policies of the New Deal are dispassionately analyzed and given academic sanction."[19] According to Ernest K. Lindley, "Their main point--that heavy public spending can no longer be regarded as emergency 'pump priming' but must be sustained--is one towards which New Deal thought has been moving."[20]

One need not look far to find the reasons for the book's popularity in Washington. It would be difficult to imagine a work more aptly designed to answer the needs of Roosevelt's partisans in 1938. In the opening paragraph the authors drew the traditional New Dealers' contrast between a nation "on the verge of complete collapse." under President Hoover, and the "feeling of collective strength and new hope for the future," brought by FDR. "We believe," the authors wrote. "that the time has come to analyze the events of the past five years against the perspective of America's historical development and, on the basis of this analysis, to formulate a program for the future--a program which is consistent, rational, and clearly linked to our democratic traditions." The authors affirmed their conviction

that the underlying objectives and methods of the

New Deal were and remain sound and necessary to the
future progress of the nation . . . The New Deal has
not failed. Rather its great weakness has been a
wavering adherence to its own principles. The duty
of true progressives is, we think, plain: to rally
around the banner of the New Deal, to recognize and
correct past errors, and to unify their ranks for
the next step forward. The analysis and proposals
which we here present are designed precisely for the
purpose of assisting them in the fufillment of this
duty.[21]

An Economic Program for American Democracy was, of course, printed
too late to be of importance in the determination of a policy to counter
the Recession. Moreover, the authors went beyond New Dealers in stating
more explicitly than had any major government official before that time
the proposition that American capitalism might be in need of permanent
government investment and continuing budget deficits to insure full
prosperity. They also suggested that government ownership of utilities
and railroads might be necessary if proposed reorganization were not
successful in solving the problems of these industries. But as they
themselves pointed out, their most important recommendation had been
adopted before the book was printed, and had begun to show positive
results. "An expanded program of government spending has already begun
to furnish support for our contention--the very backbone of this
program--that the government can, if it will, expand employment and
restore the Nation's real income of goods and services to prosperity
levels."[22] The analysis which led to these conclusions was a presentation of the Keynes of the General Theory in New Deal American garb, as
the pundits were quick to recognize.

Though the Keynesian analysis which lay behind An Economic Program
for American Democracy did not help to determine policy, it was extremely important in providing outside theoretical affirmation of the correctness of a policy already determined. And beyond that, it supported
Eccles and Hopkins in their contention that the spending program of 1938
was not just another desperate effort to "prime the pump," but rather an
integral part of a sound and coherent program. Eccles went so far as to
consider sending a copy of the book to each senator and congressman with
a covering letter. offering his opinion that "it is difficult to find in
such succinct form a more penetrating and stimulating analysis of the
nation's fiscal problems." Eccles was dissuaded by Chester Davis, a
like-minded fellow member of the Board of Governors, who argued that
intemperate references in the book to "bigoted and self-seeking members
of the Democratic party, and the proposals for government ownership of

and control of utilities would be too controversial. The study, Davis suggested, would give opponents of compensatory spending an opportunity "to say that all these things are involved in your program, and that what you have in mind is an extension of government controls far beyond the point to which the administration has heretofore gone in its declared policy."[23]

An indication of the importance of the book to Hopkins was his choice of one of the authors, Richard V. Gilbert, to head his new Division of Industrial Economics, which he organized in the Department of Commerce after being appointed Secretary of Commerce early in 1939. Another author of the book, Walter S. Salant (who did not sign the book because of a government position he held at the time of its publication) was named a staff member of the Division.

The President is reported to have recommended the book to his son, Jimmy, on February 2, 1939. Elliott Roosevelt related that FDR offered the volume as basic material for a proposed film on the economic philosophy of his Administration. According to his account. the book, "which reflected the Keynesian approach to full employment, was a bible of the New Dealers."[24] The use of the word, "bible," is particularly apt, for it captures perfectly the role the book played at that time for New Deal partisans. It provided vindication from an external authority that past actions had been right, that there was order, purpose, and meaning in what had transpired, and that with proper subsequent action a glorious future was assured.

An Economic Program for American Democracy thus began to assume a relationship with the New Deal that was later pre-empted by Keynes' General Theory of Employment, Interest and Money, itself. The authors ended their preface with the affirmation that "our basic argument and the conclusions which grow out of it become of greater importance with every day that passes, and we hope that such confirmation as the events of the past few months have afforded will help to carry this conviction to our readers."[25] Here were economists pointing to the New Deal policies of April. 1938 as a confirmation of the validity of their theoretical analysis. Many New Dealers, in turn, gladly took the theoretical analysis of economists as assurance that their policies had been correct. In subsequent years, no one noted the chicken-and-egg nature of the situation. Had Roosevelt confirmed the theories of Keynes? Had Keynes confirmed the policies of Roosevelt? To New Deal partisans in 1938, it did not seem to matter. It was enough that recovery seemed on the way again and that with recovery the salvation of democratic values in America and in the world had been so much strengthened. Thus was Keynes later to achieve a status approaching that of Roosevelt himself in the minds of those who considered themselves the bearers and preservers of the New Deal gospel for

America.

For these as for many observers, the sequence of events in 1938 carried an unmistakable message. From early 1936 to mid-1937, there was a pronounced rise in government revenues, augmented by social security taxes, and an accompanying decline in spending. A sharp economic decline followed. There was a long agony of uncertain waiting and no sign of recovery before April 1938, when the Administration announced a major renewal of spending. Within two months, the decline had been halted and recovery seemed underway. The entire scenario carried with it a dramatic quality which no doubt served well to impress its lessons upon observers sympathetic to Roosevelt. One can almost sense the expectant silence with which New Dealers awaited the results of the program and hear a sigh of relief as the statistics began to indicate that the economy was once more on the rise. Given the bitter domestic political struggle, accentuated by international ideological turmoil, the assurance of recovery meant to New Dealers no less than the preservation of liberal democracy in America and perhaps in the world. For them it must have been a splendid moment. The apparent response of the economy to the spending program did much to elevate deficit spending from a worrisome necessity to a central point of economic doctrine for New Dealers.

The manifesto of the seven Harvard and Tufts economists did not offer the only possible explanation for the Recession or for the subsequent recovery. Those who did not wish to credit the recovery to the spending program could with reason point to changes in business inventories as determining factors in the Recession and in the subsequent upswing. The economy had been on a gradual, if erratic, ascent since early 1933, a period much longer than the average of past periods of cyclical expansion. In late 1936 and early 1937, there appeared considerable inflationary pressure on both prices and wages, causing businesses to purchase excessive stocks of inventories. Eventually, a saturation point was reached resulting in a curtailment of purchasing in the summer of 1937, which precipitated the downturn. Businesses did not deplete their stocks of inventories and begin new buying until the summer of 1938. It is entirely plausible that the resultant new ordering stimulated the subsequent recovery as much as did the spending.

Morgenthau and at least one important member of his staff maintained into 1939 that a major cause of the Recession had been the increased reserve requirements imposed by the Federal Reserve System in the fall of 1936 and the spring of 1937, and that the "net cash deficit" could not have been an important factor because it had begun fifteen months before the downturn. According to an analysis prepared by George C. Haas, the rise in reserve requirements led to selling of government securities and a decline in bond prices. This eroded confidence, causing a fall in new orders for goods of all kinds, thus precipitating the subsequent recession. Haas' arguments implied that a liberalization of reserve requirements and ceasing the sterilization of gold, which Eccles reluctantly consented to in the spring of 1938, helped bring about the recovery. The Federal Reserve continued, in spite of this argument, to defend the increases in reserve requirements as measures needed in the face of unprecendented high levels of reserves to promote stability.[26]

It is almost universally admitted that a fall in business confidence was a significant factor in the Recession, as Keynes maintained in a famous set of letters written to Roosevelt that spring. But contemporary and subsequent observers have not convincingly shown why, in the fall of 1937, there was a sudden decline in confidence, or what in the summer of 1938 suddenly restored that confidence. Dozens of plausible guesses could be made, that of Haas among them. Businessmen were themselves liberal in offering Roosevelt advice as to what was causing their discouragement and what the government might do to brighten the picture. Roosevelt, however, tended to discount their suggestions as self-serving attempts to raise profits and as direct attacks upon New Deal reform. Given Roosevelt's mood, it is not surprising that he chose Eccles' spending proposals, which implied no capitulation to business demands, over those of Morgenthau. The balancing of the budget, though long an Administration goal, was losing its appeal by virtue of the fact that Roosevelt's opponents had made it their own watchcry. Thus, though it could not be denied that business confidence was a major problem, it was not clear what could be done to bolster that confidence without giving the appearance of capitulation to business demands. The occurrence of the recovery in spite of Roosevelt's April anti-monopoly message seemed to confirm Eccles' point that the best salve for business confidence would be the new orders stimulated by government additions to purchasing power. Business confidence, though important in its effects upon economic activity, is a factor which now, as then, is composed of a mixture of determinants so complex that little in the way of advice as to proper economic policy can be gained from studying it.

A COMPENSATORY FISCAL POLICY BECOMES NEW DEAL POLICY

The whole experience with the Recession of 1937 left New Dealers impressed as never before with the importance of the relationship between fiscal policy and general economic activity. Many important followers of Roosevelt came away from the crisis with a life-long conviction that the key to economic growth and stability lay in the proper management of federal accounts.

FDR was among those who, as a result of the recession crisis, began to look towards a well-managed compensatory fiscal policy as the best hope for a stable economy. The President made a low-key announcement on November 18, 1938 that he was appointing a "temporary board" to advise him "on certain fiscal and monetary subjects." The board was to include the Secretary of the Treasury, the Chairman of the Board of Governors of the Reserve System, the Director of the Budget, and the Chairman of the Advisory Committee of the National Resources Committee--Morgenthau, Eccles, Bell, and Delano. There was to be, in addition, a technical staff made up of members of the various agencies involved. The board's duties, according to the President, were to canvas systematically "the broader problems of fiscal and monetary policies in relation to national production and the national income. In other words, they will study the whole range of a great many problems that relate to fiscal and monetary policies in respect to sound and orderly recovery, and conditions essential to avoiding the peaks and valleys of booms and depressions."[27]

Morgenthau was the nominal chairman of the committee, though the idea of its establishment did not originate with him, and he had accepted the position reluctantly. The President's uncle met with Morgenthau on April 26, 1938, bringing to the Secretary's attention proposals for such a board which had been sent to the Treasury from Delano's Advisory Committee of the National Resources Committee over a year earlier. Delano reported to his colleagues, Boston industrialist Henry S. Denison, and Beardsley Ruml, that Morgenthau "thought of us as a committee that was set up to plan for spending and he had never heard of our recommendations for a Fiscal Policy Committee." Morgenthau "was not ready to accept our recommendation," Delano reported, but when it was pointed out that the proposals would but formalize meetings with men the Secretary of the Treasury must consult regularly in any case, seemed willing to give the matter careful thought. Delano thought it possible that after reflection Morgenthau would bring the matter before the President on his own, due to the fact the "he fully appreciates his great responsibility as fiscal head of the Government and would accept helpful data and advice if he was sure it was useful and helpful rather than confusing."[28]

It was Delano more than Morgenthau, however, who urged the idea upon the President, and the April 26 meeting was in all probability intended to put the Secretary in a receptive frame of mind should the suggestion come to him from higher authority. On August 12, Delano's committee sent a memo to the President, updating suggestions made in previous memos and advising him of "the necessity of coordinating Federal fiscal and monetary policies," which had hitherto been formulated "in a number of separate agencies, some of which have been set up as independent administrative establishments." The recommended board would provide information "as to the amount and character of public expenditures, the sources of Government income, the volume of private investment and savings, and the additions to buying power resulting from public spending." Delano concluded his August 1938 memo by pointing out that "such a Board is particularly important at the present moment although its continuing activity should not be minimized. To secure proper timing of present activities calls for constant watchfulness. If full benefit is to be secured from present expanded activities, the Government's taxation and spending policies must be subjected to regular analysis. Thus Government can take the lead in laying the basis for a program for the care of human need."[29]

These arguments, coming in the wake of the Recession, appealed to the President, and the Board was accordingly established in November. It became clear, as the Board began its meetings, that the point of view of those dominating the discussions was most uncongenial to that of Morgenthau. Lauchlin Currie, who became a leading figure in the technical staff, prepared a memo for Eccles during the early life of the board which showed the direction of its studies. He wrote that a proposed program of research would "pretty well boil down to: (a) What caused the downturn in 1937? (b) How can we get a high level of national income? (c) What should be done to prevent a recurrence of developments of 1937?" Currie emphasized the point that the board was "vitally interested" in these three questions and has "something to contribute to them" but should be alert to "a danger that the outside experts that might be selected may be heavily committed already on the wrong side (from our point of view)."[30] By December 15, the board had prepared a statement of policy, indicating agreement that "The objective of Federal fiscal policy and monetary policy is to assist in increasing national income, production, and employment (and to make such preparations as may seem advisable for the administration of fiscal and monetary policy toward mitigating the severity of future booms and depressions)."[31] This policy statement was appropriately timed to enter into the preparations of the January 1939 budget message, exercising a discernible influence upon it. The board prepared various spending and lending programs to stimulate the lagging economy in the spring and summer of 1939, but was eventually absorbed into the apparatus for managing the economy during wartime.

It is not immediately obvious how the board was able to function, given the widely differing opinions of its various members. There were occasions when the majority report had to be altered to satisfy

Morgenthau, causing others to offer their own dissenting opinion.[32] Undoubtedly the major part of the committee's work was done by its technical staff which included Haas, White and Currie, men of sufficiently common outlook to assure that in technical preparations, at least, a degree of unity could be obtained.[33] Morgenthau was clearly uncomfortable with some committee reports, but continued to give a degree of attention to its work until the war drew him to other concerns.[34] Certainly the fact that the President established the committee, and the tone of its various reports and proposals provide persuasive evidence for the importance of the Recession of 1937 in demonstrating the need of definite steps towards coordinating fiscal and monetary policy to stabilize economic fluctuations.

The lessons taken from the recession experience received formal approval as government policy in the budget message of January 4, 1939. The President began his message by pointing out that revenue depends upon two factors, the tax rate and the level of national income. While tax rates can be fixed by law, the President said, "we cannot by a simple legislative act raise the level of national income, but our experience in the last few years has amply demonstrated that through wise fiscal policies and other acts of government we can do much to stimulate it." A chart accompanied the message which illustrated the point by showing the estimated federal revenues at national income levels of 70, 80, and 90 billions of dollars. The President maintained that it had been necessary to increase expenditures the previous year "to check a recession" and that a formally balanced budget could not be achieved "by heavily slashing expenditures or drastically increasing taxes." In his annual message to Congress, delivered the same day, he reiterated the point that "By our common sense action of resuming government activities last spring, we have reversed a recession and started the new rising tide of prosperity and national income which we are just beginning to enjoy." The goal of an 80 billion dollar national income was stressed in both the budget message and the annual message.[35]

Eccles lost little time in pushing the President to further affirmation of the position expressed in the budget message. "As the purpose has now been formally declared," he wrote on January 11,

> to balance the budget out of increased receipts arising from an increase in national income rather than by sharply decreasing expenditures or increasing taxes on consumption at this stage, Federal deficits may be expected until such time as the budget may be balanced out of a national income of around $80 billions.

Reminding the President that this policy would evoke a hostile reaction from New Deal critics, he reiterated his conviction that it is "the only sound one that can be taken at this time which will give assurance of a continuing recovery. I feel it is of the greatest importance that our position, which I would describe as a compensatory fiscal policy, should be aggressively presented to the country."[36] Apparently the President took Eccles' advice seriously. Shortly after receiving the note, he wrote a letter to all his cabinet members asking that they take a public stance "in favor of the position taken in my annual message . . . generally known as the 'compensatory fiscal policy.' We must take our case to the country."[37] The language of the two letters could hardly have been coincidental. Eccles had indeed become, as a Washington Star cartoon of the previous month charged, the leader of the New Deal band.[38]

It was not a happy time for Morgenthau. In March 1939, he surprised the Reserve System's Director of Research and Statistics, Emmanuel Goldenweiser, with a phone call, announcing that a staff member on the way to speak to Goldenweiser was acting as his personal representative. The messenger, Eugene Duffield, asked Goldenweiser if he could supply the Treasury with any ideas or material "that would help persuade the President that Government spending was not the only factor in the situation; that it was not the decline of Government spending that brought the recession of 1937." There is considerable eloquence in the fact that Morgenthau, who had his own staff of competent researchers, quietly sought the aid of a member of Eccles' staff in his effort to dissuade the President from Eccles' interpretation of events. Goldenweiser, not overly fond of Eccles, was still less fond of Morgenthau and politely declined to offer assistance. He decided not to tell Eccles of the incident "in order not to stir up additional hostility."[39]

By that May, with the economy leveling out before even approaching the desired national income figure, Morgenthau's spirits fell to a dismal low. Lamenting the fact that Eccles had become one of FDR's chief advisors on economic policy, the Secretary bared his feelings to Mrs. Roosevelt on May 18. Mrs. Roosevelt comforted Morgenthau with the assurance that the President was not (as Morgenthau apparently feared) trying to force him out of the Administration. The Secretary explained that he wanted prosperity in 1940 for many reasons, and among them "was the fact that if we had a prosperous year the President's whole attitude, his health, etc., would be so different."[40] A month later, his spirits were momentarily revived by FDR's excitement over a proposal to make a map showing specific structures which the New Deal had contributed to each county in the United States, such as buildings, sewer lines, power lines, and CCC camps. "I haven't enjoyed any meeting that

I have had with the President as much as this one in about--it has to go back a year and a half ago," he wrote in his diary that day. "I found myself calling him Franklin for the first time."[41] Certainly for Morgenthau, as for all New Dealers, it had been a trying two years since that ebullient spring of 1937.

THE LASTING IMPORTANCE OF THE RECESSION CRISIS

What then had changed in the New Deal since the Recession swept down with sudden fury upon the followers of FDR in the fall of 1937? The recession crisis, as seen by Morgenthau and Eccles, was of major proportions, pitting the fiscal authority of the government against the monetary authority in a determined struggle for influence in the formulation of policy. Both realized, however, that more than policy was at stake, that the recession crisis might bring New Dealers to settle once and for all upon a philosophy which could safely steer their reforms between the Scylla of a regimented economy and the Charybdis of economic stagnation.

In some respects, the course of the struggle between the two men was shaped by the idiosyncrasies of each--circumstances of birth and rearing; special personality traits, gave first one the advantage, then the other. Morgenthau was the most important advisor to the President on economic policy as the Recession struck. By the time it was over, he had been supplanted by Eccles. The shift in power evoked a striking drama which illuminated the feelings of the two men about the value of their service to Roosevelt and his New Deal; and beyond this to the liberal democratic values which all three shared. Had the transition involved nothing more than the relationship of the three principals it would have been a fascinating story, well worth the telling. But far more than this was involved.

Morgenthau and Eccles each represented in the struggle ideas which had kept the New Deal divided against itself since 1933-"two contradictory philosophies" as Walter Lippmann had put it. They came from different regions of America and different New Deals, different orientations in their approach to social and economic problems.

The crisis did not precipitate the discovery of new ideas. On the contrary, it hastened and strengthened attachment to old ones. There were many who, like Morgenthau and Eccles, saw in the situation only confirmation of what they already believed. Others, however, less sure to begin with, or feeling less need to defend positions already taken, sought for more satisfactory explanations of the unexpected turn events had taken. But even for those, the exercise was one of rummaging among the lessons of past New Deal experience rather than striking out in new directions. Moreover, their search took place strictly within the limits of what was accepted and traditional in American political and social thought. Thurman Arnold wrote in 1937 that "In times of security popular opinion will always stand for more skepticism of fundamentals than in times of spiritual trouble, just as discipline in the army always relaxes in a comfortable post."[42] Opponents of Eccles felt his proposals threatened the sources of government stability and public confidence. In one sense they were correct, for the balanced budget had become for many a general symbol of national well-being, and so long as large numbers believed in its importance, Eccles' proposals did threaten to undermine the sense of security which balanced fiscal accounts brought to them. But in a larger sense, Eccles' proposals, as he constantly reiterated, were drawn as much as were those of Morgenthau from within the mainstream of American liberal traditions. Eccles' proposals relied upon taxing and spending—long accepted and legitimate powers of the federal government. He was more circumspect, in fact, than earlier New Dealers, in that he tried to avoid any direct tampering with the price and wage structure or the operations of the marketplace, which he regarded as essential to the preservation of a prosperous democratic capitalism in America. Morgenthau and Eccles were both impressed during the recession crisis with the need to hold close to fundamental values. They differed over whose policies could best defend the traditional economic and social structure of America, not over whose could best change it. By 1939, there was clearly a preponderance of opinion among New Dealers that Eccles' ideas offered the best defense.

Emerging with Eccles' victory on the budget-balancing question was a tendency for New Dealers to be more preoccupied with recovery than with reform. In January 1937, FDR had sounded the note of continued reform by declaring it his intention to bring relief to "one-third of a nation ill-housed, ill-clad, ill-nourished."[43] In January 1939, he announced that New Dealers had "now passed the period of internal conflict in the launching of our program of social reform. Our full energies may now be released to invigorate the processes of recovery in order to preserve our reforms, and to give every man and woman who wants to work a real job at a living wage."[44] No doubt the widespread belief among Roosevelt's opponents that his reforms were standing in the way of recovery, given credence by the Recession, carried a stronger message to the White House than the President would have admitted. His speeches in 1938 stressed that there would be no retreat, that reforms already accomplished would be preserved. But from that time he did not seek substantial additions to what he had achieved.

The emerging attitude towards reform was implicit in the economic philosophy Eccles had helped bring to dominance among New Dealers. Morgenthau, representative of an earlier New Deal, asked, when economic crisis threatened, "How can farmers be helped? How can jobs be found for workers? What can we do for railroads?" Eccles, representative of an emerging redefinition of New Deal economic thought, asked "What level of national income will bring full employment?" His question was precisely the question FDR emphasized in his January 1939 budget message and annual address. The first is instinctively compassionate and humane, directing policy towards the solution of specific needs. The second is technical and analytical, seeking to find causes and solutions by placing the problem insofar as possible into aggregate, and hence more abstract terms.

Of course, New Dealers did not intend that the emerging philosophy would so change their perspective. In fact, a part of its appeal lay in the promise of greater social benefits to be achieved through government expenditures. Moreover, the growing national product, the securing of jobs for everyone, would automatically eliminate many social problems. The vision which New Dealers held in adopting the new economic philosophy, in fact, was close to that of Eccles in 1933, who assured a Utah audience that "The only way to increase spending is for the Government to spend it for non-profit-yielding works for the benefit of all, for the expansion of social services of all kinds, or, "(suggesting a possibility he then proceeded to denounce) "for war."[45] It had been his self-proclaimed mission in Washington to provide New Dealers with "needed arguments on how a planned policy of adequate deficit financing could serve the humanitarian objective with which they were most directly concerned."[46] It did not occur to him or to those who became converted to his analysis that the more abstract and aggregative view of economic distress might divert them from the humanitarian objective which had been their main concern. It did not seem likely in 1938 that a future generation might concentrate so fixidly upon the growing figures of national income that they could ignore rising environmental pollution or depletion of non-renewable resources. There was no way of foreseeing that the aggregate figures of national well-being might conceal pockets of citizens who in significant numbers were not sharing in the rising prosperity. There existed real dangers in the possibility, unanticipated by New Dealers in 1938, that the need to stimulate the economy might one day determine when and where social services should be distributed more than the human needs which were Morgenthau's great concern.

Also emerging with Eccles' triumph in the wake of the Recession was a new definition of liberalism. There was a grain of truth to Senator

Byrd's jibe directly before Morgenthau's address at the Academy of Political Science meeting, that "Today at Washington a public man is a liberal in proportion to how liberal he is with other people's money."[47] In 1939 Emmanuel Goldenweiser remarked petulantly to a staff member in the research division of the Federal Reserve that Eccles had called him a conservative. Protesting that he had voted for LaFollette in 1924, he said, "if spending is [Eccles'] . . . test of liberalism . . . [I] was even a liberal on that score before . . . [Eccles]."[48] Eccles, when questioned about his Washington colleagues in his eighty-fourth year, still unhesitatingly rated their competence by the degree to which they had supported deficit spending. Perhaps more significantly, Lauchlin Currie, in recalling his role in New Deal Washington, maintained that "the New Dealers numbered probably no more than 200 or 300 people, mostly young lawyers and economists, with a scattering from other fields."[49] Clearly, a new test of liberalism was emerging--one which divided liberals from others, even "New Dealers" from others, according to how fully they accepted the new economic philosophy.

Older liberals looked to a structural reform of the economy which would obviate the need of government spending, except for temporary periods. In their view, spending was at best a palliative, which might shore up a bad situation until permanent readjustments could be made, through insuring competition, through more effective planning and administrative measures, or by other instrumental means. In the model which guided their thinking, the economy was primarily static and mechanical. The best corrective, according to this view, was to alter directly the various cogs and wheels of the mechanism to insure that it would function more smoothly. Those accepting the new philosophy shared a primarily organic and dynamic conception of the economy. The fundamental problem was how to make the organism grow. This new emphasis upon the supreme value of growth was evident in the Warm Springs memos and in the President's 1939 budget message as well. During the succeeding decades, as the new doctrine came to dominate the thinking of government policy makers, the idea of tinkering with the relationship between the various organs in the economic structure in any direct manner was given up. Nutrition is always safer than surgery, especially if the plant happens to be one as tender as democratic capitalism.

Morgenthau was schooled in an older liberal tradition, of which even his passion for balanced budgets was a legacy. During the recession crisis he characteristically thought of restructuring units within the economy--reorganizing a utility company in the fashion of the TVA, or refashioning a railroad. To Eccles the TVA was anathema, driving private capital away from the industry and preventing needed growth. He bore an equal dislike for the Agricultural Adjustment Administration, the National Recovery Administration, and of planning in general. All of this direct tampering, in his view, threatened the health of the organism.

The operative difference between what Currie called the "New Dealers" and those of Morgenthau's views was the extent to which the two groups had been exposed to the progressive reform movements in the early part of the century. Progressive reform shaped a generation with its assumptions and its biases. Morgenthau and Roosevelt were a part of that generation and could not readily escape from the convictions of their youth. Eccles was close to them in age, but had grown up in a provincial environment where the tides of reform enthusiasm could be watched with the detachment of a foreign observer and not with the passion of a participant. Perhaps his distance helped him to achieve insights denied those whose social vision had been shaped by the earlier movement. He was of a mind with the younger New Dealers Currie remembered--those who could not understand what kept the older liberals from embracing their new-found gospel. Beardsley Ruml expressed the hope of the new liberals in September of 1938. "With reasonably full employment, adequate purchasing power, and near capacity production, many problems now appearing to call for government intervention or control might solve themselves." An active monetary and fiscal policy, he proposed, "would lessen the demand and need for central government control in other parts of the economy."[50]

The changes taking place in New Deal thought in the wake of the Recession of 1937 provided the essential components of a restatement of the New Deal philosophy, turning it towards the values implicit in the "new economics", since identified with John Maynard Keynes. This new philosophy, as expressed in the language of those not trained in economics, would undoubtedly have been the same had Keynes not lived. And though clearly emerging by 1939, its ultimate triumph did not take place until after the death of Roosevelt. Those who argue that FDR never made effective use of Keynesian economics, however, and thus see Keynesian economics as a lesson later learned from New Deal failings, are missing a major point. Before deficit spending could be employed in a magnitude sufficient to make of it a potent weapon against stagnation, it needed to be accepted broadly enough among the population to command general support for the legislation required to effect it.

This, of course, was fully accomplished only after the War, partly because the experience with wartime spending strongly reinforced the economic doctrine attached to the New Deal by the recession crisis. But the Recession had already brought the new philosophy out of obscurity and into the front ranks of New Deal thought. In 1938, the President himself used that philosophy to justify past New Deal spending and make acceptable the possibility of future spending. Before his death, Roosevelt became a believing, if not a fully practicing member of the

160

new faith. Moreover, he had secured the loyalty and admiration of thousands of talented young people whose eventual domination of American politics assured that the doctrine would become the foundation of economic and social thought and policy in America, effecting as John Kenneth Galbraith once said of the Keynesian revolution "one of the great modern accomplishments in social design."[51]

Though the major emphasis of the "new philosophy" was upon recovery, the basic humanitarian impulse of New Dealers was theoretically salvaged in the expectation that the public spending which was the key stimulus to growth would be for hospitals, schools, medical research, and useful public works. This pious hope was never fully realized. The war was shortly to channel most public expenditures into the armaments effort. By the time the war was over, the habit of concentrating upon gross national product and employment figures as the prime indices of social welfare in the nation was firmly set. Expenditures for social betterment were to prove far more difficult to coax from congress than were expenditures for "defense." The one-time promise that the incremental income which deficit spending was to bring would be redistributed in favor of the consuming classes was largely neglected. In the future less emphasis would be put on redividing the pie, and more on making it ever bigger.

The change had important implications for the pronounced New Deal interest in government planning for the wise use of natural and human resources. The old liberal interest in planning had received much of its impulse and intellectual backing from the pre-Keynesian institutional economists. However, planning was as inimical to the traditional conception of a free market economy as was the collectivism of the early New Deal. Planning involves the conscious determination of how resources are best to be allocated among the various sectors of the economy and implies a coercive diversion of resources from directions the market might normally dictate into channels which the planners decide will be more socially useful. Such activity on a major scale Americans had found tolerable only in time of war. And once the war effort was over, they had dismantled the planning apparatus as rapidly as possible. As the new economics was to place more and more value upon the supreme good of growth in the gross national product, planning for wise use of natural and human resources and as a means of achieving social balance was to give way to planning as handmaiden of fiscal policy, a vastly inferior and intermittent role in terms of the hopes once held by planning advocates.

It is perhaps no coincidence that among professional economists, the star of Keynesian economics rose as that of institutional economics, with its boldly unorthodox questions and prescriptions, set. Keynesian economics promised the inestimable benefit of affirming the viability of free democratic capitalism at a most critical juncture. The eventual triumph of Keynesian thought was not to be the solitary victory of an idea which the academic scribbler had put forth into the world. It is difficult to imagine such a triumph had there not been a New Deal in America in 1938, unsure that it had command of the means to prove the viability of democracy in a world which seemed to be going all wrong. And it is equally difficult to imagine the preservation of so untarnished a memory of the New Deal had it not been for the timely comfort and rationale Keynes and those of like mind had given to its partisans.

"What is at stake is nothing less than our economic and political system," Eccles told a Harvard Business School audience in June 1939. "Let us hope for the best, but for the sake of preserving our liberty and our freedom of enterprise, let us be prepared to grapple with the worst."[52] The emergent restatement of New Deal philosophy offered Americans in a world which seemed bound for Armageddon "some assurance that we can go forward in the future."[53]

BIBLIOGRAPHIC ESSAY

Many years after he had actively participated in efforts to cope with the Recession of 1937 as an advisor to Henry Morgenthau, Jr., the eminent economist Jacob Viner pointed out that the Recession of 1937 "has never been written up as to what the issues were within the government, or what took place . . . It was more subtle and more complicated than the outside public knew, and even more so than many insiders knew." ("Reminiscences," p. 23 in the Columbia Oral History Office, Columbia University, New York City.) Historians have been slow to take up his challenge. Studies which deal specifically with the Recession have concentrated upon it as an economic phenomenon and have not gone deeply into "what the issues were within the government."

The most voluminous study of the Recession of 1937 is Kenneth D. Roose, The Economics of Recession and Revival: an Interpretation of

163

<u>1937-38</u> (New Haven: Yale University Press, 1954). Shorter, but useful studies by other economists are Douglas A. Hayes, "Business Confidence and Business Activity" A case Study of the Recession of 1937," <u>Michigan Business Studies</u> 10 (June 1951), and Melvin D. Brockie's unpublished doctoral dissertation, "The Rally, Crisis, and Depression, 1935-38," (University of California at Los Angeles, June 1948). Limiting their considerations almost solely to understanding the economic forces which led to recession and then revival, these men have not concentrated upon the interpretations which New Dealers at the time placed upon the Recession. In other words, they have studied the Recession as an economic phenomenon and not as a crisis within the New Deal community.

Historians who have included sections on the Recession in their more general studies of the New Deal have usually treated it as but one of many troubles which beset the New Deal in 1937 and 1938 and have not considered in depth the distinctive nature of the threat inherent in a New Deal recession. William E. Leuchtenberg, for example, discussed the Recession along with the attempt at court reform and labor difficulties in a chapter entitled, "A Sea of Troubles," <u>Franklin D. Roosevelt and the New Deal</u> (New York: Harper and Row, 1963). James MacGregor Burns in his <u>Roosevelt: The Lion and the Fox</u> (New York: Harcourt, Brace and World, Inc., 1956), devotes an insightful chapter to the recession crisis. Arthur Schlesinger, Jr. has not yet published the volume of his <u>The Age of Roosevelt</u> 3 vols. (Boston: Houghton Mifflin Co., 1957-60) which will deal with the Recession, though a chapter of vol. 3 <u>The Politics of Upheaval</u> (1960) dealing with "The Ideology of the Second New Deal," pp. 385-408, remains the most acute short discussion of the relationship of Keynesian economics to the ideology of the later New Deal yet published.

More recent studies of the New Deal have tended to give even less emphasis to the recession crisis than earlier accounts. Paul K. Conkin referred briefly to the new burden which the Recession added to "Roosevelt's Vale of Tears," in his <u>FDR and the Welfare State</u> (New York: Thomas Y. Crowell Company, 1967), but did not attribute shaping significance to the event. Ellis W. Hawley, in his <u>The New Deal and the Problem of Monopoly</u> (Princeton: Princeton University Press, 1966) analyzed admirably the ambiguity of Roosevelt's position when the Recession struck, but over-emphasized the importance of the anti-monopoly activities as a response. Though pointing out that compensatory spending came to be the characteristic New Deal solution to economic difficulties, he did not attempt to detail why New Dealers ultimately chose to move in this direction.

By far the best present account of the Recession and its relationship to the economic thought of New Dealers is Herbert Stein's <u>The Fiscal Revolution in America</u> (Chicago: The University of Chicago Press,

1969). Stein supports the author's contention that the recession crisis was a major force in turning New Dealers towards a compensatory fiscal policy as the foundation of their economic philosophy.

The present volume, then, is a response to Professor Viner's challenge. It is an attempt to understand the implications and consequences for New Dealers of the Recession of 1937--to see the Recession as they saw it. As such, the source material is of necessity made up primarily of documents which contain observations and reflections made by New Dealers at the time It is fortunate that the two principals in the recession controversy, Henry Morgenthau, Jr. and Marriner S. Eccles, kept rich collections of materials documenting their public careers. Both Morgenthau and Eccles were acutely conscious of the historic importance of their activities. Each left a remarkably complete record in the files of memos, letters, transcripts of meetings, speeches and personal notations which their secretaries kept for them.

The M.S. Eccles Washington File consists of over 70,000 items, most fastened into looseleaf binders. The range of materials found in the file is very broad. Chronologically, it is concentrated in the 1934-1951 period of Eccles' public career. Every conceivable type of document has been preserved--letters, memos, speeches, responses to speeches, Federal Reserve publications, clippings from newspapers and periodicals, cocktail party invitation lists, transcripts of congressional testimonies, etc. Regrettably missing are journalistic entries by Eccles himself during the period he was in Washington. But the collection is nevertheless an invaluable resource to the historian of the New Deal period. The arduous task of collecting, classifying, labeling, and binding the material was done by Miss Va Lois Egbert, Eccles' secretary throughout the Washington period of his public life. The collection is presently housed in the Marriott Library, Special Collections, University of Utah, Salt Lake City.

An excellent supplement to the Eccles collection is found in Marriner S. Eccles, Beckoning Frontiers: Public and Personal Recollections, ed. Sidney Hyman (New York: Alfred Knopf, 1951). This candid memoir catches admirably the blunt, no-nonsense style of the Utah banker. Newspaper and periodical articles provide brief, but useful supplemental material on Eccles. See, for example, "Marriner Stoddard Eccles," Fortune 11 (February 1935): 63 ff. and Paul W. Ward, "Morgenthau and his Friends," Nation 141 (August 14, 1935): 183-84. The author has also enjoyed the benefit of several interviews with Mr. Eccles, which has helped immeasurably to round out a vision of Eccles' personality and his role in the recession crisis.

There are three unpublished studies of particular aspects of Eccles' life and career. Dean L. May, "The Banking Act of 1935," (in the possession of the author) centers upon the roles of Eccles, Carter

Glass, and New York banker, George L. Harrison in the controversy surrounding the banking act. Arch O. Egbert has written on "Marriner S. Eccles and the Banking Act of 1935," (Ph.D. diss., Brigham Young University, 1967). Leonard J. Arrington's David Eccles: Pioneer Western Industrialist, published in 1975, provides significant details on Eccles' early life and career as a Utah businessman. Sydney Hyman's biography of Eccles, Marriner S. Eccles: Private Entrepreneur and Public Servant (Stanford, California, Stanford University Graduate School of Business, 1976) is regrettably little more than a paraphrase of Beckoning Frontiers.

Henry Morgenthau, Jr.'s collection of papers, known as the Morgenthau Diaries, surpass even the Eccles Washington File in the scope and volume of documents contained. Mrs. Henrietta Klotz saved nearly every item which passed over Morgenthau's desk during his Washington career, binding them in chronological order into a collection totaling several hundred volumes. Mrs. Klotz also took detailed stenographic minutes of telephone conversations and staff meetings, typing them and binding them into the volumes. In addition, Morgenthau frequently made colorful notations of his recollections of meetings with other officials and of significant daily events which were included in the diary collection. One such set of entries containing notes of Morgenthau's conversations with Roosevelt has been separately bound as the Morgenthau Presidential Diaries. Taken as a whole, the collection offers a detailed intimate insight into the activities of Morgenthau while in Washington.

The historian John Morton Blum has published three volumes based on materials taken from the Morgenthau Diaries. This set, titled From the Morgenthau Diaries 3 vols. to date (Boston: Houghton Mifflin Co., 1959-67), provides a readily available and indispensable summary of the main collection. It is also the only published source of information on Morgenthau's youth and early manhood, except for one or two page summaries in biographies of Roosevelt or general histories of the New Deal. Another publication based on excerpted material from the Morgenthau Diaries, but also containing subsequent interpretive comments by Morgenthau was serialized in Henry Morgenthau, Jr., "The Morgenthau Diaries," Colliers 120(September 7, October 4, October 11, 1947). The article by Paul W. Ward, "Henry Morgenthau and his Friends," Nation 141 (August 14, 1935): 183-185), provides a brief, useful character sketch of Morgenthau and other Treasury officials. Numerous other periodical and newspaper articles offer supplementary information on the Secretary of the Treasury.

Though the focus in this study has been upon Morgenthau and Eccles, it has been useful to seek out the widest possible range of New Deal comment on the Recession. Especially helpful collections at the

Franklin D. Roosevelt Library in Hyde Park, New York were the President's Personal File, the President's Secretary's File, and the Official File. Also useful were the Papers of Harry L. Hopkins, Aubrey Williams, and Leon Henderson. The James Roosevelt Files were disappointingly devoid of information pertinent to the Recession.

The Library of Congress collection was of value, particularly the papers of Emmanuel A. Goldenweiser, long-time director of the Division of Research and Statistics of the Board of Governors of the Federal Reserve System. The Goldenweiser papers are not voluminous, but contain candid, enlightening commentary on Federal Reserve activities. The Felix Frankfurter collection contains a lively and interesting correspondence between Frankfurter and a large number of persons sympathetic to the New Deal. His correspondence with FDR from this collection has been published as Roosevelt and Frankfurter: Their Correspondence 1928-1945, ann. Max Freedman (Boston: Little, Brown and Company, 1967).

The records of the WPA in the National Archives, Washington, D.C. provide access to the speeches and press conferences of Harry L. Hopkins during the period, but are massive in volume and not well classified so that access to items of particular interest is extremely difficult in most cases. The character of Harry L. Hopkins remains disappointingly elusive in this document collection, as in the collection of Hopkins' papers at Hyde Park. Robert E. Sherwood's Roosevelt and Hopkins: an Intimate History, rev. ed. (New York: Harper and Row, 1950) remains the most useful biography of Hopkins, though the study moves quickly through the New Deal and concentrates upon Hopkins' wartime activities.

The reminiscences in the Columbia Oral History Office offer a revealing retrospective assessment by important participants in the Recession crisis, particularly those of Jacob Viner and Mordecai Ezekial.

The author has consulted nearly every published memoir or diary of New Deal officials, books commonly cited in standard bibliographies and readily available to researchers and scholars. References to Morgenthau, Eccles, or the Recession of 1937 occur sporadically in such accounts, depending upon the proximity of the author to New Deal economic concerns or to the Treasury or the Federal Reserve. Harold L. Ickes, The Secret Diary of Harold L. Ickes 3 vols. (New York: Simon and Schuster, 1943-54) is a provocative, highly judgmental, indispensable source. Vol. 2, The Inside Struggle, 1936-1939 contains especially useful information and commentary on the recession period. The critical reflections of Raymond Moley, After Seven Years (New York: Harper and Bros., 1939) are always penetrating and instructive as are those of his colleague in Roosevelt's Brain Trust, Rexford G. Tugwell, The Democratic Roosevelt (Garden City, N.Y.: Doubleday and Co., 1957). Francis

Perkins' The Roosevelt I Knew (New York: The Viking Press, 1946) offers
the insights of a sound, sensitive observer of the New Deal scene.
These and other diaries and recollections of New Dealers have provided
valuable background material for the author's interpretations of
Morgenthau and Eccles and have generally supported the thesis that the
Recession represented a crisis of major proportions and of great consequence for New Dealers.

Essential, of course, to any study of the New Deal period is
Franklin D. Roosevelt, The Public Papers and Addresses of Franklin D.
Roosevelt, ed. Samuel I. Rosenman, 13 vols. (New York: The MacMillan
Company, 1938-1950). Particularly important were volumes 6, 7, and 8,
covering material from 1937, 1938, and 1939 respectively. Occasional
useful insights were gained from items printed in Elliott Roosevelt,
ed., FDR His Personal Letters, 4 vols. (New York: Duell, Sloan and
Pearce, 1950).

Studies which concentrate on aspects of the 1937-38 New Deal period
other than the recession crisis are helpful in providing a rounded
picture of the concerns of Roosevelt and New Dealers during the
President's second term in office. James T. Patterson, Congressional
Conservatism and the New Deal: the Growth of a Conservative Coalition in
Congress, 1933-1939 (Lexington, Ky.: The University of Kentucky Press,
1967) contains sound material dealing with the relationship of
Congressional politics to the Recession. Studies of the movement for
executive reorganization by Barry Dean Karl, Executive Reorganization
and Reform in the New Deal: the Genesis of Administrative Management,
1900-1939 (Cambridge, Mass.: Harvard University Press, 1963) and Richard
Polenberg, Reorganizing Roosevelt's Government 1936-1939: the
Controversy over Executive Reorganization (Cambridge, Mass.: Harvard
University Press, 1966) are helpful in illuminating the intellectual
currents and politics of reform during the period of the Recession of
1937.

Two books of the period were especially lucid in explaining the
conceptual difficulties characterizing New Deal social and economic
thought shortly before the recession period: Thurman Arnold, Symbols of
Government (New Haven: Yale University Press, 1935) and The Folklore of
Capitalism (New Haven: Yale University Press, 1937).

Jacob Viner was not the only observer to notice that events arising
out of the Recession of 1937 have not received adequate attention by
historians. Speaking of the triumph of Keynesian economics in America,
John Kenneth Galbraith wrote that "the history of the [Keynesian] revolution is, perhaps, the worst told story of our era." (J.K. Galbraith,
"How Keynes Came to America," New York Times Book Review, May 16, 1965.)
An underlying proposition of the present study is that the history of
the "Keynesian revolution" and the history of the New Deal met in 1937

and 1938 as Roosevelt's partisans sought to deal with the crisis which the Recession of 1937 had created. The response of Henry Morgenthau, Jr. and Marriner S. Eccles to that crisis not only illuminated the directions New Deal thought was taking as the 1930's came to a close but at the same time indicated some of the causes and consequences of the subsequent "Keynesian revolution."

Histories of economic thought in America--particularly those concerned with the growth of federal fiscal policy--are essential to understanding the recession period. Particularly important to the present study are Stein's The Fiscal Revolution in America and Lewis H. Kimmel, Federal Budget and Fiscal Policy 1789-1958 (Washington, D.C.: The Brookings Institution, 1959). Stein argues convincingly that the direction of New Deal economic policy would not have been appreciably altered had Keynes never lived. Support for his position is to be found in J. Ronnie Davis' The New Economics and the Old Economists (Ames, Iowa: The Iowa State University Press, 1971). But both men fail to consider the further question which their work opens. If Keynes did not contribute significantly to the thought which informed New Deal policy, then how and why did Keynes' name come to rank so high in the pantheon of New Deal heroes? This study, accepting the proposition that Keynes did not influence New Deal policy, builds upon the observation that Keynes has nonetheless assumed a place of cardinal importance in the memory of New Dealers. It seeks to explain how and why this came to be. The Davis study reviews thoroughly the various arguments favoring government spending to counter recessions before the growth of Keynesian thought in America. Important contemporary studies on the same theme are: Committee of the President's Conference on Unemployment, Business Cycles and Unemployment (New York: McGraw-Hill, 1923) and J.M. Clark, Economics of Planning Public Works (Washington, D.C.: United States Government Printing Office, 1935).

There is no history of the budget reform movement in the United States. Important documents, giving adequate summaries of the main arguments used by advocates of budgetary reform are William F. Willoughby, The Budget and Responsible Government (New York: The MacMillan Company, 1920) and Frederick A. Cleveland and Arthur E. Bailey The Budget and Responsible Government (New York: The MacMillan Company, 1920). The development of offical government attitudes towards both government spending and the federal budget early in the Depression are evident in Herbert Hoover, The State Papers and Other Public Writings of Herbert Hoover, ed. William Starr Myers, 2 vols. (Garden City, N.Y.: Doubleday, Doran and Co., Inc., 1934). An excellent summary of the wide range of thinking among economists, politicians, and businessmen on government expenditures in 1937 is in the Proceedings of the Academy of Political Science 17.

There is a vast literature on Keynes and Keynesian economics. The author of this study has been especially interested in the transit of Keynesian thought to America. A pioneering work devoted to this problem is John Kenneth Galbraith, "How Keynes Came to America," New York Times Book Review 62 (May 16, 1965). An excellent set of papers and discussions of the subject by professional economists is in The American Economic Review 62(May 1972):116-141. Several authors have made similar contributions to the history of Keynesian economics in America, but these remain primarily accounts by participants, valuable documents in themselves,but by no means systematic historical studies. See, for example, Herbert Feis, "Keynes in Retrospect" Foreign Affairs 29(July 1951): 564-77 and Seymour Harris, ed., Schumpeter: Social Scientist (Cambridge, Mass.: Harvard University Press, 1951), especially the essay by Paul M. Sweezy. A central document in this literature in Seymour E. Harris, ed., The New Economics (New York: Alfred A. Knopf, 1948). An illuminating analysis of the development of Keynesian economic thought is by Axel Leijonhufvud, On Keynesian Economics and the Economics of Keynes (New York: Oxford University Press, 1968).

It is hoped that the present study, in emphasizing the importance of the Recession of 1937 as a critical experience preparing the minds of New Dealers for their subsequent attachment to the new economics as taught by Keynes has taken an initial step towards a fuller study of the growth of Keynesian economics in America. To a great extent New Deal and Keynesian thought were joined by the circumstances of their meeting in the recession crisis. They emerged to give form to politics, social thought, and economic thought in America for decades to come.

CHAPTER ONE, PAGES 1-16

1.   Attempts to define the term "New Dealer" precisely lead inevitably to sterile disputes over where such lines as New Dealer/non-New Dealer most aptly should be drawn. Here I am referring to persons who saw themselves as advocates of Franklin D. Roosevelt and most of his policies and were sufficiently informed on economic matters to have opinions on national fiscal policy and its relationship to the economy.

2.   Franklin D. Roosevelt, *The Public Papers and Addresses of Franklin Roosevelt*, ed. Samuel I. Rosenman, vol. 6 (New York: The MacMillan Company, 1941), p. 165; in a speech delivered April 20, 1937.

3.   Ibid. 8:9-10; the message was delivered January 4, 1939. See also John Morton Blum, *From the Morgenthau Diaries*, 3 vols., vol. 2, *Years of Urgency, 1938-41* (Boston: Houghton-Mifflin Company, 1965), p. 33.

4.   See FDR, *Public Papers*, 8:36-53, especially pp.36 and 37. Budget messages prepared in January include estimates for the fiscal year beginning July 1 of that calendar year and ending June 30 of the next calendar year. A fiscal year takes the name of the calendar year in which it ends. Thus the budget message delivered in January 1939 contained estimates for fiscal 1940, which was to begin July 1, 1939 and end June 30, 1940.

5.   C.K. Berryman, "The Sour Note," *Washington Star*, December 4, 1938.

6.   Harrison became Senate Finance Committee Chairman in 1933.

7.   The percentages are computed by the author from monthly figures adjusted for seasonal variation, with the 1923-1925 average

equal to 100, in the Board of Governors of the Federal Reserve System, Twenty-fifth Annual Report (Washington, D.C.: U.S. Government Printing Office, 1939), p. 69. See also Douglas A. Haynes, "Business Confidence and Business Activity: a Case Study of the Recession of 1937," Michigan Business Studies (June 1951) 10:9-18; and Broadus Mitchell, The Depression Decade from New Era through New Deal, 1929-41 (New York: Rinehart and Winston, 1947), p. 447.

8. Bernard Bailyn and Gordon Wood have asked how and why men in crisis were brought to replace old values and ideals with new ones during the period of the American Revolution. My question is similar to theirs—that is, not how ideas are created, but how events give special significance to certain ideas. See Bernard Bailyn, The Ideological Origins of the American Revolution (Cambridge: Harvard Univ. Press, 1967) and Gordon S. Wood, The Creation of the American Republic 1776-1787 (Chapel Hill, North Carolina: Institute of Early American History and Culture, 1969).

9. Most obvious, of course, are James M. Burns' two volumes, Roosevelt, the Lion and the Fox (New York: Harcourt and Brace, 1956) and Roosevelt: Soldier of Freedom (New York: Harcourt and Brace, 1970).

10. See, for example, Frank Freidel's summary, The New Deal in Historical Perspective, 2nd ed. (Washington, D.C.: American Historical Association Service Center for Teachers of History, 1965), p. 20.

11. FDR, Public Papers, 6:359-362.

12. "A Program to Combat the Recession" memo dated October 31, 1937 in the Marriner S. Eccles WHITE HOUSE FILE #4 under "Material Furnished, 1934-1937." The M.S. Eccles Washington file consists of over 70,000 items, most of them fastened into looseleaf binders. Most binders are labeled and the contents of each is further indicated by dividers within the binder. In citing materials from the Eccles file, I will capitalize the title of the binder and indicate titles of any further divisions with quotation marks (ie. MSE, WHITE HOUSE FILE #4, "Material Furnished, 1934-37"). The collection is presently housed in The Marriott Library, Special Collections, University of Utah, Salt Lake City.

13. Transcript of Group Meeting, 9:30 A.M., October 14, 1937, The Morgenthau Diaries, Vol. 92, p. 113, Franklin D. Roosevelt Library. Hereafter cited as MD 92:113. The Morgenthau Diaries surpass the Eccles Washington File in the scope and volume of documents contained. In addition to materials similar to those contained in the Eccles file, they contain verbatim transcripts of telephone conversations and Treasury Department meetings as well as frequent candid journal entries of Morgenthau, himself. John Morton Blum's three volumes, From the Morgenthau Diaries (Boston: Houghton and Mifflin, 1957-69), provide an indispensable summary of the contents of the collection.

14. An excellent discussion of the relationship of the Recession to Congressional politics can be found in James T. Patterson's _Congressional Conservatism and the New Deal: the Growth of a Conservative Coalition in Congress 1933-1939_ (Lexington, Kentucky: Univ. of Kentucky Press, 1967), especially see Chapter 7, "Recession Politics, 1938."

15. Harold L. Ickes, _The Secret Diary of Harold L. Ickes_, vol. 2, _The Inside Struggle, 1936-39_ (New York: Simon and Schuster, 1954), pp. 251-53.

16. From Morgenthau's notes on a cabinet meeting held November 12, 1937, MD 98:12.

17. Thurman Arnold, _Symbols of Government_ (New Haven: Yale Univ. Press, 1935), pp. 106-110.

18. Henry Morgenthau, Jr., speech, "Federal Spending and the Federal Budget," November 10, 1937 in _Proceedings of the Academy of Political Science_ (January 1938) 17:353.

19. Thurman Arnold, _Symbols of Government_, p. 106.

20. Frankfurter to Roosevelt, Nov. 10, 1937 in _Roosevelt and Frankfurter: Their Correspondence 1938-1945_, annotated by Max Freedman (Boston: Little, Brown and Company, 1967), pp. 438-39.

21. Journal entry, November 8, 1937, MD 94:154.

22. Treasury Department Meeting, November 4, 1937, MD 94:54-60.

23. Transcript of a September 30, 1937 meeting with Treasury staff members, MD 95:13-14.

24. Ickes, _Secret Diary_, 2:240.

25. Memo, Haas to Morgenthau, February 28, 1938, MD 112:335.

CHAPTER TWO, PAGES 17-37

1.   Harold L. Ickes, The Secret Diary of Harold L. Ickes, 3 vols. (New York: Simon and Schuster, 1953-54), vol. 1 The First Thousand Days (1953), pp. 223-24.

2.   Paul W. Ward in The Nation 141 (August 14, 1935): 182.

3.   See Arthur M. Schlesinger, Jr., The Age of Roosevelt, 3 vols. (Boston: Houghton Mifflin Co., 1957-60) vol. 2 The Coming of the New Deal, (1959), p. 538 for references to the resentment of Morgenthau on the part of other administrators and officials.

4.   Brief accounts of Morgenthau's early life are found in Frank Freidel, Franklin D. Roosevelt, 4 vols. to date (Boston: Little Brown and Company, 1952-   ) vol. 2 The Ordeal (1954), pp. 115-16. Schlesinger, The Coming of the New Deal, pp. 243-44 and in John Morton Blum, From the Morgenthau Diaries 3 vols. to date, vol. 1 Years of Crisis, 1928-38 (Boston: Houghton Mifflin, 1959), pp. 1-21. Blum's account is the most complete and has been the major source of biographical information (though not of interpretation) for this study.

5.   Blum, From the Morgenthau Diaries, pp. 2-3.

6.   Ibid., p. 5.

7.   Ibid., pp. 7-13; the quotation is on page 13.

8.   Ibid., p. 21.

9.   See the Morgenthau Presidential Diaries, vol. 1, pp. 101-103, in the Franklin Roosevelt Library, Hyde Park, N.Y. These diaries consist

of short notes which Morgenthau wrote from memory shortly after meetings with FDR. They will hereafter be cited MPD 1:101-03.

10. Frances Perkins, The Roosevelt I Knew (New York: The Viking Press, 1946), p. 120. See also Schlesinger, The Coming of the New Deal, p. 542 for further documentation of Roosevelt's frequent reference to himself as "Papa."

While no attempt is here made to offer a psychoanalytical study of the relationship between the two men, it is worth pointing out that there is abundant material for such a study, especially in Morgenthau's records. Very seldom have the public and private expressions of a high government figure been so candidly and thoroughly recorded.

11. The Morgenthau Diaries, vol. 92, pp. 45-46 in the Franklin D. Roosevelt Library, Hyde Park, N.Y., hereafter cited as MD 92:45-46. This quotation is from the transcript of a regular Treasury staff meeting (held each morning at 9:30 a.m.) for October 12, 1937.

12. MD 94:74.

13. Blum, Years of Crisis, p. vii.

14. Ibid., p. 22.

15. Ibid., p. 49.

16. Ibid., p. 34.

17. Frank Freidel, Franklin D. Roosevelt, vol. 4, Launching the New Deal (Boston: Little, Brown, and Company, 1973), p. 241.

18. Reports detailing the issues involved and the positions of various political groupings on the proposed constitution are in the New York Times October 8; 13; 16; 30; 31; 1915.

19. A competent brief review of the history of federal accounting procedures is found in Arthur Smithies, The Budgetary Process in the United States (New York: McGraw-Hill Book Co., Inc., 1955), pp. 48-89. See also E.E. Naylor, The Federal Budget System in Operation (Washington, D.C.: Columbus Univ., 1941), pp. 9-30, and Lewis H. Kimmel, Federal Budget and Fiscal Policy 1789-1958 (Washington, D.C.: The Brookings Institute, 1959), pp. 1-142. See especially Naylor, pp. 20-21.

20. See Kimmel, Federal Budget, pp. 315-16 for charts prepared from source material in the Annual Report of the Secretary of the Treasury on the State of the Finances for the Fiscal Year Ended June 30, 1956, pp. 318-21.

21. W.F. Willoughby, The Movement for Budgetary Reform in the States (New York: D. Appleton and Co., 1919), pp. 3-4.

22. Hearings before the Select Committee on the Budget of the House of Representatives on the Establishment of a National Budgetary System, Sixty-Sixth Congress, First Session (Washington, D.C.: U.S. Government Printing Office, 1919), p. 669.

23. Ibid., p. 665.

24. Willoughby was Director of the Institute for Government Research, a Washington-based citizens' group advocating "scientific study of government with a view to promoting efficiency and economy in its operations and advancing the science of administration." The quotation is from Willoughby, _Movement for Budgetary Reform_, pp. 1-2, 5.

25. _The New York Times_, October 31, 1915.

26. Frederick A. Cleveland and Arthur Eugene Buck, _The Budget and Responsible Government_ (New York: The MacMillan Co., 1920).

27. Ibid., pp. 1, ff.

28. The Democratic Party Platforms for 1916 and 1920 are in _The New York Times_, June 17, 1916; July 3, 1920.

29. Hoover, _State Papers_, 1:167-79, especially p. 179.

30. Ibid., pp. 441-459. See also Kimmel, _Federal Budget_, p. 319, for a convenient summary of the budget figures.

31. Ibid., 1:456.

32. Ibid., p. 457.

33. The war debt figure is from Kimmel, _Federal Budget_, p. 319.

34. Hoover, _State Papers_, 2:57-72, especially p. 59.

35. See _The New York Times_, April 1, 1931 and T.R.B., Washington Notes," _New Republic_, June 10, 1931, p. 97, for examples.

36. Hoover, _State Papers_ 2:105-6.

37. Ibid., p. 194. The quotation is from a letter to Herbert S. Crocker of the American Society of Civil Engineers in response to their suggestion that public works be expanded as an anti-depression measure. It is worth noting that Hoover, in listing the measures the federal government could take to counter the depression, listed "the quick, honest balancing of the Federal Budget" first. Earlier, in the fall of 1929 there was no mention of maintaining a balanced budget as an important anti-depression measure. Indeed, the President proposed that the Administration demonstrate confidence by undertaking tax reduction. "Every dollar so returned," he had said, "fertilizes the soil of prosperity." See vol. 1 of the _State Papers_, pp. 133-34 and p. 142.

38. Ibid., 2:307.

39. Kimmel, _Federal Budget_, pp. 315-19.

40. Ibid., pp. 317-18.

41. Quoted in Herbert Stein, _Fiscal Revolution_, p. 36 from Jacob Viner, _Balanced Deflation, Inflation or More Depression?_ (Minneapolis: Univ. of Minnesota, 1933), pp. 18-19.

42. The statistics are from Kimmel, _Federal Budget_, pp. 318-19.

43. Ibid., 3:16-24. Herbert Stein's _Fiscal Revolution_ contains an insightful discussion of Roosevelt's 1934 "plan" and subsequent fiscal developments in the 1930's. See especially pp. 68-73.

44. Ibid., 5:402-408.

45. Blum, _Years of Crisis_, pp. 274-75.

46. The incident was recalled by Henry Morgenthau, Jr. in "The Morgenthau Diaries: The Fight to Balance the Budget," _Colliers_ 120 (September 27, 1947), p. 82.

47. Ibid., p. 12.

48. Ibid., p. 82.

CHAPTER THREE, PAGES 37-66

1.   Gulick to Eccles, July 7, 1937; Eccles to Gulick, July 12, 1937; in M.S. ECCLES' FILE (FEDERAL RESERVE), "Comments." In Marriott Library, Special Collections, University of Utah, Salt Lake City, Utah.

Eccles was probably unaware that Gulick had made major contributions to the budgetary reform movement of the 1920's, thus adding substantially to the chain of developments which had endowed the balanced budget with the remarkable healing powers many Americans of Henry Morgenthau's generation presumed it to possess.

2.   Eccles to Frederic A. Delano, May 6, 1938, in M.S. ECCLES' FILE (FEDERAL RESERVE), "Letters (Prominent People)."

3.   Leonard J. Arrington, David Eccles, Pioneer Western Industrialist, (Logan, Utah: Utah State University Press, 1974), chapter 2.

4.   Marriner S. Eccles, Beckoning Frontiers: Public and Personal Recollections, ed. Sydney Hyman, (New York): Alfred Knopf, 1951), pp. 36-37.

5.   Leonard J. Arrington argues this thesis in his Great Basin Kingdom: an Economic History of the Latter-day Saints, 1830-1900 (Cambridge, Mass.: Harvard Univ. Press, 1958). See also Hamilton Gardner, "Cooperation Among the Mormons," Quarterly Journal of Economics 31 (May 1917): 461-99; Hamilton Gardner, "Communism Among the Mormons," Quarterly Journal of Economics 37 (November 1922): 134-37; and Leonard J. Arrington, Feramorz Y. Fox and Dean L. May, Building the City of God: Community and Cooperation Among the Mormons (Salt Lake City: Deseret

Book Company, 1976).

6. Arrington, "David Eccles," chapters 8, 12, 14.

7. Ibid., chapters 13 and 15; Eccles, _Beckoning Frontiers_, pp. 23-25.

8. Arrington, "David Eccles," chapters 10-12; _The Ogden Evening Standard_, December 7, 1912.

9. Arrington, "David Eccles," chapters 14, 15.

10. Eccles, _Beckoning Frontiers_, p. 27.

11. Ibid., p. 51.

12. Ibid., p. 71.

13. Biographical data form parts II and III of Eccles, _Beckoning Frontiers_. The quotation is from p. 104.

14. Memo of Henry Edmiston to M.S. Eccles, July 17, 1939 in M.S. ECCLES' FILE (FEDERAL RESERVE) "Correspondence, Lauchlin Currie (Confidential)." The character sketch is partly the author's own impressions from several meetings with Eccles. It also draws from Paul W. Ward, Morgenthau and his Friends," _Nation_ 141 (August 14, 1935): 184; and "Marriner Stoddard Eccles," _Fortune_ 11 (February 1935): 65.

15. M.S. Eccles to Frank F. Brooks, March 28, 1939 in M.S. ECCLES' FILE (FEDERAL RESERVE) "Comments."

16. Quoted in Eccles, _Beckoning Frontiers_, pp. 124-125.

17. Ibid., p. 102.

18. John Clive and Bernard Bailyn, "England's Cultural Provinces: Scotland and America" _William and Mary Quarterly_ 11 (April 1954): 213.

19. Senate Finance Committee, _Investigation of Economic Problems_, 72nd Congress 2nd Session (1933), p. 705.

20. Ibid., p. 730.

21. Eccles, _Beckoning Frontiers_, p. 116.

22. Quoted in Ibid., pp. 124-25.

23. Ibid., p. 131.

24. Eccles memo of May 21, 1936 in M.S. ECCLES' FILE (FEDERAL RESERVE), " Addresses, June 1925-5/8/36."

25. Eccles, _Beckoning Frontiers_, p. 148.

26. Ibid., p. 159.

27. Eccles' account is in _Beckoning Frontiers_, pp. 165-66. _The New York Times_ speculated on candidates other than Eccles August 22, p. 27, col. 6 and September 29, p. 23, col. 2. References relating to Eccles' appointment are also in Vol. II, pp. 71-ff. of the Morgenthau Diaries in the Franklin D. Roosevelt Library, Hyde Park, New York, hereafter cited as MD.

28. Dean L. May, "The Banking Act of 1935," MS, in the author's possession.

29. Eccles, _Beckoning Frontiers_, p. 132.

30. _New York Times_, November 25, 1934, Section VIII, p. 2.

31. March 26, 1931 address at a bank management conference in Salt Lake City, in M.S. ECCLES' FILE (FEDERAL RESERVE) "Addresses June 1925-5/8/36."

32. Quotes are from Eccles' June 17, 1932 speech before a Utah state bankers' convention, in M.S. ECCLES' FILE (FEDERAL RESERVE) "Addresses June 1925-5/8/36."

33. October 27, 1933 address before the Utah Education Association, in MS. ECCLES' FILE (FEDERAL RESERVE) "Addresses June 1925-5/8/36."

34. See Leonard J. Arrington and Thomas G. Alexander, A Dependent Commonwealth: Utah's Economy from Statehood to the Great Depression, ed. Dean L. May (Provo, Utah: Brigham Young University Press, 1974).

35. See, for example, the essays by Wesley C. Mitchell in the Committee of the President's Conference on Unemployment, Business Cycles and Unemployment (New York: McGraw-Hill, 1923), pp. 1-18. The classic study of business cycles is Wesley C. Mitchell, Business Cycles (Berkeley, California: Univ. of California Press, 1913). Other important books of the period are Alvin H. Hansen, Cycles of Prosperity and Depression (Madison, Wisconsin: 1921) and G.H. Hull, Industrial Depressions (New York: Frederick A. Stokes Company, 1911).

36. June 1932 speech before the Utah State Bankers Convention in M.S. ECCLES' FILE (FEDERAL RESERVE) "Addresses June 1925-5/8/36."

37. Eccles, Beckoning Frontiers, pp. 54-55.

38. October 27, 1933 address before the Utah Education Association, in M.S. ECCLES' FILE (FEDERAL RESERVE) "Addresses June 1925-5/8/36."

39. June 17, 1932 speech before a Utah State Bankers Convention, in M.S. ECCLES' FILE (FEDERAL RESERVE) "Addresses June 1925-5/8/36."

40. Eccles, Beckoning Frontiers, p. ix.

41. Basil Rauch, "Memoirs of an Agile Banker," The New Republic (July 30, 1951), p. 19.

42. John Morton Blum, Roosevelt and Morgenthau: a Revision and Condensation of 'From the Morgenthau Diaries' (Boston: Houghton-Mifflin, 1970), pp. xii, xiii.

43. Leon H. Keyserling, "Discussion," American Economic Review 62 (May 1972): 134-35.

44. MD 4:10; 118-123.

45. Currie to Eccles, December 12, 1936, M.S. ECCLES' FILE (FEDERAL RESERVE) 'Correspondence, Lauchlin Currie."

46. Quoted from the Morgenthau Diaries in John Morton Blum, From the Morgenthau Diaries 3 vols. to date, vol. 1 Years of Crisis. 1928-38 (Boston: Houghton Mifflin Co., 1959), pp. 280-281.

47. Morgenthau's account of his call to the Treasury Department on November 13, 1933 is in Blum, Years of Crisis, p. 73.

48. MD 92:152, for example.

49. Eccles, Beckoning Frontiers, pp. 327-330.

50. Ibid.

51. Steven Early to Marvin McIntyre, Memo of December 13, 1935 in File 90, Miscellaneous Memos, Franklin D. Roosevelt Library, Hyde Park, New York.

52. Eccles to Delano, May 25, 1936 in M.S. ECCLES' FILE (FEDERAL RESERVE) "Addresses June 1925-5/8/36."

53. See Eccles to J.I.H. Herbert, December 20, 1935; Stuart Chase to Eccles, May 22, 1936; Dorothy Keller to Eccles, December 18, 1935; Frederic A. Delano to Eccles, December 18, 1935; George T. Ross to Eccles, November 30, 1935; Delano to Eccles, May 22, 1936; W.I. Myers to Eccles, May 16, 1936; Herbert Gaston to Eccles, May 16, 1936; Lippmann to Eccles, May 17, 1936; and others, all in M.S. ECCLES' FILE (FEDERAL RESERVE) "Addresses June 1925-5/8/36."

54. Eccles recounted his meetings with Delano, Denison, Flanders and Ruml in an interview with the author; March 13, 1974.

55. October 27, 1933 address before the Utah Education Association, in M.S. ECCLES' FILE (FEDERAL RESERVE), "Addresses June 1925-5/8/36."

CHAPTER FOUR, PAGES 67-90

1.   See Lewis H. Kimmel, Federal Budget and Fiscal Policy 1789-1958 (Washington: The Brookings Institution, 1969), especially pp. 16-25 and 70-75 for discussion of the problem of surpluses. The controversy over internal improvements as it relates to fiscal policy is reviewed on pp. 29-37.

2.   For an example of the type of argument used against public works spending in the nineteenth century, see the veto message of Chester A. Arthur, August 1, 1882 in James D. Richardson, A Compilation of the Messages and Papers of the Presidents, 19 vols. and suppl. (Washington, D.C.: 1901-02) 8: 120-22.

3.   A review of the history of work relief can be found in J.M. Clark, Economics of Planning Public Works (Washington, D.C." United States Government Printing Office, 1935), pp. 2-12. See also Leah H. Fedel, Unemployment Relief in Periods of Depression (New York: Russell Sage Foundation, 1936).

4.   Sidney and Beatrice Webb, The Prevention of Destitution (London and New York: Longmans, Green and Co., 1911) and "Report on the Poor Laws and Relief of Distress," 1909, Ld. 4499, p. 1159, cited in Committee of the President's Conference on Unemployment, Business Cycles and Unemployment (New York: McGraw-Hill, 1923), p. 237.

5.   The book was published with a Foreward by Herbert Hoover and was unanimously approved by the prominent industrialists, bankers, and economists serving as members of the Committee. It consisted of articles written by several authors on various problems involving the relationship between business cycles and unemployment. Particularly important to this study are the Introduction and "Business Cycles" (pp. 1-18) by Wesley C. Mitchell, then of the National Bureau of Economic Research and a chapter on "The Long-Range Planning of Public Works" (pp.

231-61) by Otto T. Mallery, Member of the Pennsylvania State Industrial Board.

6. The Mitchell quotations are all from _Business Cycles and Unemployment_ (in order of use in the text), pp. 5, 8, 10, and 7.

7. See Mallery's chapter on "The Long-Range Planning of Public Works" in _Business Cycles and Unemployment_, pp. 231-61.

8. Cited in _Business Cycles and Unemployment_, p. 237 from the "Report of the Royal Commission on the Poor Laws and Relief of Distress," 1909, Ld. 4499. p. 1159.

9. _Business Cycles and Unemployment_, p. 243.

10. Quotations are from Mallery's chapter in _Business Cycles and Unemployment_, in order of use in the text, pp. 243, 244, 232-233.

11. Ibid., pp. 236-37.

12. Hoover endorsed the "Prosperity Relief Bill" in 1928 and authorized the proposal of a "3 billion reserve fund" program to a Conference of Sate Governors in the spring of 1929. Both of these were aimed at reserving funds during prosperity to be applied to public works in depression. See Herbert Stein's _The Fiscal Revolution in America_ (Chicago: The Univ. of Chicago Press, 1969), pp. 10-14.

For a more detailed review of attitudes towards public works during the 1920's see E.J. Howenstine, Jr., "Public Works Policy in the Twenties," _Social Research_ 13 (1946): 478-500.

13. Herbert Hoover, _The State Papers and Other Public Writings of Herbert Hoover_, ed. by William Starr Meyers, 2 vols. (New York: Doubleday, Doran and Co., Inc., 1934) 1:137.

14. Ibid., p. 292.

15. Ibid., p. 346.

16. Ibid.

17. Ibid., pp. 358-359.

18. Ibid., p. 411.

19. Ibid. pp. 432-33.

20. The most carefully-prepared exposition of President Hoover's attitude on further expansion of public works in 1932 is a letter of May 21, 1932, to Herbert S. Crocker, President of the American Society of Civil Engineers. The letter is in Ibid., 2:189-195.

21. Ibid., 2:505-531. Quotation is from p. 513. The President did not state what the amount of the reduction would be and the published budget figures do not single out public works as a category of expenditure.

22. Ibid., p. 347.

23. Ibid., p. 195.

24. Franklin D. Roosevelt, _Public Papers_, 1:8.

25. The Hoover Administration did not approve of federal relief legislation until July of 1932. This legislation underlined Hoover's

belief that relief was purely a local responsibility. It provided for loans to states from the Reconstruction Finance Corporation, to be repaid by deductions from future highway grants. See "Note" in Franklin D. Roosevelt, Public Papers, 2:83.

26. Ibid., 1:625.

27. An outline of Administration thinking on the Civilian Conservation Corps is found in Franklin D. Roosevelt, Public Papers, 2:80-84. The President also discussed the proposed CCC in Ibid., pp. 67-70. See also John A. Salmond, The Civilian Conservation Corps, 1933-1942: a New Deal Case (Durham, N.C.: Duke Univ. Press, 1967).

Administration aims for this and other work programs are well explained in pertinent documents and accompanying notes in the Public Papers.

28. Items and notes pertaining to the Federal Emergency Relief Administration can be found in Public Papers 2:80-84; 183-185; 237-242. See also Harry L. Hopkins, Spending to Save (New York: W.W. Norton and Co., 1936).

29. Arthur M. Schlesinger, Jr., The Age of Roosevelt, 3 vols. (Boston: Houghton Mifflin, 1957_1960) vol. 2 The Coming of the New Deal (1959), pp. 282-287.

30. Numerous pertinent references to the Public Works Administration and the National Recovery Administration can be found in vols. II and III of Public Papers. See also Hugh Johnson, The Blue Eagle from Egg to Earth (Garden City, N.Y.: Doubleday, Doran, and Co., 1935) and Harold L. Ickes, Back to Work: Story of the PWA (New York: MacMillan, 1935).

31. See item and notes in Public Papers 2:454-459. The quotations are from pp. 457 and 459, respectively. See also Schlesinger, 2:270 and Robert E. Sherwood, Roosevelt and Hopkins (New York: Grosset and Dunlap, 1948), p. 52.

32. See the explanatory note in Public Papers 3:108-111.

33. Ibid., 4:15-25, especially pp. 19-20.

34. The President's Executive Order establishing the WPA is in Public Papers, 4:163-167 and an accompanying note is on pp. 168-78. See also Hopkins' Spending to Save and Donald S. Howard's The WPA and Federal Relief Policy (New York: Russell Sage Foundation, 1943).

35. Eccles' memo, The Pump-Priming Deficit for 1933-34" is in ECCLES' SCRAPBOOK "Miscellaneous Memos and Letters, Feb. 1933-June 1951," in the Special Collections, Marriott Library, University of Utah, Salt Lake City, Utah.

36. Speech delivered before the Commercial Club of Boston, February 16, 1935, in M.S. ECCLES' FILE (FEDERAL RESERVE) "Addresses June 1925-5/8/36.

37. Eccles Memo, "The Pump-Priming Deficit for 1933-34," in M.S

ECCLES' SCRAPBOOK.

38. Public Papers, 5:17-18.

39. Ibid., pp. 643-44.

40. A brief review of the debate between Eccles and Morgenthau during the winter of 1936-37 is in John Morton Blum, From the Morgenthau Diaries 3 vols., vol. 1, Years of Crisis, 1928-29. (Boston: Houghton Mifflin Co., 1959), pp. 279-283. The quotation is on p. 282.

41. Statement released April 12, 1937 in M.S. ECCLES' WASHINGTON FILE (FEDERAL RESERVE) "TREASURY 1934-48."

42. Message to Congress, April 20, 1937 in Public Papers 6: 165. This statement was drafted by Herbert Gaston, Assistant to the Secretary of the Treasury, and included in the President's speech at Morgenthau's suggestion. See Blum, Years of Crisis, pp. 191-196.

CHAPTER FIVE, PAGES 91-114

1. The President retained this goal at least in his communication with Morgenthau, as late as mid-September. See John Morton Blum, From the Morgenthau Diaries, vol. 2 Years of Crisis 1928-1938 (Boston: Houghton-Mifflin, 1959), p. 381. Hereafter cited as Blum, Years of Crisis.

2. Quoted in Blum, Years of Crisis, p. 382.

3. The Morgenthau Diaries, vol. 95 p. 1-5, Franklin D. Roosevelt Library, Hyde Park, New York. Hereafter cited as MD 95:1-5.

4. Memo, Haas to Morgenthau, August 18, 1937, MD 80:82.

5. Memo, Morgenthau to Roosevelt, September 5, 1937. In the President's Secretary's File, Box #66, Departmental Correspondence, Treasury Department, Henry Morgenthau, Jr. 1933-37, 1938-1939-1940. Franklin D. Roosevelt Library, Hyde Park, New York.

6. A transcript of the September 30 meeting is in MD 95: 6-25.

7. MD 95:18.

8. MD 95:16.

9. MD 95:10.

10. MD 95:13-14.

11. MD 95:17, 13-14.

12. "Tax Revisions Studies, 1937"--General Statement to Mr. Magill from Mr. Haas. August 31, 1937, in MD 81:84.

13. The speech draft is in MD 95:78-99. Quoted portions in order of use are on pp. 86, 88, 89, 99.

14. Morgenthau to Roosevelt, October 5, 1937, in President's Secretary's File, Box #66, Henry Morgenthau Jr. 1933-1937. The President was urging, among other things, the passage of wages-and-hours legislation, executive reorganization, and the establishment of the Agricultural Adjustment Administration activities on a permanent,

financially sound basis.

15. October 12, 1937. Memo of Morgenthau in MD 92:57. Morgenthau frequently made observations on a day's events in the form of a "memo to self," or under other designations. All are essentially journal entries, some obviously made moments after the meeting or conference to which they refer. See also MD 91:191-205.

16. From Morgenthau's notes on an October 12, 1937 meeting, with Doughton, Vinson, and the President in MD 92:43-44.

17. See MD 91:228-229, 260.

18. Transcript of phone call, 9:58 a.m., October 12, 1937 in MD 92:18-20.

19. In a 9:30 a.m. group meeting, October 14, 1937, MD 92:113-114.

20. MD 92:115.

21. MD 92:114-115.

22. MD 95:116.

23. An example of Morgenthau's sense that he was doing a needed service for Roosevelt is in MD 95:50. The quote is in MD 95:320-21.

24. MD 95:20 in an October 14 meeting concerning the address.

25. MD 95: 53-54.

26. MD 95:54.

27. Henry Morgenthau, Jr., "The Morgenthau Diaries: the Fight to Balance the Budget," Colliers (September 27, 1947), p. 12.

28. MD 95:37-40.

29. MD 95:50.

30. MD 95:126. Riefler had been a member of the Federal Reserve Staff under E.A. Goldenweiser and had served as economic advisor to FDR.

31. MD 95:127.

32. MD 95: 140-41.

33. MD 95:396-97.

34. In a journal entry of November 4, 1937, MD 94:49-50.

35. In a meeting held the afternoon of November 4, MD 95:477.

36. MD 94:52-53, Morgenthau's notes on a cabinet meeting of November 4.

37. MD 94:54-60. Transcript of a phone conversation between Morgenthau and Eccles, November 4, 1937 at 10:48 a.m.

38. Transcript of a meeting held November 4, 1937 in MD 95:470-71.

39. MD 95:473.

40. MD 95:476.

41. MD 94:154.

42. These changes are written in the President's hand on drafts of the speech found in MD 96:28-48 and 50-72. This particular change is on p. 64 of the diary. The most conveniently available printed form of the speech is in the Proceedings of the Academy of Political Science 17 (January 1938): 534-42. This particular reference is on p. 539.

43. P. 69 of the diary, p. 541 of the Proceedings.

44. P. 76 of the diary, p. 542 of the Proceedings.

45. MD 96:80.

46. MD 94:166-67, 187.

47. For a list of program committee members see the Proceedings, p. iii. Attendance figures were reported in Time, November 22, 1937, p. 16.

48. MD 98:35-36.

49. Proceedings, pp. 526, 532-33. Audience reaction was reported in the New York Times, November 11, 1937.

50. For Gilbert's introduction, see the Proceedings, pp. 432-33. For audience reaction to Morgenthau's speech, see the New York Times, November 11, 1937.

51. In a staff meeting of November 15, 1937, MD 98:35-36.

52. Time, November 22, 1937 p. 16.

53. New York Times, Sunday, November 14, 1937, Section IV.

54. New York Times, November 12, 1937, p. 1, col. 8, and pp. 5 and 6.

55. Roswell Magill's notes on a Cabinet meeting of November 12, 1937, MD 98:12-13.

56. Twenty-fifth Annual Report of the Board of Governors of the Federal Reserve System (Washington: 1939), p. 69.

57. MD 94:116. In a Treasury meeting of November 5, 1937.

58. MD 95:140-41.

59. MD 100:355-77.

60. John Morton Blum, Roosevelt and Morgenthau (Boston: Houghton-Mifflin, 1970), pp. xii, xiii.

61. FDR, Public Papers, 6:493, in a November 15 message to the Extraordinary Session of Congress.

62. Ibid., 7:8, in the President's Annual Message of January 3, 1938.

63. MD 103:160.

CHAPTER SIX, PAGES 115-140

1.   Frankfurter to Roosevelt, November 10, 1937 in <u>Roosevelt and
Frankfurter: their Correspondence 1938-1945,</u> ann. Max Freedman (Boston:
Little Brown and Company, 1967), pp. 438-39.

2.   The Morgenthau Diaries, vol. 99, p. 217, Franklin D. Roosevelt
Library, Hyde Park, New York. Hereafter cited as MD 99:217.

3.   Editorial, "The New Deal and the 'Recession'," <u>Common Sense</u> 7
(January 1938): 3.

4.   MD 110:190-92.

5.   Morgenthau memo dated December 6, 1937 in MD 101:69-70.

6.   Memo of Eccles to FDR, "Summary of Program to Combat the
Recession," October 31, 1937 in M.S. ECCLES' WHITE HOUSE FILE, "M.S.E.
Material Furnished 1934-37." In Marriott Library, Special Collections,
University of Utah, Salt Lake City, Utah.

7.   Henderson to Eccles, December 20, 1937; Cohen to Eccles, December 20, 1937;   Eccles to Chester C. Davis, December 23, 1937; all in
M.S. ECCLES' FILE (FEDERAL RESERVE) "Addresses 5/30/36-6/16/39."

8.   M.S. ECCLES' FILE (FEDERAL RESERVE) "Testimonies--June 14,
1938-March 24, 1941."

9.   Testimony of MSE before a Senate Special Committee to Investigate Unemployment and Relief, January 4, 1938 in M.S. ECCLES' FILE
(FEDERAL RESERVE) 'Testimonies--June 14, 1938-March 24, 1941.

10.   <u>The Washington Star,</u> February 7, 1938.

11.   Eccles to FDR, Memo, "The Immediate Need for More Spending,"
June 16, 1938, in M.S. ECCLES' WHITE HOUSE FILE, "M.S.E. Material
Furnished 1934-37."

12.   See Paul Appleby, "Reminiscences," pp. 143-44 in the Columbia
Oral History Office, Columbia University, New York City; also Mordecai
Ezekial, "A Memorandum for members of Informal Discussion Group," April

15, 1938 in M.S. ECCLES' FILE (FEDERAL RESERVE) "Monetary and Fiscal Policy Committee." There is some discrepancy in the two accounts. Appleby remembers meetings taking place before the Recession began and continuing through the winter with Hopkins participating. The Ezekial memo mentions meetings only after January 1 and does not include Hopkins. The Ezekial memo is contemporary, and more likely to be correct in details, though the author considers it unlikely that Appleby would have misremembered so important a detail as the presence of Harry L. Hopkins. It is altogether possible that the earlier meetings remembered by Appleby, which could have included Hopkins, did take place but that Ezekial did not participate and that the gatherings became more formalized in January as mentioned in the Ezekial memo.

13. Eccles, Beckoning Frontiers, p. 130.

14. Mordecai Ezekial, "A Memorandum for members of the Informal Discussion Group," April 14, 1938 in M.S. ECCLES' FILE (FEDERAL RESERVE) "Monetary and Fiscal Committee."

15. Paul Appleby, "Reminiscences," pp. 143-44 in the Columbia Oral History Library.

16. See John Morton Blum, From the Morgenthau Diaries 3 vols. to date,, vol. 1 Years of Crisis, 1928-38 (Boston: Houghton Mifflin Co., 1959), pp. 422-23; 438; also MD 101:69-70.

17. Currie, Henderson, and Lubin memo, "Causes of the Recession," November 8, 1937 in M.S. ECCLES' WHITE HOUSE FILE "M.S.E. Material Furnished 1934-37."

18. See Robert E. Sherwood, Roosevelt and Hopkins (New York: Grosset and Dunlap, The Universal Library, 1950), pp. 92-95.

19. Eccles to Hopkins, December 18, 1937; Hopkins to Eccles, January 10, 1938; both in M.S. ECCLES' FILE (FEDERAL RESERVE) "Letters (Prominent People)".

20. Blum, Years of Crisis, p. 406.

21. Transcript of Morgenthau/Wallace phone conversation, February 17, 1938 in MD 111:181-83. The words are Morgenthau's.

22. Morgenthau memo of conversation with Eccles, February 14, 1938 in MD 11:55.

23. Transcript of an Interdepartmental Meeting, February 15, 1938 in MD 110:183-204 and 193-94.

24. Memo, Haas to Morgenthau, February 28, 1938, "Opportunity for Next Monetary Step?" in MD 112:335.

25. Eccles to James Roosevelt, memo of February 1, 1938; Currie to Eccles, memo of February 1, 1938; both in M.S. ECCLES' WHITE HOUSE FILE No. 6, "Political Material Furnished M.S.E. 1935-48."

26. M.S. ECCLES' FILE (FEDERAL RESERVE) "Addresses 5/30/36-6/16/39."

27. Eccles to FDR, Memo of March 8, 1938 in M.S. ECCLES' WHITE

HOUSE FILE, 'M.S.E. Material Furnished 1934-47." See also MD 94:152-54 and 101:266; Harry L. Hopkins Papers, Box 5, Speeches of July 16, 1938 and October 8, 1938, Franklin D. Roosevelt Library, Hyde Park, New York; also numerous public pronouncements of FDR beginning October 5, 1937. A large number of the President's speeches during this period make reference to the challenge of totalitarianism. He later entitled his Fireside Chat of April 14, announcing the new spending program, "Dictatorships Do Not Grow out of Strong and Successful Governments, but out of Weak and Helpless Ones." See FDR, Public Papers, vols. 6, 7, 8.

28. Memo in MD 117:447.

29. Hopkins to David Lynch in Harry L. Hopkins Papers, Box 79, Franklin D. Roosevelt Library, Hyde Park, New York. This undated letter is an account of the Warm Springs meeting prepared by Hopkins for David Lynch, who was doing a study of the incident for a University of Iowa degree.

30. Western Union Telegram to Beardsley Ruml, April 1, 1938 in Harry L. Hopkins Papers, box 50, "Miscellaneous," Franklin D. Roosevelt Library.

31. Henderson-Ruml memo, April 1, 1938, Harry L. Hopkins Papers, Box 50, "Leon Henderson memos 1937-38."

32. Senator Pat Harrison in a speech delivered April 3, 1938 in MD 118:40-43.

33. See the Hopkins to David Lynch letter cited in footnote 29, above.

34. MD 118:196-97.

35. The series of memos, Haas to Morgenthau and White to Morgenthau, April 8, 1938 are in MD 118:225-39.

36. MD 118:247-48.

37. The Morgenthau Presidential Diaries, April 11, 1938, 1:0005. These are a series of memos written by Morgenthau describing conversations with the President. Hereafter cited as MPD.

38. Transcript of Treasury Staff Meeting, April 11, 1938, MD 118:266-86.

39. Ibid., p. 277.

40. Ibid., p. 283.

41. Luncheon meeting in Morgenthau's office, April 12, 1938 in MD 118:343-47 and Morgenthau's notes on the meeting on p. 348.

42. Taylor to Morgenthau memo, April 12, 1938 in MD 118:387-89.

43. Notes on an April 13, 1938 meeting with FDR in MPD 1:0020.

44. MD 119:30-40; the quote is on p. 38.

45. MD 119:44-45.

46. FDR, Public Papers 7:236-47.

47. Ibid., pp. 236-248.

CHAPTER SEVEN, PAGES 141-162

1. Henderson-Ruml memo, undated, Harry L. Hopkins Papers, Box 50, "Leon Henderson memos 1937-38" Western Union Telegram to Beardsley Ruml, April 1, 1938 in Harry L. Hopkins Papers, box 50, "Miscellaneous," Franklin D. Roosevelt Library, Hyde Park, New York.

2. FDR, Public Papers, 7:236-47.

3. April 8, 1938 statement before a Special Committee of the Congress to Investigate Unemployment and Relief, In Harry L. Hopkins Papers, Box 5, Franklin D. Roosevelt Library.

4. Both the speech and the letter are in the Harry L. Hopkins Papers, Box 5, Franklin D. Roosevelt Library; other speeches made by Hopkins during the summer are in the same location.

5. Eccles to A.H. Coate, May 25, 1938; Eccles speech before the New Jersey Bankers' Association Convention, May 13, 1938; Eccles to Gerard Swope, May 27, 1938; Eccles speech to officers and directors of the Federal Reserve Bank of Richmond, Virginia, May 19, 1938; all in M.S. ECCLES' FILE (FEDERAL RESERVE), "Addresses 5/30/36-6/16/39," in the Marriott Library, Special Collections, University of Utah, Salt Lake City, Utah.

6. Eccles to FDR memos: "The Next Steps in the Recovery Program," April 27, 1938 and "The Immediate Need for More Spending," June 6, 1938; both in M.S. ECCLES' WHITE HOUSE FILE, "M.S.E. Material Furnished 1934-37."

7. Taylor-Morgenthau memo, April 12, 1938 in The Morgenthau Diaries 118:387-89, Franklin D. Roosevelt Library, Hyde Park, New York.

8. Morgenthau memo, December 6, 1937 in MD 101: 69-70.

9. Lippmann to Eccles, May 17, 1936; Eccles speech at a March 2,

1938 Washington meeting of Reserve officials, in M.S. ECCLES' FILE (FEDERAL RESERVE), "Addresses June 1925-5/8/36."

10. Board of Governors of the Federal Reserve System, _Twenty-fifth Annual Report . . . for the Year 1939)_ (Washington, D.C.: U.S. Government Printing Office, 1939), p. 69.

11. Berle to FDR, August 16 1938, President's Secretary's File, Box 61, Franklin D. Roosevelt Library.

12. Eccles to Robert J. Bulkley, October 4, 1938, M.S. ECCLES' FILE (FEDERAL RESERVE), "Senators and Representatives (Correspondence)."

13. Blum, _From the Morgenthau Diaries_, vol. 1 _Years of Crisis_, p. 449.

14. Herbert Stein, _The Fiscal Revolution in America_, p. 168.

15. See Marriner S. Eccles, _Beckoning Frontiers_, pp. 316, 321.

16. FDR, _Public Papers_ 8:45 in the Annual Budget Message, January 5, 1939.

17. _New York Times_, January 23, 1939; January 30, 1939; February 6, 1939. The book went into a second printing on January 27. See James Henle to Paul M. Sweezy, January 27, 1939, in a file on _An Economic Program for American Democracy_ in the possession of Mr. Sweezy.

18. _Washington D.C. Star_, March 5, 1939.

19. _Boston Globe_, January 12, 1939.

20. _Washington D.C. Post_, December 4, 1938.

21. Richard V. Gilbert, et al., _An Economic Program for American Democracy_ (New York: Vanguard Press, 1938), pp. 15; ix.

22. Ibid., p. vi.

23. Davis to Eccles, January 5, 1939; the draft letter to the Congressmen is included with Davis' reply to Eccles in M.S. ECCLES FILE (FEDERAL RESERVE), "Correspondence, Chester Davis." Numerous copies of the book were still in Eccles' library at the time of his death in 1977.

24. Reported by Herbert Stein, _Fiscal Revolution_, p. 487. Stein also cites in this place the notation of Elliott Roosevelt, in Elliot Roosevelt (ed.), _FDR: His Personal Letters_ 4 vols. (New York: Duel, Sloan and Pearce, 1950), 4:857-58.

25. Gilbert, et al., _Economic Program_, p. vi.

26. See the statements of the Board of Governors, July 14, 1936, January 30, 1937, and March 15, 1937, explaining their action with regard to the raising of reserve requirements. M.S. ECCLES' SCRAPBOOK, "Published Articles-Interviews-Press Releases, etc." The Haas memo, with Currie's comments, dated January 18, 1939, is in M.S. ECCLES' FILE (FEDERAL RESERVE) "Treasury 1939-47."

27. FDR, _Public Papers_ 7:601-02.

28. Memo, Delano to Ruml and Denison, April 27, 1938, in MD 121:213-14.

29. Memo of the Advisory Committee of the National Resources

Committee to FDR, August 12, 1938, M.S. ECCLES' FILE (FEDERAL RESERVE) "monetary and Fiscal Policy Committee."

30. Currie to Eccles memo, February 6, 1939, M.S. ECCLES' FILE (FEDERAL RESERVE), "Monetary and Fiscal Policy Committee."

31. Monetary and Fiscal Advisory Board, statement of policy, December 15, 1938. M.S. ECCLES' FILE (FEDERAL RESERVE), "Monetary and Fiscal Advisory Committee."

32. Monetary and Fiscal Advisory Board, memo of December 19, 1938. M.S. ECCLES' WHITE HOUSE FILE, 'Fiscal and Monetary Committee, 1934-1939."

33. Currie to Eccles, February 16, 1939, M.S. ECCLES FILE (FEDERAL RESERVE), "Monetary and Fiscal Policy Committee."

34. Blum, From the Morgenthau Diaries, vol. 2 Years of Urgency, p. 32.

35. FDR, Public Papers, 8:37; 45-47; 10.

36. Eccles to FDR memo, January 11, 1939, M.S. ECCLES' WHITE HOUSE FILE, "Material Furnished 1934-37."

37. Blum, Years of Urgency, p. 33.

38. C.K. Berryman, "The Sour Note," Washington Star, December 4, 1938.

39. Goldenweiser memo of March 25, 1939 in Goldenweiser Papers, "Personal and Confidential Notes," C7, Library of Congress.

40. Morgenthau Presidential Diaries, 1:99-100; 102-103, Franklin D. Roosevelt Library. Hereafter cited as MPD.

41. MPD 1:113-16.

42. Thurman Arnold, The Folklore of Capitalism (New Haven: Yale University Press, 1937), p. 28.

43. FDR, Public Papers 60:5.

44. Ibid., 8:7.

45. Address, "Reconstructing Economic Thinking," given before a meeting of the Utah Education Association, October 27, 1938, in M.S. ECCLES' FILE (FEDERAL RESERVE), "Addresses June 1925-5/8/36."

46. Eccles, Beckoning Frontiers, p. 131.

47. Proceedings of the American Academy of Political Science 17 (January 1938): 521.

48. Edmiston to Eccles memo July 17, 1939, in M.S. ECCLES' FILE (FEDERAL RESERVE), "Correspondence, Lauchlin Currie, etc."

49. Lauchlin B. Currie, "Discussion," American Economic Review 62 (May 1972): 139.

50. Ruml memo on compensatory fiscal policy, September 5, 1938, Harry L. Hopkins Papers, Box 79, Franklin D. Roosevelt Library.

51. John Kenneth Galbraith, "Came the Revolution," New York Times, May 16, 1965.

52. Eccles Address at Harvard Business School, June 16, 1939, in

M.S. ECCLES' FILE (FEDERAL RESERVE) "Addresses, 5/30/36-6/16/39."

    53.   Eccles Address to Washington, D.C. meeting of Reserve Officials, March 2, 1938, M.S. ECCLES' FILE (FEDERAL RESERVE) "Addresses, 5/30/36-6/16/39."

Hildebrand, (con't)
  Economic Program for American
  Democracy, 147
Hitler, Adolph, 130
Hoover, Herbert C., 7, 30, 53,
  55-56, 66-67, 73, 88, 117;
  budget messages of, 31-33;
  difference from Roosevelt on
  public works spending, 76;
  instigates public works
  spending conference, 69; on
  positive effects of public
  works spending, 73-74; policies seem as antithesis of
  New Deal, 12-13; promotes
  balanced budget as recovery
  measure, 33-34; sees limits
  to useful public works, 74-75
Hopkins, Harry, 2, 17, 37, 83,
  98, 117, 135, 141; administers CWA and WPA, 80, 82;
  attends informal anti-recession meetings, 123; chooses
  Gilbert for Commerce post,
  148; close to FDR, 125-126;
  death of wife, 126; Eccles
  meets, 50; meets FDR at Warm
  Springs, 131-134; places high
  value on national income,
  142-143; relationship to
  Eccles, 126; surgery at Mayo
  Clinic, 126
Housing industry, 118, 122, 127
Howe, Louis, 18, 124
Ickes, Harold L., 82, 98, 117,
  137; administers PWA, 79;
  describes Morgenthau, 17-18;
  says President has no program, 15; "spender" in Berryman cartoon, 2-3; view of
  1940 elections, 9
Institute for Advanced Study,
  102
Institutional economics, 161-
  162
Jackson, Robert H., 117, 123,
  133
J.P. Morgan, Co., 109
Kahn, R.F., 59
Keynes, John Maynard, 55, 58-
  59, 146, 151, 160-162

Keynesian Economics. See Keynes
Keyserling, Leon H., 59
King, William H., 45
LaFollette, Robert, Jr., 123
Lamont, Thomas S., 109
LeCron, James, 123
Liberalism, 130-131, 158-161
Lindley, Ernest K., 147
Lippmann, Walter, 65, 145, 156
"Liquidity preference," 59
Logan, Utah 44
Lubin, Isadore 123-124
McAdoo, William G., 61
McIntyre, Marvin, 63
McKay, David O., 42
McReynolds, William, 106
Magill, Roswell, 106, 110, 135
Mallery, Otto T., 70-72
Marshall, Louis, 28
Massachusetts: experience of
  with relief work, 72
Merriam, Charles E., 38
Mills, Ogden, 34, 44, 108
Ministry of Labor (British), 69
Mitchell, Charles, 44
Mitchell, Wesley C., 69
Monetary Fiscal and Advisory
  Committee, 153-154
Morgan, J.P., 44
Morgenthau, Eleanor Fatman, 20
Morgenthau, Henry, Sr., 19-21,
  30
Morgenthau, Henry, Jr., 8, 17,
  46, 51, 56, 63, 82, 88, 115,
  116, 125, 133, 145; accepts
  chair of Monetary and Fiscal
  Advisory Committee, 151;
  advocates farmers'
  cooperatives, 21; believes
  increased reserve requirements caused Recession, 150;
  in Berryman cartoon, 2-3;
  appointments: head of Federal
  Farm Board, 22; New York
  State Conservation Commissioner, 21; Secretary of
  Treasury, 22; and budget reform movement, 29-30; character sketch of, 18-19;
  closeness to FDR, 61, comment
  on Douglas resignation, 37;

200

New Jersey Bankers' (con't)
Association, 143
New York City, 46, 47; Academy
meeting to be held in, 92;
bankers of oppose New Deal
reforms, 98; business and
financial leaders of hear
Morgenthau's speech, 108-113;
Eccles visits Tugwell in, 49
New York Times, 28, 53, 103,
110
NRA. See National Recovery
Administration
Ogden, Utah, 43
Oliphant, Herman, 8, 98, 109-
110, 137
Oregon, 40, 41
Oregon Lumber Company, 43
Parliament (British):
establishes public works
committee, 69
Paynter, Henry, 147
Pennsylvania State Industrial
Board, 70
Perkins, Frances, 22
Perpetual Emigrating Fund, 40
Phillips Exeter, 20
Presidential campaign of 1936,
8, 13, 36
President's Committee on
Administrative Management, 38
President's Conference on
Unemployment, 69, 70, 72
President's Monetary and Fiscal
Advisory Committee, 124, 153-
154
Progressive reform, 71, 73, 89
"Propensity to consume", 59
Public works spending: as anti-
depression measure, 68; early
concepts of, 68; differences
of Hoover and Roosevelt on,
75-76; differentiated from
"work relief," 68; Hoover
praises effects of, 74; levels of in Hoover administration, 74; Parliament establishes committee for, 69; a
part of new spending program,
136; rationale for in
depression, 70-72

Public Works Administration
(PWA), 79-81, 125
Quarantine speech: of FDR, 2
Railroad reorganization, 105,
122, 129, 135, 148
Randall, Samuel J., 27
Rauch, Basil, 58-59
Recession of 1937: economic
indicators of, 4; inter-
national implications of, 5-
6; political implication of,
7-9; possible explanations
of, 150; questions raised by,
65-66
Reconstruction Finance
Corporation (RFC), 47, 122
"Reform" session, of congress,
2, 96
Relief Work, 68-69, 72, 77
Resettlement Administration, 81
Richmond, Virginia, 143
Riefler, Winfield, 102
Roosevelt, Eleanor, 155-156
Roosevlet, Elliott, 149
Roosevelt, Franklin D., 18, 56,
82; announces details of
spending program, 138-139;
announces reform session of
congress, 80; asks Morgenthau
to talk to Eccles, 104; believes businessmen sabotaging
his programs, 103; bound by
Recession crisis, 13; budget
messages, 35, 87, 110, 153,
154; campaign address, 36;
changes draft of Morgenthau's
speech, 107; decides to increase government spending,
133; differs from Hoover on
public works spending, 76-77;
discusses Recession with cabinet, 104; disregards distinction between public works
and relief work, 77; Eccles
sees as "pharoah," 47; establishes monetary and fiscal
advisory committee, 152;
leaves for Warm Springs, 128,
131; photograph of with
Eccles, 62; photograph of
with Morgenthau, 25; plans to

202